500

CACTI

500

CACTI

Ken Preston-Mafham

Species and Varieties in
Cultivation

FIREFLY BOOKS

A FIREFLY BOOK

Published by Firefly Books Ltd. 2007

Copyright © 2007 The Brown Reference Group plc

First printing

Publisher Cataloging-in-Publication Data (U.S.)
Preston-Mafham, Ken.
    500 Cacti: species and varieties in cultivation / Ken Preston-
Mafham.
[528] p. : col. photos. ; cm.
Includes bibliographical references and index.
Summary: An account of 500 species of cultivated cacti,
including their description, natural distribution, and habitat.
ISBN-13: 978-1-55407-261-3
ISBN-10: 1-55407-261-1
1. Cactus. I. Five hundred cacti. II. Title.
583.56 dc22   QK495.C11.P747 2007

Library and Archives Canada Cataloguing in Publication
Preston-Mafham, Ken
    500 cacti : species and varieties in cultivation / Ken Preston-
Mafham.
Includes bibliographical references and index.
ISBN-13: 978-1-55407-261-3
ISBN-10: 1-55407-261-1

    1. Cactus. I. Title. II. Title: Five hundred cacti.

QK495.C11P74 2007   583'.56   C2006-904851-7

Published in the United States by
Firefly Books (U.S.) Inc.
P.O. Box 1338, Ellicott Station
Buffalo, New York 14205

Published in Canada by
Firefly Books Ltd.
66 Leek Crescent,
Richmond Hill, Ontario L4B 1H1

For The Brown Reference Group plc:
Editorial Director: Lindsey Lowe
Project Editor: Graham Bateman
Editor: Virginia Carter
Design: Steve McCurdy

All Photographs within the book:
    Premaphotos Wildlife

Page 1: *Notocactus rudibuenekeri*
Pages 2–3: *Rebutia fulviseta*

Cover Photos

Front Cover: *Opuntia species*, Jamie Farrant
Spine: *Echinocereus viereckii morricallii*, Premaphotos Wildlife
Back Cover: *Mammillaria species*, Rewat Wannasuk

Printed in China

Contents

CONTENTS

CONTENTS

Introduction

500 Cacti describes more than 500 species of cacti that are generally available for enthusiasts from specialist nurseries, including some from more general garden stores. While it is difficult to choose what to include or exclude from this large group of plants, it can be said that anyone obtaining all the plants in this book (or a reasonable selection) would end up with a well-balanced collection of diverse, interesting, and rewarding cacti.

The final list contains as many genera as reasonably possible, even if they have only a single example. Popular genera, or those that seem to be gaining numerous new devotees at present and that are not always covered well elsewhere (for example, the *Opuntia* group) have been dealt with rather more fully than some people might think they deserve. Genera that have few fans, such as some of the long pendant epiphytes, or many large-growing, columnar kinds (cerei), or those whose members are difficult to grow on their own roots (such as *Blossfeldia*), have been omitted.

To assist the reader who is a complete beginner with cacti and is wrestling with a confusion of names on a mail order list, a selection of genera that are not included here, along with brief reasons why, is given on page 516.

The plants in this book are all members of a single family (the Cactaceae), most of which have succulent stems used for storing water. Numerous other kinds of plants are also succulent and are very popular with collectors, for example, living stones (*Lithops*) in the family Aizoaceae or *Stapelia* in the milkweed family (Asclepiadaceae). These and many other succulent plants do not belong to the family Cactaceae, and so are not included in the following pages.

NAMING CACTI

The cactus family has been subject to a great deal of study recently, leading to many name changes. These have not been universally acclaimed or accepted, and a number of genera that have recently been combined are included here separately, in contrast to some other modern treatments. That is because this is not a work of academic botany, but a book designed to allow the reader to see plants under the names where they are most likely to be found in lists of cactus plants or seeds for sale, or on the label on a pot.

The owners of cactus nurseries tend to be conservative where generic names are concerned. Genera such as *Pseudolobivia*, *Soehrensia*, *Helianthocereus*, *Acantholobivia*, *Aylostera*, *Krainzia*, *Bartschella*, *Navajoa*, *Submatucana*, *Eriocactus*, and *Brasiliparodia*, (among others) are still used routinely, long after they have been abandoned elsewhere. As for the generic names used in this book, the author does not for one moment believe, for example, that *Lobivia*, *Trichocereus,* and *Echinopis* are three distinct genera, but for practical purposes it is convenient to treat them as such here. Similarly, *Notocactus* has not been subsumed in *Parodia*; *Sulcorebutia* and *Weingartia* have been kept separate from *Rebutia*; and *Neoporteria* and *Pyrrhocactus* are not included in *Eriosyce*—all in contravention of the latest botanical thinking. However, the most recent name is mentioned where possible in the species entry.

SPECIES DESCRIPTIONS

Each species description comprises three elements: *Data, Background Information,* and *Photograph*.

Data. Included for each species is a description of the basic characteristics of the plant. In the main, this information has been gleaned from the initial description, when the plant (type specimen) was originally named. In many instances the often rather basic description has been amplified, partly because of the author's own experience or that of other workers, and partly because several other species have often been included within the original one since its initial description.

To begin with, the basic structure of each cactus is described under the headings *Form*, *Spines*, and *Flower*. You will find definitions of the small number of technical terms used in the *Glossary* (page 517).

Included in *Flower* there is usually a mention of when it can be expected to appear, either in cultivation or in habitat (sometimes both). The dates given under cultivation are those experienced by the author in southern England. Flowering dates in other areas, such as California or the south of France, may differ from these—as will those in the southern hemisphere. Flowering dates in habitat are based mainly on the author's own observations. Unfortunately, information on the time when flowering occurs in habitat is somewhat scarce.

Flowering time from seed is based on the author's own methods of seed-raising and subsequent cultivation. Other people may find that their plants flower after a shorter or longer period, depending on their methods. This information is therefore included as a helpful guide to complete beginners who have no idea about how long plants from various genera take to flower from seed.

Distribution indicates the known areas where the plants are to be found in the wild.

Background Information covers a range of topics relevant to each species. This may include species synonyms (names under which the species may have been described or listed before or proposed for the future), similar species, features of the plant in the wild (often as observed by the author), cultivation hints, and much more.

Photographs were all taken by the author either of plants in their natural habitat or in his collection, often of plants grown on from seed collected from the wild. Most photographs show the plants in full flower.

Code Numbers. Frequently in the texts code numbers such as PM140, RBC397, and Lau 025 are cited. When cactus enthusiasts collect seeds or plants from habitat, they normally allocate a number that is subsequently used in plant lists and should always be kept with the plant. See table opposite for further information.

CACTUS COLLECTORS

The cacti that we grow and enjoy today have almost all been discovered by enthusiastic amateurs. Several names stand out, appearing over and over on photos of documented plant material, as in this book. Friedrich Ritter left his native Germany in the 1950s to spend much of the rest of his life exploring for cacti, firstly (but only briefly) in Mexico, and then for several decades in South America. He discovered hundreds of new species, not all of which have stood the test of time, but including current favorites such as *Notocactus magnificus* and *Rebutia albiflora*.

South America was also the lure for the Austrian Walter Rausch, who made his first trip in the early 1960s. A great deal of Rausch's material has survived to this day as vegetative propagations, especially in *Lobivia*, *Rebutia*, and *Sulcorebutia*. As with Ritter, many of Rausch's new names have since been lumped into earlier names—often by

Rausch himself, who has changed his ideas about species as his knowledge has grown.

Perhaps the best-known name in the whole of the cactus world, because it is linked to so many discoveries both in Mexico and South America, is Alfred Lau, commemorated in plants such as *Copiapoa laui* and *Echinocereus laui*. He is renowned for being tireless in his determination to seek out new plants or track down the lost localities of old ones. He is also famed for having a "nose" for where exciting new plants could be, often turning up amazing novelties in areas that to anyone else would seem absolutely barren and unpromising.

For Ritter, Rausch, and Lau, the physical difficulties in actually getting to see the plants, especially in South

Collectors' Codes and Abbreviations

The origin and ownership of the plant material in this book is referred to by a collector's code and number. Abbreviations of names are as follows:

LB Lüdwig Bercht	**ML** Michel Lacoste
RBC Ramirez Brothers Cacti	**PM** Ken Preston-Mafham
DJF Dave Ferguson	**GN** Gert G. Neuhuber
RMF Roger Ferryman	**WP** Wolfgang Papsch
AH Andreas Hofacker	**WR** Walter Rausch
ZJ Zlatko Janeba	**FR** Friedrich Ritter
HK H. Kuenzler	**HS** Heinz Swoboda
FK F. Kühhas	**HT** Hans Till
KK K. Knize	

An Argentinian landscape high in the Andes to the east of Yavi, Jujuy, covered with magnificent Oreocereus celsianus *cacti.*

America, were far greater than they are today. Roads were less developed, or did not exist at all, and vehicles were not like modern four-by-fours. The number of hobbyists who can live their dream and see their beloved plants in their natural home seems to grow every year, and numerous names have recently become familiar, attached to material that is widespread in cultivation and that usually originates from seed collected in habitat. It is not uncommon for people to make the pilgrimage to South America or Mexico every year, and it is now often easier to find good pictures of plants in habitat than in cultivation—the reverse of the situation 20 years ago.

Among the more recent names quoted on plants illustrated in this book, two of the most familiar are Andreas Hofacker, who leaves his native Germany most years to travel in Brazil, and Roger Ferryman, who has traveled extensively over many years in Chile and Argentina from his home in England. A full list of numbers and plants covering most of the best-known collectors is available on the Cactus Mall website (see page 518). Lists for Alfred Lau have been printed in the form of booklets giving additional habitat details. These may be obtained from dealers specializing in cactus books.

CULTIVATION

Composts. The descriptions accompanying each plant seldom mention composts. This is because the types of composts available will depend largely on where the reader lives, often being proprietary products that are only available in certain countries. In the United Kingdom a popular mix (used by the author) consists of one-third coarse grit (not limestone), one-third peat-free compost (a composted bark product is best), and one-third John Innes (a mix containing, among other things, loam, grit, and fertilizer). Some people use a similar combination but in different percentages, often adding perlite granules. Various brands of baked-clay granules are also available, giving good results for some people, but not working at all for others—something that also applies to vermiculite.

In Europe and North America pumice granules are very popular, often used on their own, while in the United Kingdom some people use various types of grit, on their own or combined with a coarse sand. The advantage of these purely mineral composts is said to be that repotting can be quite infrequent, whereas in organically based composts, such as the coir/peat-free/perlite mix used with great success by some commercial growers, repotting needs to be done each year for the plants to thrive.

Potting. With the author's preferred mix, repotting is recommended every two to three years, but many species are still growing well in the author's somewhat neglected collection after five to six years. When repotting, all the old compost should be thoroughly removed from the roots, especially if changing compost types (for example, from a peat-free/coir mix to a more mineral-based medium).

If the roots are very long and bushy it can be useful to trim them back so they do not lie in a lank mass in the new compost, which should be used in a relatively dry (but not dusty) state. Try cutting up old newspapers to fit in the bottom of the pot. This keeps soil from falling out of the drainage hole but allows water to drain through. It also gives you a good idea of whether or not the compost has fully dried out. Look under the pot: if the paper is dry, you can be pretty sure that the whole of the compost is, too.

Cactus cultivation is often carried out on a large scale, as in this specialized nursery.

When repotting your plant always use the next pot size up, rather than jumping one or two sizes, since many cacti refuse to settle into a pot that is much too big for them. Plastic pots are the norm.

Watering. Watering overhead with a rose is quickest, but it gives you little control over how much each plant receives. You may prefer to water each plant individually with a can, which allows you to check it for general health and the presence of pests such as red spider mites. In the author's experience the best method is to ensure that the compost is thoroughly wetted, then wait for it to dry out completely, although this is not so essential when using organic composts such as coir/composted-bark mixes.

Roots that are not allowed to dry out completely do not seem to rot as readily in these mediums as in those containing loam. In the temperate northern hemisphere most people withhold water completely from late September to mid-March (or early to mid-April if the weather is dull). If organic or purely mineral composts are used, you will need to add a suitable fertilizer to your water supply, preferably one that dissolves fully. Most proprietary composts already have a fertilizer added, but topping it up after a few months when watering will give better growth.

Light and Ventilation. In habitat a surprising number of cacti live in fairly deep shade beneath trees and bushes, although the shade is often only temporary, when the trees leaf out during the wet season. In dull temperate climates the sun comes and goes, with searingly hot sunny days following suddenly after weeks of dull misery. This makes managing the greenhouse very difficult, and a portable form of shading, such as netting, is the best answer. The alternative of painting a water-soluble shade mix onto the glass is less satisfactory—it makes matters worse because it is still there throughout the dull periods when maximum light is needed. (In regions with almost constant sun, however, this is not a problem.)

Cacti growing near the glass are particularly vulnerable to scorching in hot weather, which at the least can disfigure a specimen plant, and at worst will kill it. Good ventilation can help minimize this. Fans are the best solution, but since they use electricity they are not very environmentally friendly. In really hot summers the only answer may be the temporary removal of several panes of glass.

Not everyone has a greenhouse. Some people are obliged to keep their cactus collection on a windowsill,

which should be as sunny as possible, otherwise growth may become deformed and flowering inhibited. In winter it is best not to keep your plants on a windowsill next to a radiator: they will dry out too thoroughly and may have problems getting back into growth come springtime.

Winter Care. Most cacti are surprisingly hardy and can withstand relatively prolonged periods of frost. Certain species, particularly those from the United States or Patagonia, can cope with long periods at very low temperatures. Damp can be more of a problem, and it is vital to remove all fruits or dead flowers throughout the winter, to prevent mildew from making its way into the plant and killing it. De-fruiting your mammillarias is crucial,

The brown areas on this Ferocactus macrodiscus *are the result of damage caused by exposure to low temperatures.*

as is taking off any dead flowers from late-flowering parodias (if your climate is damp, take them indoors if the flowers cannot be detached). Really winter-tender cacti include all species of *Melocactus*, *Pilosocereus*, and *Uebelmannia*. Other winter-tender species are mentioned in the text. Frost does not always kill the plant, but can so disfigure it that it is not worth keeping, as evidenced by the unsightly brown marks on the *Ferocactus macrodiscus* illustrated here. The author keeps his greenhouse at about 40°F (4°C), which seems fine for everything except the more tender types. As long as these are not too numerous, the simplest thing is to take them indoors for the winter.

Growing Cacti from Seed. A collection of plants that you have raised yourself from seed undoubtedly gives the maximum satisfaction and is very easy to achieve. Cactus seed generally germinates well, and though often very small, the seedlings are surprisingly tough. For the first few weeks the compost should never be allowed to dry out and should be kept shaded at all times. At this stage the main enemies are damping off (use adequate ventilation and don't make the compost *too* wet) and fungus gnats, whose tiny maggotlike larvae chew into the tender seedlings.

Easy-to-Grow Cacti for the Beginner

Aporocactus flagelliformis	*Mammillaria bocasana*
Austrocylindropuntia subulata	*Mammillaria elongata*
Cleistocactus straussii	*Mammillaria petterssonii*
Copiapoa coquimbana	*Matucana aureiflora*
Echinocactus grusonii	*Notocactus herteri*
Echinocereus coccineus	*Notocactus magnificus*
Ferocactus hystrix	*Oreocereus trollii*
Gymnocalycium monvillei	*Oroya peruviana*
Gymnocalycium schickendantzii	*Parodia chrysacanthion*
Lobivia pentlandii	*Rebutia albiflora*
Mammillaria albata	*Rebutia flavistyla*
	Stenocactus crispatus
	Sulcorebutia crispata
	Thelocactus rinconensis

Insecticidal drenches are often disappointingly ineffective, and the best answer (as used by a large-scale commercial grower) is to sprinkle aquarium-type grit onto the surface of the compost a week or two after all the seedlings have germinated. The grit inhibits the egg-laying females, since they prefer moist, highly organic egg-laying sites, but does not seem to affect the seedlings adversely—even when buried, they eventually grow up through the grit.

How to Sow Seed. Sprinkle the seeds thinly on a suitable growing medium, but do not cover any seeds, (except very large ones, such as opuntias). Maintain at a temperature of 64 to 75ºF (18–24ºC) and keep moist but not wet. Water by gentle overhead spraying or part-immersion of the container in water until it just starts to wet the whole surface. Prick out the seedlings into fresh compost at about one year old.

Vegetative Propagation. Plants can also be increased vegetatively. Offsets or stem segments can be detached, either by pulling on them—when they often break free relatively easily—or by cutting through the narrowest point of attachment with a sharp knife. In the latter case, dry the cut surface for a few days before rooting up in your normal growing medium. Several cuttings crowded in closely together often seem to root far more readily than lone cuttings.

Pests. Unfortunately, pests tend to be cosmopolitan and we all suffer equally, wherever we may be. As with composts, pesticides have local names, so there is not much point in going into details here, except to say that the recent advent of some very effective systemic compounds (that are actively absorbed by the plant via its roots) has brought about more effective control of mealy bug and root

mealy bug than has hitherto been possible. Red spider mite remains a problem, partly because its presence may not be suspected until damage has been done, as is obvious from the scarred apex of a *Lobivia saltensis* illustrated here. Over the last few years western flower thrip has spread around the world, adding yet another problem to those already suffered by the cactophile. This small blackish insect attacks the flowers and nibbles at the apex of certain

The scarring on the apex of this Lobivia saltensis *was caused by red spider mites.*

cacti when they are in fresh growth, or during the winter when flowers are not available. In the author's collection the apex of *Gymnocalycium monvillei* is constantly attacked, as are the tender growing points of most species of *Escobaria*. Once again, excellent new treatments are available, but you need to keep on top of the problem.

PURCHASING TIPS

Until you gain experience it is probably best to buy only plants that you can see. After that, you may wish to use mail order. Never buy plants that you know to have been collected from the wild: this is usually both illegal and environmental vandalism. The only exception is when plants are removed legally from development sites. Even then, good seed-grown plants are almost always far more attractive and do much better in cultivation.

Acanthocalycium spiniflorum violaceum

Form: Simple. 11.8 in (30 cm) high or more; 5.1 in (13 cm) across.

Spines: Numerous, yellowish, up to 1.6 in (4 cm) long. Radials and centrals intermixed and difficult to distinguish.

Flower: Various shades of lilac to almost white. To 1.6 in (4 cm) broad. In cultivation June–August; in habitat November–December.

Flowering time from seed: 5–6 years.

Distribution: Argentina (Córdoba, e.g., around Quines, Yacanto, and Mina Cavera).

The white-flowered *Acanthocalycium spiniflorum* is often found in abundance in the woodlands of southern Córdoba and northern San Luis. Its variability has led to it being described by various names, such as *A. klimpelianum* and *A. peitscherianum*. These are better considered as forms, as with *violaceum*, which was also originally described as a separate species. The color of the flowers varies a little from place to place and even among the plants in a single locality.

The plant illustrated is growing near Salsacate, Córdoba, Argentina. Note the dead fern fronds from the previous year. When the new fronds are fully grown, they will probably cover the plant to a large extent.

Ancistrocactus scheerii

At various times this plant has been included in *Ferocactus*, *Pediocactus*, and *Sclerocactus*. Given this lack of consistency, it is perhaps best to give it its own genus—*Ancistrocactus*—in which it is most often listed by specialist dealers. It can be a little tricky to grow, since it tends to rot off at the roots. It therefore needs to be kept relatively dry, except perhaps for the first two months of growth after its winter rest, when it puts on a spurt. It then slows to a crawl for the hottest part of the summer, at which time water should be given only sparingly—just enough to prevent any shriveling.

The plant illustrated below was grown from seed that was collected at Ojo Caliente, New Mexico.

DATA

Form: Simple. Up to 3.9 in (10 cm) high and 2.4 in (6 cm) across.

Spines: Radials 15–18; whitish. Centrals 3–4; hooked; 0.8–2 in (2–5 cm) long.

Flower: Greenish yellow. 1 in (2.5 cm) long. In cultivation April–May.

Flowering time from seed: 4–5 years.

Distribution: Northern Mexico; United States (Texas).

17

Aporocactus flagelliformis

Form: Stems clumping, thin, pendant. Length up to 6.6 ft (2 m).

Spines: Weak, bristly, and relatively dense; brownish yellow.

Flower: Bright pink. 2.4–2.8 in (6–7 cm) long. Open for several days, appearing over a long period in spring and early summer in cultivation.

Flowering time from seed: Not available; normally grown from cuttings.

Distribution: Mexico (Hidalgo).

This plant, often called the rat's-tail cactus, is best grown in a hanging basket, allowing the long thin stems to hang down freely. Water can be given generously during warm weather. Seed is not normally available, propagation being from cuttings that root easily if taken in early summer. In the latest botanical treatments this plant is listed under *Disocactus*.

The illustration shows a vegetative propagation from a plant originally collected north of Zimapán, Hidalgo, Mexico.

Ariocarpus retusus

Form: Up to 9.8 in (25 cm) broad, usually smaller and relatively flattened, with a large taproot. The plant is covered with more or less erect, broadly based gray tubercles that taper upward to a fine tip.

Spines: None.

Flower: White to pale pink. 1.6 in (4 cm) across. Appears in late fall in cultivation (late August–early October in habitat).

Flowering time from seed: 15 years on average.

Distribution: Mexico. Widespread and often common from north of Saltillo, Coahuila, southward to San Luis Potosí city.

This splendid plant usually grows among loose limestone rubble, making it very hard to spot in its natural surroundings. Plants from the northern part of its range (as illustrated) tend to have convex-topped tubercles with sharpish tips, and are sometimes known as *Ariocarpus furfuraceus*; in those from the south the tubercles are flat topped and blunt tipped.

The plant illustrated was growing on limestone hills south of Matehuala, San Luis Potosí.

Armatocereus matucanensis

Form: Treelike, gray green, branching, with a woody trunk. Up to 20 ft (6 m) high or more.

Spines: Radials 4–7; centrals 1–3. To 5.9 in (15 cm) long.

Flower: White. 2.8–3.5 in (7–9 cm) long.

Flowering time from seed: 20 years plus.

Distribution: Central Peru, e.g., valleys east of Lima.

For many years nobody saw much of these large-growing plants in cultivation, but in recent times many hobbyists have visited Peru and brought back seeds collected in habitat from the large, very spiny fruits. Whereas flowers are not likely to be seen under glass in cultivation, the plants themselves are distinctive and interesting. They have plump gray-green segments, with a new one added each year so that the stems resemble a string of sausages. The plants are not very hardy, however, and should be kept in a warm greenhouse.

The plant illustrated is in the Eulalia valley near Lima. Note the large spiny fruits on the tips of the branches.

Arrojadoa rhodantha

Arrojadoas are noted for their cylindrical flowers, which are produced from brushlike tufts of long bristles situated at the ends of the stems. Although individually not spectacular, the flowers are striking when produced in numbers, as in the accompanying illustration. Like all cacti from the tropical regions of Brazil, arrojadoas should be kept well above freezing in winter. A number of attractive forms have been described, including subspecies *canudosensis* and *aureispina*.

The plant illustrated was grown from commercial seed of unknown provenance.

DATA

Form: Shrubby, often sprawling. Stems up to 6.6 ft (2 m) high; 0.8–1.2 in (2–3 cm) across.

Spines: Radials and centrals mixed; about 20. To 1.2 in (3 cm) long.

Flower: Pinkish to bluish red. To 1.4 in (3.5 cm) long; 0.6 in (1.5 cm) across. June–July in cultivation.

Flowering time from seed: 5–6 years.

Distribution: Brazil (Bahia, Piauí, and Pernambuco).

Astrophytum capricorne

DATA

Form: Spherical at first, becoming elongated. To 14 in (35 cm) high; 6 in (15 cm) across.

Spines: Brown. Up to 10, very flexible and interlacing, eventually being shed from the oldest areoles. To 2.8 in (7 cm) long.

Flower: Glossy yellow with a carmine center. To 2.8 in (7 cm) long. Lasts several days; appears mostly June–August in cultivation and in habitat.

Flowering time from seed: 4–5 years.

Distribution: Mexico (Coahuila).

Plants of this lovely species are usually covered in a variable amount of white flock. This is particularly dense in var. *niveum*, which also has shorter, more rigid spination. In *Astrophytum senile*, now generally regarded as a form of *A. capricorne*, the flock is so sparse that the body appears more or less green, while the lowermost spines are not shed with age. These plants are all very intolerant of overwatering and overpotting, so beware of both.

The plant illustrated was grown from seed collected 16 miles (26 km) west of Saltillo, Coahuila.

Astrophytum myriostigma

Form: Up to 11.8 in (30 cm) or more high; 5.9 in (15 cm) across.

Spines: None.

Flower: Satiny yellow, often with a reddish throat. Sweetly scented. 1.2–2.4 in (3–6 cm) across. Produced from May through August in cultivation.

Flowering time from seed: 3–4 years.

Distribution: Widespread but scattered in the northern and central highlands of Mexico.

The dense white scales that cover the body of most specimens of this popular plant act as an effective sunscreen as well as being very decorative. This is the easiest member of the genus to grow, although it is intolerant of overwatering. Various named forms are often listed, varying in body size, number of ribs—usually 5, sometimes 4, but occasionally only 3—and size of flower. The most distinctive form is the plain shiny green var. *nudum*.

The plant illustrated above was grown from seed collected near Buenavista, San Luis Potosí.

Austrocylindropuntia floccosa

Form: In habitat forms cushions up to 6.6 ft (2 m) across, but smaller in cultivation. Individual segments to over 3.9 in (10 cm) long and 1.2 in (3 cm) across.

Spines: Yellowish. Usually 1–3, sometimes absent. 0.4–1.2 in (1–3 cm) long. Variable amounts of tangled white hairs are intermixed with the spines.

Flower: Yellowish to orange or red. Up to 1.2 in (3 cm) long; 1.4 in (3.5 cm) across. Mostly flowering December–March in habitat.

Flowering time from seed: 10–20 years.

Distribution: Peru to northern Bolivia, on the altiplano at between 11,500 and 15,000 ft (3,500–4,600 m).

This beautiful species is grown for its often dense ornament of white hairs rather than for its flowers, which are seldom produced in cultivation. In habitat adjacent mounds can be densely hairy or quite naked, looking like separate species. The most attractive white-woolly clone widely available in cultivation seems to be HS30a from Morochata, Bolivia. Because of its high-altitude habitat, this species is completely hardy in winter if kept dry. Seed can be difficult (sometimes impossible) to germinate; propagation is usually by cuttings.

The plant illustrated was growing near Huaras in the Cordillera Blanca, Peru.

Austrocylindropuntia shaferi

This cold-resistant species forms a much stouter plant than the similar *Austrocylindropuntia vestita* and makes a handsome and fast-growing specimen in cultivation, since it is less likely to sprawl. Most plants offered by dealers are vegetative propagations derived from seed collected in habitat. Curt Backeberg's *A. humahuacana* and *A. weingartiana* seem to be simply forms of this species.

The plant illustrated below was seen growing in the Quebrada de Humahuaca, Jujuy, Argentina.

DATA

Form: Branched, upright plants to 23.6 in (60 cm) or more high; stems to 2 in (5 cm) broad.

Spines: Centrals 3–5; to 2.4 in (6 cm) long; sharp. Radials up to 15 or more, mixed with sparse white hairs.

Flower: Violet red. Up to 1 in (2.5 cm) across. Mainly seen during July in cultivation but November–December in habitat.

Flowering time from seed: 6–8 years.

Distribution: From southern Bolivia (around Tupiza) to northern Argentina.

Austrocylindropuntia subulata

Form: An erect mass of shrubby branches up to 13.2 ft (4 m) high with a woody trunk 2.4–3.9 in (6–10 cm) across; in cultivation much smaller.

Spines: 1–2 or more, up to 3.2 in (8 cm) long, but usually poorly developed in cultivated specimens. The areoles also bear cylindrical leaves up to 4.7 in (12 cm) or more long.

Flower: Reddish, but rarely seen in cultivation. Up to 2.8 in (7 cm) long.

Flowering time from seed: 10–20 years.

Distribution: Widespread in Peru.

Although often sneered at by more advanced hobbyists, this has always been a popular plant with beginners and is still supplied in numbers to retail outlets in order to satisfy the constant demand. It will do reasonably well on a windowsill, is tolerant of poor treatment, shrugs off cold weather, and grows easily from cuttings.

The illustration shows the kind of plant that is turned out in its thousands each year from cuttings to supply the "windowsill" trade.

Austrocylindropuntia verschaffeltii

DATA

Form: Clumps growing to 7.8–19.6 in (20–50 cm) across, consisting of numerous pencil-thin, upright stems each reaching 4–7.9 in (10–20 cm) high.

Spines: Sparse, bristly, whitish. Up to 1.2 in (3 cm) long.

Flower: Orange to red, very lustrous. 0.8–1.6 in (2–4 cm) across.

Flowering time from seed: 5–6 years.

Distribution: Bolivia to northern Argentina.

This species is usually offered in the form of propagations from field-collected plants (rather than from seed). Cultivated plants are generally spindly, but growing them in a 50–50 mixture of coir and composted bark (peat-free compost) gives stouter bodies and longer spines than when using gritty composts. Some clones are more free-flowering than others, so ask before you buy.

The plant illustrated was growing on the Abra de Infernillo, Tucumán, Argentina.

Bolivicereus samaipatanus

DATA

Form: Groups of erect or sprawling branching stems up to 5 ft (1.5 m high) and 1.4–1.6 in (3.5–4 cm) across.

Spines: 13–22, thin, brownish, yellowish, or pale gray. 0.2–1.2 in (4–30 mm) long.

Flower: Deep blood red with a purple sheen. Up to 1.6 in (4 cm) long.

Flowering time from seed: 4–5 years.

Distribution: Bolivia (Santa Cruz, near Samaipata).

When out of flower it can be a temptation to throw out this rather scruffy plant to make some space. Any such thoughts are immediately swept away by the sheer extravagant beauty of the brilliant red tubular blooms with their subtle violet sheen, designed mainly to attract hummingbirds as pollinators. Although growing well enough from seed, many plants are vegetative propagations from habitat-collected material.

The plant illustrated is a typical commercial specimen of unknown origin.

Browningia candelaris

With its long, straight, densely spined trunk surmounted by a tuft of wavy stems, a mature plant of this species in habitat is like no other cactus. Unfortunately, we cannot grow specimens to this size under glass in cultivation, but seedlings have become available in recent years as more and more collectors have visited the South American cactus habitats and brought home supplies of seed. Seed-grown plants are reasonably handsome but they are slow-growing and prone to rot off if left too wet. They are also not very hardy against the cold.

The plant illustrated was growing in northern Chile, beside the road from Arica into Bolivia.

DATA

Form: Treelike, grows to 16.4 ft (5 m) high; trunk woody, to 19.6 in (50 cm) across.

Spines: In mature plants only on the trunk. To 5.9 in (15 cm) long.

Flower: White or flushed pink. 3.2–4.7 in (8–12 cm) long.

Flowering time from seed: 30 years plus.

Distribution: Northern Chile to Tinajas Canyon south of Lima, Peru.

Cephalocereus senilis

DATA

Form: Only infrequently branching. To 49 ft (15 m) high; 17.7 in (45 cm) across.

Spines: 3–5 yellowish or gray spines up to 1.6 in (4 cm) long, mixed with 20–30 white floppy hairs.

Flower: Pale yellowish white. To 3 in (7.5 cm) broad.

Flowering time from seed: Up to 50 years.

Distribution: Mexico (Hidalgo, near Metztitlán).

Popularly known as the "old man cactus," the typical commercial specimen illustrated here used to be an old favorite and was grown in large numbers. Lately, however, it seems to have fallen out of fashion. It was always grown for its shaggy-dog appearance rather than its flowers, which are most unlikely to be seen in cultivation, since they are produced only on plants 19.6 ft (6 m) or so tall. Don't be afraid to shampoo the hairs when they get dirty, using a dilute detergent followed by a good rinse. Winter can be a problem—keep temperatures above 46°F (8°C).

Cereus repandus

Formerly included in the genus *Subpilocereus* (and often still listed as such), this is a tropical plant that needs to be maintained in a warm environment during winter. As with many of the cereoid cacti, seed from habitat has been freely available in recent years and produces seedlings that are distinctive and extremely handsome, with attractive neat spination. In habitat the fruits are eagerly eaten by parakeets, orioles, and other birds that spread the seeds in their droppings.

The plant illustrated is growing on Bonaire, PM140.

DATA

Form: Treelike, strongly branching. To 39 ft (12 m) high.

Spines: Radials 7–13. Centrals 1–7; up to 2.6 in (6.5 cm) long.

Flower: White, greenish white, or pinkish. 2.4–4.3 in (6–11 cm) long.

Flowering time from seed: 20 years.

Distribution: Grenada; Netherlands Antilles; coastal areas of Venezuela and Colombia.

Cintia knizei

Form: Simple, with a long carrotlike taproot. Grows to 1.2–1.6 in (3–4 cm) across.

Spines: Absent, but the areoles bear short whitish wool.

Flower: Yellow. 1.2–1.6 in (3–4 cm) across. April–May in cultivation.

Flowering time from seed: 3–4 years.

Distribution: Bolivia (Dept. Chuquisaca near Otavi) at 13,000 ft (4,000 m).

This plant was discovered in 1969 but did not receive a name until 1996. Since then it has become a "must" for any collectors who have a liking for plants that are both miniature and supposedly rare. In the early days, after its initial discovery, relatively high prices were paid for specimens. These days it is more freely available from specialist nurseries. Many people have little success with this plant on its own roots, and grow it on a graft, but cuttings thrive in a mix of coir and composted bark (peat-free) with some additional perlite.

The plant illustrated above is a vegetative propagation from a plant collected near the type locality.

Cleistocactus baumannii

This is one of a small number of cacti that inhabit the very hot lowlands on the eastern side of the Andes. These relatively flat areas are dominated by thorny trees and scrub, beneath which the cacti grow. The stems of this species start off by growing upright but soon begin to flop over. You may want to stake the stems to keep them upright. In cultivation flowers are produced less freely than in some other members of the genus. *Cleistocactus bruneispinus* and *C. flavispinus* are synonyms. *Cleistocactus chacoanus* and *C. horstii*—with thinner, more sprawling stems—are much more free-flowering and are both now treated as subspecies of *C. baumannii*.

The plant illustrated below was seen growing in habitat near Cruz del Eje in northwestern Argentina.

DATA

Form: Stems erect, then sprawling. To 3.3 ft (1 m) or more long; 1–1.2 in (2.5–3 cm) across.

Spines: Radials 15–20, to 0.6 in (1.5 cm) long. Centrals 1; to 1.2 in (3 cm) long; yellowish to dark brown.

Flower: More or less tubular, flame red. To 2.8 in (7 cm) long. Produced May–June in cultivation; October–November in habitat.

Flowering time from seed: 5–8 years.

Distribution: Lowland areas of northwestern Argentina; also Uruguay and Paraguay.

Cleistocactus brookeae

DATA

Form: To 19.6 in (50 cm) high; 1 in (2.5 cm) across.

Spines: Numerous, yellow. Up to 0.4 in (1 cm) long.

Flower: Dark reddish orange; S-shaped. About 2 in (5 cm) long. Occurring May–June in cultivation.

Flowering time from seed: 5–6 years.

Distribution: Bolivia (Santa Cruz, near Pozo No. 4, Camiri).

With its dense golden spination, this is one of the most handsome members of the genus. The very distinctive flowers arise near the apex of the stems and, although not produced in the large numbers that are seen in some other species, are well worth seeing. *Cleistocactus wendlandiorum* appears to be identical.

The plant illustrated above is a vegetative propagation from a plant collected at the type locality.

Cleistocactus candelilla

Few people would bother growing this plant for its looks, but during its satisfyingly long flowering period it is transformed into a real stunner. The very distinctive and highly flamboyant flowers are dispensed in great masses, adorning the stems for some distance down from the growing apex. Tall plants start to lean and may break off if left to their own devices. Either stake them or start again by taking a good-sized topcut—say 11.8 in (30 cm). It should root easily enough.

The plant illustrated below is a vegetative propagation from a plant that was collected near Cochabamba.

DATA

Form: Stems erect, then prostrate. To 3.3 ft (1 m) high; 0.8–1.2 cm (2–3 cm) across.

Spines: Radials 13–15, 0.2 in (5 mm) long. Centrals 3–4, slightly flattened. All glassy whitish.

Flower: Tubular; petals purple with a white border; sepals yellow tipped, projecting. 1.2–2 in (3–5 cm) long. In cultivation flowering occurs continuously over several weeks in May and June.

Flowering time from seed: 5–6 years.

Distribution: Bolivia (province of Florida, Pampa Grande).

Cleistocactus hyalacanthus

Form: Clumps of erect
stems up to 3.3 ft (1 m)
high; 1.6 in (4 cm) across.

Spines: Fairly dense.
Radials 25–30, whitish.
Centrals stouter, brownish
to yellowish, 1.2 in (3 cm)
or more long.

Flower: Tubular, scarlet.
To 1.6 in (4 cm) long.
Produced during May
and June in cultivation;
October–December
in habitat.

**Flowering time from
seed:** 4–6 years.

Distribution: Argentina
(Jujuy and Salta).

This plant has numerous merits. It is quick to flower from seed, flowers freely over a long period, and is handsome enough to earn a place in the collection even when sterile. Backeberg's *Cleistocactus jujuyensis* appears to be simply a redescription, while *C. tarijensis* from around Tarija in Bolivia seems to be nothing more than a slightly smaller form with shorter but otherwise identical flowers.

*The plant illustrated is growing in the
Quebrada del Toro, Salta, PM320.*

Cleistocactus smaragdiflorus

DATA

Form: Stems mostly sprawling; up to 3.3 ft (1 m) long and 1.4 in (3.5 cm) across.

Spines: Fairly dense, glassy yellowish. Variable in length from one locality to another.

Flower: Tubular; tube and ovary reddish pink, limb greenish yellow. To 2 in (5 cm) long. Produced during May and June in cultivation; October–December in habitat.

Flowering time from seed: 3–4 years.

Distribution: Paraguay and northern Argentina.

It is the eye-catchingly bicolored nature of the flowers that makes this otherwise undistinguished plant worth having in a collection. Fortunately, the flowers are freely produced over a long period. The stems tend to stay a little thin and may need staking with age, although it is probably easier to take a few cuttings and start afresh. *Cleistocactus ferrarii* from cliff faces north of Salta appears to be simply a form of this species with denser, shorter spination; the flowers seem to be identical, although perhaps slightly shorter.

The plant illustrated above was seen growing on the Cuesta de Portezuelo, Catamarca, PM286.

Cleistocactus strausii

DATA

Form: In habitat to 5 ft (1.5 m) high, but much larger when planted out in a bed in cultivation. Stem 1.6–3.2 in (4–8 cm) across.

Spines: Radials 30–40, hairlike, white; to 0.7 in (1.7 cm) long. Centrals 4, yellowish; to 0.8 in (2 cm) or more long.

Flower: Tubular, dingy wine red with brown hairs. 3.2–3.5 in (8–9 cm) long. Produced June–July in cultivation; October–November in habitat.

Flowering time from seed: 8–9 years.

Distribution: Southern Bolivia (near Tarija).

"Nice plant, pity about the flowers" probably sums up many people's opinions of this highly ornamental plant, the best of the bunch within the genus. Unlike most of its relatives, it looks good all year around. The flowers, although large and distinctively shaped, are a dullish shade of red. Old plants tend to get tatty lower down, so you may want to chop off a few heads and start again.

The plant illustrated was growning near the Condor Pass, PM189.

Cleistocactus viridiflorus

DATA

Form: Clumping. Stems to 5 ft (1.5 m) high; 0.9 in (2.2 cm) across.

Spines: Radials 15–18; to 0.4 in (1 cm) long. Centrals to 0.9 in (2.2 cm), scarcely distinguishable.

Flower: Green. About 1.4 in (3.5 cm) long. Produced over a long period in summer in cultivation.

Flowering time from seed: 5–6 years.

Distribution: Bolivia (Ayata).

This is a strongly growing, relatively handsome plant that flowers in great profusion for some distance along its stems. Although not brightly colored, the fact that the flower is green holds a certain fascination because of its rarity within the cactus family. Like many members of this genus, cultivated plants are not as sturdy as those in habitat, and unless supported in some way they may break off when they get too tall to support their own weight. Some people regard this species as merely a form of *Cleistocactus palhuayacensis*.

The plant illustrated above was grown from seed that was collected near Ayata, La Paz, RBC397.

Cleistocactus vulpis-cauda

Form: Pendant, branching from the base. Stems to 6.6 ft (2 m long) and 0.8–2 in (2–5 cm) across.

Spines: Consist of about 50 flexible reddish to whitish hairs 0.4–0.8 cm (1–2 cm) long.

Flower: Red and orange. Up to 2.4 in (6 cm) long. Produced over a long period in summer in cultivation.

Flowering time from seed: 5–6 years.

Distribution: Bolivia (province of Tomina, on sheer cliffs at Puente Acero).

This plant is closely related to *Cleistocactus brookeae*, but while that species grows upright, the long stems of *C. vulpis-cauda* hang down, reflecting its habit of growing on almost inaccessible cliff faces. Consequently, it should be grown in a hanging pot in cultivation, where it makes a handsome specimen, especially when covered in its attractive long-lasting flowers.

The plant illustrated is a vegetative propagation from a plant that was collected from the type locality.

Cochemiea maritima

For some time *Cochemiea* was subsumed into *Mammillaria*, but recent DNA evidence has indicated that is deserves to be treated as a separate genus after all. (It is often demoted to a subspecies of *C. pondii*.) *Cochemiea maritima* is one of the most free-flowering members of the genus, although some plants are less obliging than others in this respect. As is typical of *Cochemiea*, propagations from old field-collected material flower best.

The plant illustrated is a vegetative propagation from a plant that was collected at Santa Rosalillita, Baja California, Lau 025.

DATA

Form: Dense colonies. Stems bluish green; 20 in (50 cm) high and 1.2–2.8 in (3–7 cm) across.

Spines: Reddish brown. Radials 10–15; 0.4 in (1 cm) long. Centrals 4, the lowest one hooked; to 2 in (5 cm) long.

Flower: Scarlet. About 1.2 in (3 cm) long. Mainly produced in springtime in cultivation and often again in late summer.

Flowering time from seed: 8–10 years.

Distribution: Mexico (Baja California, Punta Blanca).

Cochemiea pondii

DATA

Form: Usually branching strongly from the base. Stem to 7.8 in (20 cm) high; 1.2–1.6 in (3–4 cm) across.

Spines: Radials 15–25. Centrals 8–11 (1–2 of which are hooked); up to 1.2 in (3 cm) long.

Flower: Scarlet. 2 in (5 cm) long. Usually produced in springtime in cultivation—often in early April, sometimes later—and again in late summer.

Flowering time from seed: 8–10 years.

Distribution: Mexico (Baja California, Cedros Island).

With its denser spination and neater mode of growth, this is a more attractive plant than *Cochemiea maritima*. It tends to be even more generous with its flowers, which usually appear as scarlet clusters at the tips of the stems. However, as with *C. maritima*, propagations from old field-collected plants flower more freely and reliably than 8- to 10-year-old seed-grown specimens. In its natural home dry arroyo beds are the favored habitat.

The plant illustrated is a vegetative propagation from a plant that was collected at Punta Norte, Cedros Island, Lau 008.

Copiapoa bridgesii

With its densely woolly areoles, especially in the crown, and its long strong spines, *Copiapoa bridgesii* is probably the most handsome specimen of any of the green-bodied copiapoas. Like most members of the genus, however, it is fairly slow-growing. However, as long as it is not overwatered, it should make steady progress and is not likely to loose its roots or suffer from any of the other little problems that afflict many more temperamental cacti. These days *C. bridgesii* is often treated as a subspecies of *C. marginata*.

The plant illustrated was growing in the hills north of Chañaral Airfield, PM261.

DATA

Form: Body green, clumping from the base. 7.8–15.8 in (20–40 cm) high; 2–3.2 in (5–8 cm) thick.

Spines: Radials 5–10, short, awl-like; 0.4–0.8 in (1–2 cm) long. Centrals 1–3, strong and relatively thick, curved upward; 0.6–2 in (1.5–5 cm) long.

Flower: Yellow. Up to 1.2 in (3 cm) across. Mainly June–July in cultivation.

Flowering time from seed: 5–6 years.

Distribution: Chile (hills to the north of Chañaral).

Copiapoa calderana

Form: Simple or clumping; grayish green. To 3.9 in (10 cm) across; 15.8 in (40 cm) or more high.

Spines: Radials 5–7; to 0.6 in (1.5) cm. Centrals 1–2; to 1.2 in (3 cm).

Flower: Yellow, scented. 1.2 in (3 cm) across. June–July in cultivation; mainly November–January in habitat.

Flowering time from seed: 8–10 years.

Distribution: Chile (coast north of Caldera).

Like so many cacti, this is a very variable plant. In some localities the plants form clusters of relatively tall heads and the body surface is covered with a grayish bloom, contrasting with blackish spines. Take a half-hour drive and you will see tiny plants with gray-green bodies and golden spines. The name *Copiapoa lembckei* is sometimes used for one of the more distinctive forms, but this is not really justified. In cultivation, growth is slow but relatively trouble-free, but the eventual result does tend to become more narrowly cylindrical than would be typical in habitat.

The plant illustrated is a dwarf form growing south of Barquito and seems to correspond to Ritter's var. spinosior.

Copiapoa cinerascens

DATA

Form: Body more or less globular, strongly clumping. Grayish green (normal green in cultivation). To 3.2 in (8 cm) or more across.

Spines: Radials up to 8; about 0.4 in (1 cm) long. Centrals mostly 1; up to 1 in (2.5 cm) long; thicker than radials.

Flower: Yellow. 0.8–1.2 in (2–3 cm) across. May– July in cultivation.

Flowering time from seed: 5–6 years.

Distribution: Chile (from near Barquito to Pan de Azúcar National Park, northwest of Chañaral).

In habitat this plant forms large mounds, mainly on gravelly and sandy coastal flats. It varies considerably, however, over a small area. For example, Ritter's var. *intermedia* clumps very sparingly and grows mainly among rocks. *Copiapa grandiflora* from Esmeralda, which has very pale yellow flowers up to 2.4 inches (6 cm) across and a more gray-green (often almost blackish) body, is simply a form of *C. cinerascens*. They all grow well and flower freely in cultivation.

The plant illustrated was grown from seed collected near Chañaral, PM210.

Copiapoa cinerea

DATA

Form: Usually forms clumps; body generally chalky white, sometimes green. To 4.3 ft (1.3 m) high; 8 in (20 cm) or more thick.

Spines: Usually 2 black spines 0.7–0.8 in (1.8–2 cm) long. Variable—sometimes many, longer, thinner, and paler spines; occasionally absent.

Flower: Yellow. 1.4 in (3.5 cm) across. May–July in cultivation, but can be shy with its flowers.

Flowering time from seed: Usually 8–10 years or more.

Distribution: Chile (to the north and south of Taltal).

With their chalky-white bodies, plants in habitat are a spectacular sight. Unfortunately, in the duller parts of Europe, such as the British Isles, seed-grown plants fail to develop this white coat to any great extent, although they are still attractive. The variety *columna-alba* from the coast around Pan de Azúcar and Esmeralda remains solitary and is even more slow-growing in cultivation. Despite the name, seedlings of var. *albispina* can have either white or black spines, but are good, vigorous growers.

The plant illustrated was growing near Taltal.

Copiapoa coquimbana

This plant is so variable that every population is distinct not only in appearance but also in the rate of growth from seed. In cultivation, plants derived from seed collected in different localities only a short distance apart may vary in size by a factor of 10 or more at 20 years old. Some forms also begin to offset when they are still young, while others remain solitary after 20 years or more. However, one thing they all have in common is that they flower freely in cultivation. The most distinctive form is probably the slow-growing var. *fiedleriana* from east of Huasco.

The plant illustrated was grown from seed collected near Punta Hornos, north of La Serena, PM403.

DATA

Form: Green, clumping to form large mounds. Single heads to 3.9 in (10 cm) across.

Spines: Very variable. Radials 8–10, thinnish. Centrals 1–2; thicker, often curved.

Flower: Yellow. To 1.2 in (3 cm) across. June–July in cultivation.

Flowering time from seed: 5–6 years.

Distribution: Chile (along the coast from south of Frai Jorge to north of Huasco and inland up the coastal valleys such as the Elqui).

Copiapoa dealbata

Form: Whitish, grayish, or green; strongly clumping to form huge mounds. Individual heads 3.2–4.7 in (8–12 cm) thick.

Spines: Radials 4–7; to 1.2 in (3 cm) long. Centrals 0–1; to 1.6 in (4 cm); black.

Flower: Yellow. To 1.2 in (3 cm) across. June–July in cultivation.

Flowering time from seed: 6–8 years.

Distribution: Chile (on the coast, from about 15 miles/25 km north of Huasco to about 18 miles/30 km north of Carrizal Bajo.

The gently rolling coastal hills near Carrizal Bajo, Chile, covered with thousands of large clumps of this magnificent cactus, must rank as one of the botanical wonders of the world. As can be seen from the illustration, the plants are in perfect condition despite the arid climate. In cultivation, growth is so slow that one can only wonder at the age of the largest clumps—up to 10 feet (3 m) across—in habitat. Ritter also described *Copiapoa carrizalensis* from this area, and this name is often used in the literature, but the plants do not differ significantly from *C. dealbata*. As with other members of the white- or gray-bodied group of copiapoas, the attractive surface bloom is scarcely developed in cultivation in some temperate areas.

Copiapoa echinata

DATA

Form: Often clumping profusely. Heads to 3.9 in (10 cm) high and broad; grayish green to blackish.

Spines: Black then gray. Radials 7–12; 0.2–0.6 in (0.5–1.5 cm) long. Centrals 4–10; 0.6–1.6 in (1.5–4 cm) long. All strong and relatively thick.

Flower: Yellow. 1.2 in (3 cm) across. May–July in cultivation.

Flowering time from seed: 8–9 years.

Distribution: Chile (along the coast north of Huasco and inland as far as Monte Amargo).

This species, often now treated as a variety of *Copiapoa megarhiza*, is one of the slowest-growing copiapoas of all. Seedlings may take as long as 10 years or more to fill a 2-inch (5-cm) pot. Nevertheless, the black-spined forms are most handsome and flowers can always be relied on year after year. Near the coast large mounds are formed, while Ritter's var. *borealis* from near Monte Amargo grows in a very arid habitat and only manages to make small clumps, or remains solitary.

The plant illustrated was grown from seed collected near Totoral Bajo, PM220.

Copiapoa echinoides

Form: Clumping; green or brownish. Heads to 7.8 in (20 cm) or more high; 7 in (18 cm) across.

Spines: Strong. Radials 6–10; to 1 in (2.5 cm) long. Centrals 0–3, very thick and strong; to 2 in (5 cm) long.

Flower: Yellow; scented. 1.2 in (3 cm) across. June–August in cultivation.

Flowering time from seed: 5–6 years.

Distribution: Chile (near the coast from a few miles north of Huasco to Totoral).

This plant is most often seen offered for sale under the more recent name of *Copiapoa dura*. It is a very slow-growing species and is also very variable, such that seedlings from each population soon become distinctive in cultivation. Ritter bestowed the name *C. cuprea* upon plants from a population with a high percentage of brown-bodied individuals. Despite its slow growth, it should eventually make an attractive specimen in cultivation and is fairly problem-free, with good strong roots. It is also very generous with its flowers.

The plant illustrated was grown from seed collected south of Totoral, PM221.

Copiapoa gigantea

This plant is often listed as *Copiapoa haseltoniana*, but *C. gigantea* was described much earlier and has priority. That said, they are not identical and are easily told apart at a glance. They are not sufficiently different to be regarded as separate species, however. Both are often treated as varieties of the very variable *C. cinerea*, which is a much slower-growing plant. Seed-grown plants of *C. gigantea* in the author's collection have formed splendid clumps some 10 times larger than *C. cinerea* of the same age, which have remained as relatively small, solitary heads.

The plant illustrated was growing near the sea at Paposo, PM202, and would conform to C. haseltoniana. *Typical* C. gigantea, *a much darker-looking plant, grows in the hills to the east, well above the sea.*

DATA

Form: Offsetting to form large clumps. Whitish gray. Stems to 3.3 ft (1 m) high and 7.8 in (20 cm) broad.

Spines: Arising from large areoles 0.3 in (9 mm) across. Radials 7–9. Centrals 1–2; to 1.6 in (4 cm) long; yellowish. The crown of the plant is covered in attractive orange wool.

Flower: Yellow. 0.8–1.2 in (2–3 cm) across. May–June in cultivation.

Flowering time from seed: 8–12 years.

Distribution: Chile (to north and south of Paposo).

Copiapoa humilis

DATA

Form: Heads 0.8–2 in (2–5 cm) across; to 5.9 in (15 cm) long; blackish or brownish green to dark green; usually clumping to form substantial mounds with a large taproot.

Spines: Variable, but all thin. Radials 8–14; 0.1–0.6 in (0.3–1.5 cm) long. Centrals 1–4; 0.4–0.6 in (1–1.5 cm) long.

Flower: Yellow. To 1.2 in (3 cm) across. May–July in cultivation; December–February in habitat.

Flowering time from seed: 3–4 years.

Distribution: Chile (from Copiapó in the south northward to Tocopilla).

This plant has been around for a long time, having been described in 1860, and is one of the easiest copiapoas to grow and flower from seed. Several forms now considered to be subspecies were originally described as species, the most attractive of them probably being the very dark-bodied var. *tenuissima*, a little gem that is ideal for someone with limited growing space—although it does need a pot big enough to accommodate its large taproot.

The plant illustrated was grown from seed collected from a plant growing near the sea at Paposo, PM200.

Copiapoa krainziana

With its striking thatch of bristly white spines, this species—often treated as a subspecies of *Copiapoa cinerea*, incorrectly so in the author's opinion—has always been one of the most sought-after members of the genus. Growth from seed is slow, but at 20 years old a plant can be expected to have several heads and fill a 7.8-inch (20-cm) pan. A pan should be used in preference to a deep pot because the roots do not like to hang wet for long. For this reason, you should always go easy on the watering—this is a plant that does not like to be hurried.

The plant illustrated was growing in the Quebrada San Ramón, Taltal, PM206.

DATA

Form: Clumping; grayish. Heads to 3.3 ft (1 m) high; 4.7 in (12 cm) across.

Spines: Very flexible and bristly. Radials 10–12; 0.4–0.8 in (1–2 cm) long. Centrals 14–20; 0.8–1.2 in (2–3 cm) long. All spines glassy whitish.

Flower: Yellow. 1.2 in (3 cm) across. Seen sparingly in cultivation.

Flowering time from seed: 10–15 years.

Distribution: Chile (in canyons north of Taltal).

Copiapoa laui

Form: Strongly clumping, with a large taproot. Heads 0.4–0.8 in (1–2 cm) across.

Spines: Insignificant.

Flower: Yellow. 0.8 in (2 cm) across. Throughout the summer in cultivation.

Flowering time from seed: 3–4 years.

Distribution: Chile (Guanillos, near Esmeralda).

Although it grows well from seed, many plants of this diminutive species are vegetative propagations of plants collected from habitat. In some areas of the Guanillos valley thousands of these plants occur on the hillsides, while a smaller form, usually covered with fine gravel, occurs farther south along the coast. In cultivation growth is slow but sure, except when mealy bugs manage to build up a large population out of sight beneath the close-packed heads, which may suddenly dry up and die as a result.

The plant illustrated was grown from seed collected in Guanillos.

Copiapoa longistaminea

This is arguably the most beautiful of all copiapoas. The thousands of mounds scattered across the open desert floor near Esmeralda make a never-to-be-forgotten sight. The bodies in habitat can be white or greenish, but remain fairly dull in cultivation. After a long period when neither seed nor plants were available, both have suddenly appeared in recent years. Growth is very slow, however, and plants in cultivation (at least in some areas, such as the British Isles) seldom, if ever, flower. (They hardly ever seem to flower or set seed in habitat either, hence the shortage of material.) This species has been treated as a variety of both *Copiapoa cinerea* and *C. calderana*; the first certainly incorrect, the second probably so.

The plant illustrated was seen at Esmeralda, Guanillos.

DATA

Form: Dense clumps up to 3.3 ft (1 m) or more across. Individual heads up to 19.6 in (50 cm) high and 5.9 in (15 cm across).

Spines: Radials 4–5; 0.4–1.2 in (1–3 cm) long. Centrals 0–1. All spines dark chestnut to more or less black; almost crimson in the crown when young.

Flower: Yellow. 1.2 in (3 cm) across. June–July in cultivation.

Flowering time from seed: 12–15 years.

Distribution: Chile (only Guanillos, near Esmeralda).

Copiapoa marginata

Form: Individual heads to 23.6 in (60 cm) or more long; to 4.7 in (12 cm) wide.

Spines: Dense. Radials 5–9; 0.4–0.6 in (1–1.5 cm) long. Centrals 1–3; 1–1.6 in (2.5–4 cm) long; dark brown to blackish.

Flower: Yellow. 1–1.4 in (2.5–3.5 cm) long. May–June in cultivation.

Flowering time from seed: 6–8 years.

Distribution: Chile (on the Morro Copiapó near Caldera).

This is a much slimmer, darker-bodied (almost black), and more profusely clumping plant than the closely related *C. bridgesii,* which is often treated as a subspecies of *C. marginata*. In *C. marginata* the spines around the growing point are usually so long and densely packed that the flowers are scarcely able to open. Even so, on the Morro Copiapó—where the plant illustrated was growing—the author observed bees forcing their way in to gain access to the abundant nectar and pollen. Being unable to open fully does not seem to disadvantage the flowers.

Copiapoa rupestris

DATA

Form: Individual heads to 15.8 in (40 cm long) and 4.3 in (11 cm) across, remaining single or forming small- to medium-sized clumps.

Spines: Brownish. Radials 6–8; 0.4–0.8 in (1–2 cm) long. Centrals 1–3; 0.8–2.4 in (2–6 cm) long.

Flower: Pale yellow, usually with pale red edges to the petals. 1.2–1.6 in (3–4 cm) long, scarcely opening because of the spines. Flowering May–July in cultivation; December–February in habitat.

Flowering time from seed: 10–15 years.

Distribution: Chile (from Cifunchos to just north of Taltal).

This green-bodied plant is one of the few copiapoas to have a flower that is not just plain yellow. It is extremely slow-growing, has a large taproot, and should certainly not be pushed too hard or overpotted. In fact, the author has had plants in the same relatively gritty compost for nearly 10 years without repotting, with no problems. They grow and flower happily every year. In the closely related and even more slow-growing *C. desertorum,* the flower is pure red.

The plant illustrated was grown from seed that was collected in the Quebrada San Ramón, Taltal, PM203.

Copiapoa serpentisulcata

DATA

Form: Heads to 10 in (25 cm high) and 5.9 in (15 cm) broad, forming clumps to 3.3 ft (1 m) across.

Spines: Radials 6–10; to 0.8 in (2 cm) long. Centrals 1–4; to 1.2 in (3 cm).

Flower: Yellow, scented. To 1.2 in (3 cm across). June in cultivation; mainly November–December in habitat.

Flowering time from seed: 15–20 years.

Distribution: Chile (near Chañaral).

In habitat this is a relatively scarce plant that shares its rocky and very arid domain with numerous many-headed mounds of *Copiapoa cinerascens*. Although superficially similar at first glance, a closer look soon reveals major differences between the two species. In cultivation any similarity seems to disappear, and at a few years from seed the two species are very distinct. Unfortunately, *C. serpentisulcata* is rarely offered for sale, either as seed or as plants. The latter are slow-growing and a little reluctant to flower, which may explain the lack of seed.

The plant illustrated was growing on a rocky outcrop near the sea in Pan de Azúcar National Park near Chañaral, PM212.

Corryocactus brevistylus

While not likely to flower in the average small greenhouse, plants that have been given free root-run in a large pot or, even better, planted out in a bed are quite handsome and may flower if allowed to grow large enough. The lemon-yellow flowers are relatively large and well worth seeing. Seed from named localities has become widely available in recent years as more and more cactophiles have tramped the hills of South America. As a result, acquiring plants with a good pedigree has become easier.

The plant illustrated below was found growing 9 miles (15 km) east of the city limits of Arequipa, PM460.

DATA

Form: Branching from a woody trunk. To 13.2 ft (4 m) high; branches to 7.8 in (20 cm) across.

Spines: About 15; 0.4–9.5 in (1–24 cm) long.

Flower: Yellow. To 3.9 in (10 cm) across. Mainly November–December in habitat.

Flowering time from seed: 15–20 years.

Distribution: Southern Peru (common around Arequipa).

Corryocactus melanotrichus

Form: Clumping. Stems to more than 4 ft (1.2 m) tall; 1.2–2.8 in (3–7 cm) across.

Spines: 10–14. Radials and centrals similar; 0.3–1.2 in (0.7–3 cm) long.

Flower: Red. 2.4 (6 cm) across. May in cultivation; October–December in habitat.

Flowering time from seed: 8–12 years.

Distribution: Bolivia (around La Paz and onward to Cochabamba).

Seed of this species has been available for years and, given a large enough pot, a seedling will fairly rapidly grow into a good-sized plant that may well flower in cultivation. This is even more likely to happen if the plant is given a really good root-run by being planted out in a bed. Coming from a relatively high altitude, reasonably cold winters should not be a problem for this species.

The plant illustrated was growing in hills near the university at La Paz.

Corryocactus squarrosus

Along with several other species of relatively small-growing corryocacti, this plant is often listed in the genus *Erdisia*, which does not differ significantly from *Corryocactus* and is therefore not treated separately in this book. This is one of the best members of the genus to grow under glass, since it is quick to flower from seed or cuttings and it is also free-flowering—something that is not typical of all the smaller members of the genus.

The plant illustrated was grown from seed that was collected at Tarma by Carlos Ostaleza, OST84273.

DATA

Form: Stems to 9.8 in (25 cm) long and 0.8–1 in (2–2.5 cm) across, with a large taproot.

Spines: Radials 9–11; to 0.5 in (1.2 cm) long. Centrals mostly 1; up to 1.2 in (3 cm) long.

Flower: Yellowish to reddish. To 1.8 in (4.5 cm) long. July–August in cultivation.

Flowering time from seed: 4–5 years.

Distribution: Central Peru (Tarma).

Coryphantha calipensis

DATA

Form: Clumping to form large mounds. Individual heads globular; up to 4.7 in (12 cm) across.

Tubercles: Large and broad; curved upward.

Spines: Radials 10–16; 0.4–0.6 in (1–1.5 cm) long. Centrals 1; a little thicker; 0.6–0.8 in (1.5–2 cm) long.

Flower: Yellow. 2.4 in (6 cm) across. July–August in cultivation and in habitat.

Flowering time from seed: 4–5 years.

Distribution: Mexico (Calipan near Tehuacán, Puebla; also widespread in the woodlands on the road to Oaxaca for some distance from Calipan).

Although relatively slow-growing, in 15 to 20 years this species will make a very attractive clump. As with most coryphanthas, red spider mites can be a problem, so keep an eye on your plant and spray at the first sign of infection. Some people can spot these tiny mites with the naked eye, but using a magnifying glass is more reliable. In many coryphanthas an unsightly black mold develops on the sugary liquid secreted from extrafloral nectaries on the tubercles. However, this is less of a problem in this species than in some others.

The plant illustrated was growing in open woodland between Oaxaca and Calipan.

Coryphantha cornifera

This is a very variable species and probably grades into several others, making it difficult to decide where one stops and another begins. That is probably why most plants and seeds listed as *Coryphantha* sp. turn out to be just *C. cornifera*. At least they all have the merit of flowering well under glass. In cultivation growth is fairly slow, and black mold can be a problem, so a good wash may be in order from time to time. Fortunately, red spider mites seem slightly less attracted to this species than to most others.

The plant illustrated was one of thousands in flower near Zimapán, Hidalgo.

DATA

Form: Body globular, up to 4.7 in (12 cm) high. Often offsetting at the base to form small clumps.

Tubercles: Up to 1 in (2.5 cm) long.

Spines: Radials 7–20; whitish; to 0.9 in (2.2 cm) long. Centrals 0–1; brown; up to 0.6 in (1.5 cm) long; sometimes more or less hooked at the tip.

Flower: Lemon yellow. To 2 in (5 cm) broad. July–August in cultivation and in habitat.

Flowering time from seed: 4–5 years.

Distribution: Mexico (widespread in Hidalgo and Querétaro).

Coryphantha durangensis

Form: Cylindrical. Individual heads up to 3.9 in (10 cm) long and 1.6 in (4 cm) across, usually sprouting from the base or offsetting around the sides to form small clumps.

Tubercles: Grayish green.

Spines: Radials 6–8; to 0.4 in (1 cm) long. Centrals 1; black, fading to gray.

Flower: Pale yellow. To 1.6 in (4 cm) across. July–August in cultivation and in habitat.

Flowering time from seed: 5–6 years.

Distribution: Mexico (Durango).

This is one of the most slow-growing members of the genus, but eventually it makes an attractive small clump. It is distinctive for its pale grayish green body and very woolly crown from which the relatively small, pale flowers arise. Fortunately, red spider mites seem far less attracted to this species than to some other members of the genus and are rarely a problem. Because of its slow growth rate, more care is perhaps needed in watering than in some of the lusher species, such as *Coryphantha elephantidens*.

The plant illustrated below is a vegetative propagation from a plant that was collected near Nazas.

Coryphantha elephantidens

DATA

Form: Simple or clumping. Heads to 5.5 in (14 cm) high and 7.5 in (19 cm) broad.

Tubercles: Broad and fat. To 1.6 in (4 cm) long; up to 2.4 in (6 cm) across at the base.

Spines: Radials 5–8; to 0.8 in (2 cm) long. Centrals 0.

Flower: From yellow to vivid magenta, with every shade in between. To 3.9 in (10 cm) across. August–September in cultivation and in habitat.

Flowering time from seed: 4–6 years.

Distribution: Mexico (Morelos, Guerrero, Michoacán, Zacatecas, and Veracruz).

As currently conceived this consists of a very variable and widespread species incorporating several former names, including *Coryphantha bumamma*, *C. garessii*, and the very popular and attractive *C. greenwoodii*. The latter is a much more vigorous grower than the other two. These three all have yellow flowers, the transition to pink and magenta occurring only within a limited area. Being relatively lush green plants that usually grow among grass (often under bushes), they need to be generously watered during the growing season.

The plant illustrated was grown from seed collected in Morelos.

Coryphantha guerkeana

Form: Generally simple. 2.4–3.2 in (6–8 cm) high and broad.

Tubercles: Plump. 0.4–2 in (1–5 cm) long.

Spines: Very open. Radials 7; 0.6 in (1.5 cm) long. Centrals 2–3; 0.6–0.8 in (1.5–2 cm) long.

Flower: White or very pale yellow. To 1.4 in (4 cm) across. July–August in cultivation.

Flowering time from seed: 5–6 years.

Distribution: Mexico (Durango, near Durango City and southward to Zacatecas).

With its bright green body, open spination, and white flower, this is one of the few coryphanthas that can be easily recognized on sight. Unfortunately, it suffers badly from blotches of black mold on the body, so it needs washing regularly to keep it looking good. It seems to appreciate extra amounts of water in hot weather.

The plant illustrated was grown from seed that was collected at El Salto, Monte Escobedo, Zacatecas, Lau 1162.

Coryphantha pallida

With its black central spines contrasting against the dense white radials and abundantly woolly crown, this is one of the neatest and most attractive plants in the genus. It is slow-growing and remains solitary for many years, which makes it ideal for a small greenhouse. Even relatively small plants flower well every year over a number of weeks during summer.

The plant illustrated below was grown from seed that was collected near Tehuacán, Puebla, CH154.

DATA

Form: Globular. 2.4–4.7 in (6–12 cm) across. Simple or forming clumps of up to 10 heads.

Tubercles: Short, plump.

Spines: Radials 20 or more; white; 0.4 in (1 cm) long. Centrals up to 3 or more; curved; black; up to 0.4 in (1 cm) long.

Flower: Yellow. 2–2.8 in (5–7 cm) broad. July–August in cultivation and in habitat.

Flowering time from seed: 5–6 years.

Distribution: Mexico (Puebla, near Tehuacán).

Cumulopuntia boliviana

Form: Segments ovoid to oblong. Up to 3.9 in (10 cm) long and 1.6 in (4 cm) broad. Forming large mounds.

Spines: Mostly on the upper part of the segment. 1–5; yellowish to brownish or blackish; up to 2.8 in (7 cm) long.

Flower: Yellow to orange. To 2 in (5 cm) across. June–July in cultivation; October–December in habitat.

Flowering time from seed: 6–8 years.

Distribution: Over a vast area of mountainous terrain in Bolivia and Argentina.

As currently interpreted, *Cumulopuntia boliviana* is a dumping ground for a huge assortment of forms, many of which do not resemble each other very much and vary in every character (particularly the spines) in a perplexing way. This means that there is no such thing as a "typical" *C. boliviana*, and the real enthusiast will obtain dozens of clones from different localities in order to show the full range. Unfortunately, one thing that they all seem to have in common is that they are not always very obliging with their flowers in cultivation.

The plant illustrated above was seen growing on the Cuesta de Capillitas, Catamarca, Argentina.

Cumulopuntia chichensis

The description (right) applies to plants from near Potosí in Bolivia. The illustration below is of a plant growing near Tres Cruces in Argentina, a long way from Potosí. It is assumed that this plant, with its spectacular spination (although nearly half the plants in this population were almost spineless), is conspecific with *Cumulopuntia chichensis*, but in the absence of any definite intermediate populations, this is not certain. However, as the only alternative would be to coin a new name, it seems wiser to use *C. chichensis*, given the strong resemblance. Propagations from the Tres Cruces plant are now becoming wildly popular with enthusiasts, especially since the spines in cultivation are every bit as long as in habitat—up to 5.5 inches (14 cm) on the author's plant.

DATA

Form: Segments to 3.7 in (9.5 cm) long and 1.8 in (4.5 cm) across, forming clumps to 3.3 ft (1 m) broad.

Spines: 11–16; to 2.4 in (6.2 cm) long.

Flower: Yellow. 1.8 in (4.5 cm) long.

Flowering time from seed: 8–10 years.

Distribution: Bolivia (near Potosí) to northern Argentina (Jujuy).

Cumulopuntia ignescens

DATA

Form: Segments
1.2–2.4 in (3–6 cm)
long and 0.6–1.2 in
(1.5–3 cm) thick; forming
clumps composed of
hundreds of stems to
15.8 in (40 cm) or
more high.

Spines: Dense. Yellow or
golden brown. To 3.2 in
(8 cm) long.

Flower: Red to orange.
1.4–2 in (3.5–5 cm)
across. Mostly November–
December in habitat.

**Flowering time from
seed:** 10 years or more.

Distribution: Southern
Peru and northern Chile,
at high altitudes.

As can be seen from the photograph below, among the glories of the Lauca National Park in northern Chile are hundreds of superb mounds of this spectacular species. They are scattered around near the clear blue lakes on the high cold altiplano (at more than 13,200 feet/4,000 m), against a backdrop of two perfect snow-covered volcanic cones. The plants in such a high-altitude habitat have a much longer and denser spination than those from lower down and than those grown under glass in cultivation. This species is also less free-flowering in cultivation than some of its relatives.

Cumulopuntia pampana

DATA

Form: Densely clumping. Segments 1.6–3.5 in (4–9 cm) long; 0.8–2 in (2–5 cm) thick.

Spines: Brown to golden yellow. 5–12 (sometimes up to 16). 0.8–3.2 in (2–8 cm long).

Flower: Golden yellow. 2 in (5 cm) across. Produced in June in cultivation; November–December in habitat.

Flowering time from seed: 5–6 years.

Distribution: Argentina (Jujuy, Abra Pampa).

The plethora of *Cumulopuntia* forms on the high plains around Abra Pampa, Argentina, is very confusing, and some people dump them all into the hold-all species *C. boliviana*. With its long spines and tendency to remain small in cultivation, *C. pampana* is one of the best members of this grouping to grow in a greenhouse with restricted space. Most plants in cultivation are vegetative propagations from field-collected material, as with the plant in the photograph above, collected originally at Azul Pampa, FK91-13-237. The author has two clones with this number, one of which flowers every year (as here), the other of which has never yet bloomed.

Cumulopuntia rossiana

Form: Forming low, flattened cushions of short, crowded segments.

Spines: 5–6. Whitish. 0.5 in (1.25 cm) or more long.

Flower: Yellow, bright red or brick red, or brownish. Up to 1.7 in (4.2 cm) across. July–August in cultivation; November–December in habitat.

Flowering time from seed: 5–6 years.

Distribution: Widespread in the highlands of Bolivia and Argentina.

Some people regard the plant illustrated as a variety of *Cumulopuntia pentlandii*, as it was originally described by Backeberg, but the basis for this seems doubtful. Like all members of the genus, it is a highland plant and is very hardy in cultivation, being immune to temperatures well below freezing. The low, sometimes almost spineless mounds are very attractive and free-flowering in cultivation, and this species is highly recommended.

The plant illustrated was one of hundreds of a relatively long-spined form seen flowering near Iturbe, Jujuy, Argentina.

Cumulopuntia sphaerica

As with most members of the *Opuntia* group, this species is normally propagated from cuttings rather than seed. For many years it was incorrectly known as *Opuntia* (or *Tephrocactus*) *berteri*, while its great variability has given rise to numerous other names, such as *Cumulopuntia kuehrichiana*, *C. multiareolata*, and *C. tubercularis*. Whatever their names, all these plants have the great merit of flowering well in cultivation. The downside is that the tips of the spines are barbed and readily cling to human flesh, so be careful. The segments also fall off very easily, instantly reducing your specimen plant to a mere vestige of its former glory.

The plant illustrated is a vegetative propagation from a plant collected near Nazca, Peru, KK764. This came as Tephrocactus mirus—*yet another name—but is easily the most handsome of all the forms and well worth having.*

DATA

Form: Segments to 3.2 in (8 cm) or more long; globular to elongate-oval; forming large clumps.

Spines: 5–12. To 1.4 in (3.5 cm) long.

Flower: Yellow to pale orange. 1.2–1.6 in (3–4 cm) across. June–July in cultivation; mainly November–December in habitat.

Flowering time from seed: 5–6 years.

Distribution: Widespread in Chile and Peru.

Cylindropuntia bigelovii

Form: Forming a small shrub to 3.3 ft (1 m) high. Individual segments to 5.9 in (15 cm) long; plumpish.

Tubercles: Not very prominent. 4-sided.

Spines: Dense, glassy yellowish white. To 1 in (2.5 cm) long.

Flower: Mainly whitish. 1.6 in (4 cm) across. Flowering in April in habitat.

Flowering time from seed: 8–10 years.

Distribution: United States (Nevada, Arizona, and California); Mexico (northern Baja California).

In habitat this species forms spectacularly spiny clumps, and it is probably one of the most attractive members of the genus. In cultivation it tends to get rather big, so it is best grown hard to keep the rate of growth to a minimum, although flowers tend to be produced somewhat shyly. As with all these so-called chollas, the spines have barbed tips that attach themselves to human skin at the merest touch, so always handle your plant with strong gardening gloves.

The plant illustrated was seen in southern Arizona.

Denmoza rhodacantha

With its strong, colorful spination this cactus makes a fine sight even when not in flower. The eventual size of the plant varies from one locality to another. Those in the south, around Mendoza, tend to be the largest, while those in the north, in the Quebrada de Cafayate in Salta province, may reach less than 19.6 inches (50 cm) in height. Seed from these smaller-growing forms is more likely to produce plants that will flower in cultivation. *Denmoza erythrocephala* is a synonym.

The plant illustrated was grown from seed collected from distinctive yellow-spined plants at Agua de Toro, Mendoza, DJF186.

DATA

Form: To 5 ft (1.5 m) tall and 11.8 in (30 cm) across.

Spines: Mostly red, sometimes yellow, often mixed with a few long white bristly hairs. 10–30; up to 2.4 in (6 cm) long; variable in thickness.

Flower: Red. 2.8 in (7 cm) long. July–August in cultivation; October–December in habitat.

Flowering time from seed: 12–20 years.

Distribution: Argentina (from Mendoza to Salta).

Disocactus echlamii

Form: Bushy, branching from the base. Stems to 8.7 in (22 cm) long and 1.8 in (4.5.cm) wide.

Spines: Absent.

Flower: Red. 2.4–2.8 in (6–7 cm) long. June–July in cultivation.

Flowering time from seed: 4–5 years.

Distribution: Guatemala (near Santa Lucia).

Like most epiphytic cacti, cuttings rather than seed are the normal method of propagation for this species. In their native home the plants grow on the branches of trees in forest, a reasonably shady habitat, so in greenhouse cultivation many people place them underneath the staging, well out of the burning summer sun. A windowsill will be equally suitable, where flowering should occur quite easily.

The plant illustrated is a vegetative propagation from a plant collected near Santa Lucia.

Echinocactus grusonii

DATA

Form: To 4.2 ft (1.3 m) high and 31 in (80 cm) across.

Spines: Yellow. Radials 8–10; to 1.2 in (3 cm) long. Centrals mostly 4; to 2 in (5 cm) long. The crown of the plant is covered in dense white wool.

Flower: Yellow. To 2 in (5 cm) across.

Flowering time from seed: 15–20 years or more.

Distribution: Mexico (San Luis Potosí, Hidalgo, Querétaro, and Guanajuato).

Never very common in habitat, the numbers of this beautiful species, often known as the "golden barrel cactus," have been further reduced by construction of a dam in one of its best habitats. Cultivated plants grow rapidly, but need to be a considerable size before they will flower. Beware of cold—for some reason this species marks badly with rust-colored blotches if the temperature drops too low— keep above 46°F (8°C).

The plant illustrated above was grown from seed that was collected at Rancho Nuevo, Guanajuato.

Echinocereus bonkerae

DATA

Form: Stems to 7.8 in (20 cm) long and 2.4–2.8 in (6–7 cm) broad, clumping from the base.

Spines: 12–15. Centrals 1; up to 0.4 in (1 cm) long, often much shorter.

Flower: Brilliant magenta. To 2.5 in (6.25 cm) across. April–May in habitat; slightly later in cultivation.

Flowering time from seed: 4–5 years.

Distribution: United States (central and southeastern Arizona).

After having been treated for many years as a form of both *Echinocereus fendleri* and *E. fasciculatus*, this attractive plant has once again emerged as a species in its own right, although how long this will last is anyone's guess. With its short, almost comblike spination, it is certainly a very distinctive plant and is spectacular when in flower. Unfortunately, in cultivation it tends to grow in rather a lumpy and misshapen fashion, far removed from the perfect specimens that can be seen in its sunny natural habitat.

The plant illustrated above was one of hundreds seen in flower on a rocky hillside near Globe.

Echinocereus coccineus

Until relatively recently this cactus was widely regarded as a form of *Echinocereus triglochidiatus* (as var. *melanacanthus*), but it is now once again considered to be a distinct species. It is one of the most winter-hardy of all cacti and can withstand remarkably low temperatures. The brilliant red flowers individually last a week or more and occur prolifically on older plants, although some clones are more free-flowering than others. In one form from the Jarilla Mountains in New Mexico the flowers are a striking shade of salmon pink. Well worth getting!

The plant illustrated was seen in Utah.

DATA

Form: Clumping to form mounds that may reach 3.3 ft (1 m) or more across, with up to 500 heads. Heads 2.4–2.8 in (6–7 cm) high; 1.2–2 in (3–5 cm) across.

Spines: 6–14, including 1–3 centrals. Up to 2.4 in (6 cm) long but usually much shorter.

Flower: Red. 2–2.8 in (5–7 cm) long. Produced in springtime in cultivation and in habitat.

Flowering time from seed: 4–6 years.

Distribution: United States (widespread in the southwest).

Echinocereus engelmannii

DATA

Form: Clumping from the base. Stem to 17.7 in (45 cm) long and 2.4 in (6 cm) broad.

Spines: Very variable—whitish, yellowish, or brownish to almost black; straight or wavy; stiff or flexible. Radials 6–14. Centrals 2–7; to 2.8 in (7 cm) or more long, but mostly 0.8–1.2 in (2–3 cm).

Flower: Pink to purple. To 3.5 in (9 cm) across. Produced in late spring both in cultivation and in habitat.

Flowering time from seed: 8–9 years.

Distribution: Widespread in the southwest United States; also found in northwest Mexico.

Although a very easy plant to grow, this is a very difficult species to get to flower, at least in certain areas. Because the very variable spination is attractive in its own right, this is not a huge problem. A few flowers would be a bonus, though, especially since individually they last a week or more, as with most members of this genus. Several varieties have been named (mostly based on spination), but these names have recently been discarded because of the incredible variablility of the plants even within a single locality.

The plant illustrated was growing in Joshua Tree National Monument in California.

Echinocereus enneacanthus brevispinus

DATA

Form: Large clumps. Stems to 2 in (5 cm) across and 6.6 ft (2 m) long.

Spines: Radials 6–13; to 1.5 cm. Centrals usually 1; up to to 1.6 in (4 cm) long.

Flower: Magenta. To 3.9 in (10 cm) or more across. June in cultivation.

Flowering time from seed: 6–7 years.

Distribution: United States (southern Texas; southern New Mexico; northern Mexico).

Included here for its magnificent flowers, it has to be admitted that this is not the most attractive plant you are ever likely to grow. The stems are a little straggly, they often look ragged and tatty with age, and they form untidy clumps. None of this matters when the flowers, each of which lasts a week or more, put in their annual, more or less guaranteed appearance. By contrast, *Echinocereus enneacanthus enneacanthus* (formerly known as *E. dubius*) is much less obliging, often not managing to produce even a solitary bloom on a large, ancient clump—although its much longer spination does help earn its place in the collection.

The plant illustrated is a vegetative propagation from a plant that was collected in the Devil's River Canyon in Texas.

Echinocereus fasciculatus

DATA

Form: Clumping. Stems 6.9–17.7 in (17.5–45 cm) long and 1.6–2.4 in (4–6 cm) across.

Spines: 10–15, of which 1–3 are centrals; the lowermost up to 3 in (7.5 cm) long.

Flower: Magenta. 2.4–3.5 in (6–9 cm) across. May–June in cultivation; April in habitat.

Flowering time from seed: 4–5 years.

Distribution: United States (Arizona and New Mexico); Mexico (Sonora).

A clump of this cactus in full flower in the Sonoran desert in April makes a magnificent sight. It is equally free-flowering in cultivation, unlike *Echinocereus engelmannii*, with which it has been linked by some people. But while the latter is easy to grow, *E. fasciculatus* can be a real problem. It often loses its roots and forms misshapen stems, problems that link it closely with the similarly afflicted *E. bonkerae*.

The plant illustrated was growing near Tucson, Arizona.

Echinocereus fendleri

DATA

Form: Small clumps. Stems to 6 in (15 cm) high and 2.4–3.9 in (6–10 cm) broad.

Spines: Centrals 1, curving upward; to 1.5 in (3.7 cm) long. Radials 9–11; shorter.

Flower: Magenta. To 2.8 in (7 cm) or more across. Produced in late spring both in cultivation and in habitat.

Flowering time from seed: 4–5 years.

Distribution: United States (Arizona and New Mexico); Mexico (Sonora and Chihuahua).

This species often has a spectacularly large flower in relation to the size of the plant. It takes a good many years to form even a small clump, making it one of the best members of the genus to acquire if you want magnificent, large, long-lasting flowers on small plants. These have the additional merit of being perfectly hardy in winter. *Echinocereus hempelii* and *E. kuenzleri* are now regarded as mere forms of this species, differing only in minor details.

The plant illustrated was growing near Farmington, New Mexico.

Echinocereus klapperi

DATA

Form: Large mounds.
Heads 2.4–2.8 in
(6–7 cm) long; 0.8–1.2 in
(2–3 cm) across.

Ribs: 8–11.

Spines: Golden yellow; up
to 0.5 in (1.2 cm) long.

Flower: Scarlet. To 1.6 in
(4 cm) long. May–June
in cultivation.

**Flowering time from
seed:** 6–10 years.

Distribution: Mexico
(Sonora, Sierra de la
Ciénega).

At first thought to be a distinct and strikingly yellow-spined form of the variable *Echinocereus polyacanthus*, this distinctive plant was eventually described as a species in its own right. The combination of numerous smallish heads, yellow spines, and abundant scarlet flowers—each lasting for several days—makes it one of the most desirable members of the genus. Like most of its relatives, it is also winter-hardy.

The plant illustrated above was grown from seed that was collected at the type locality, Lau 1544.

Echinocereus knippelianus

This has always been a sought-after plant, seldom offered in quantity by dealers. In relatively recent times two varieties have been described. Glass and Foster introduced var. *kruegeri*, a strongly clumping form from southern Nuevo León, with a smaller stem and whitish flowers borne near the apex. A little later Alfred Lau described var. *reyesii* with a larger, deeper purplish pink flower. Both of the variants seem to be offered for sale more often than the type.

The plant illustrated was grown from seed collected south of General Cepeda.

DATA

Form: Individual heads to 3.9 in (10 cm) high and 1.2 in (3 cm) across, with a huge taproot. In habitat remains simple and almost buried in the ground, but in cultivation it forms clumps.

Spines: Weak; generally dropping off in age. Usually 0–4; 0.4–0.8 in (1–2 cm) long.

Flower: Light pink. 1.6–2.4 in (4–6 cm) across. Appearing in springtime in cultivation and in habitat.

Flowering time from seed: 3–4 years.

Distribution. Mexico (Coahuila). In mountains; widely scattered and generally rare.

Echinocereus longisetus

Form: Branching from the base to form clumps of up to 30 stems. Stems up to 11.8 in (30 cm) long and 1–3 in (2.5–7.5 cm) across.

Spines: Dense; glassy whitish. Radial spines 15–25; 0.6 in (1.5 cm) long. Centrals 4–7; to 2.2 in (5.5 cm) long.

Flower: Magenta. 2.4–2.8 in (6–7 cm) across. Usually produced May–June in cultivation.

Flowering time from seed: 6–8 years.

Distribution: Northeast Mexico, on limestone hillsides on the eastern flanks of the Sierra Madre Oriental.

For many years the identity of this plant was uncertain, but genuine material is now available, mostly of Lau 1538 from the Sierra de Cármen, Coahuila, as depicted in the illustration. This plant was grown from seed collected by Alfred Lau at this locality. In subspecies *delaetii* (usually seen for sale as *Echinocereus delaetii*) the stems and flowers are larger, and the central spines are wavy and hairlike and up to 3.9 inches (10 cm) long. These are two of the more shy-flowering members of the genus, and some plants seldom, if ever, flower in cultivation.

Echinocereus nicholii

Distinctive with its pale spines and usually rather small, very pale flower, this species was once regarded as a form of *Echinocereus engelmannii*. The fact that the two often grow together without interbreeding is a clear sign that they are two distinct species, and they are now treated as such. In cultivation in a temperate climate, one key difference lies in the fact that *E. nicholii* is very free-flowering whereas *E. engelmannii* is one of the most shy-flowering members of the genus. Both plants are very hardy.

The plant illustrated was growing in southern Arizona.

DATA

Form: Clumping. Stems stout, to 11.8 in (30 cm) long, and 3 in (7.5 cm) across.

Spines: Clear yellow to almost white. Lowermost centrals are the longest, usually 0.8–1.2 in (2–3 cm).

Flower: Pale lavender. To 3.5 in (9 cm) across, usually much smaller. April in habitat; May–June in cultivation.

Flowering time from seed: 5–8 years.

Distribution: Mexico (northwest Sonora); United States (central-southern Arizona—easy to see around Tucson and in Organ Pipe Cactus National Monument).

Echinocereus ortegae

Form: Clumping. Stems 5.9–7.8 in (15–20 cm) long and 1–1.6 in (2.5–4 cm) across.

Spines: Numerous and dense; pale. To 0.4 in (1 cm) long.

Flower: Scarlet. About 2.8 in (7 cm) long and 2.4 in (6 cm) across. May–June in cultivation.

Flowering time from seed: 4–5 years.

Distribution: Mexico (southern Sinaloa and western Durango). On cliffs in forest at 2,000–8,000 ft (600–2,400 m) in the mountains between Mazatlán and the city of Durango.

For many years after its description from near the Río Tamazula, this species remained unknown in cultivation and was dismissed as a form of the familiar *Echinocereus scheerii*. Lau 1143 from the same general area was described as a new species, *E. koehresianus*, before it was realized that it conformed more or less to the old *E. ortegae* (although it is still regarded by some people as a variety of that species). As a cultivated plant it has some merit: although it does not grow as large as other members of the genus, it has strikingly beautiful, freely produced flowers.

The plant illustrated above was grown from seed that was collected by Alfred Lau at the original locality.

Echinocereus pamanesiorum

With its large flowers and ease of cultivation, this attractive discovery by Alfred Lau has rapidly become popular with collectors, although it can be somewhat prone to infection by red spider mites. If these cause scarring that ruins the plant (often around the lower half), it is easy enough to cut off the unaffected upper half, dry it off for a week or so, and then root it up as a cutting, leaving the base to produce fresh new offsets.

The plant illustrated below was grown from seed that was collected at the type locality, Lau 1247.

DATA

Form: Stem to 13.8 in (35 cm) high and 3.2 in (8 cm) across; sparingly branched.

Spines: Radials 9–12, to 0.4 in (1 cm) long; yellowish to white. Centrals 0–2; to 0.9 in (1.7 cm) long; brownish, with darker tips.

Flower: Pink. To 3.5 in (9 cm) across. June–July in cultivation.

Flowering time from seed: 4–5 years.

Distribution: Mexico (Zacatecas, Río Huaynamota valley).

Echinocereus polyacanthus huitcholensis

DATA

Form: Clumping. Stems 5.9–7.8 in (15–20 cm) long and 0.8–2 in (2–5 cm) across.

Spines: Radials 9–15, 0.08–0.4 in (2–10 mm) long. Centrals 1–7, to 0.4–0.6 in (10–15 mm) long.

Flower: Deep pink, orange red, or scarlet. To 3.2 in (8 cm) long. May–June in cultivation.

Flowering time from seed: 4–6 years.

Distribution: Mexico (Nayarit, Sinaloa, southwest Durango, and northwest Jalisco), on rocks and cliffs in mountain forests.

This is another plant that remained more or less unknown until long after it was first described (as *Echinocereus huitcholensis*), and yet another that was introduced to cultivation through the tireless exploits of Alfred Lau. His distinctive plant from Plomosos in Sinaloa (Lau 768, shown above) was originally regarded as a form of *E. scheerii*, but was eventually considered to belong to the widespread and variable *E. polyacanthus*. Some experts still regard it as a subspecies of *E. acifer*, itself only recently rescued from obscurity after having been buried for a long time in *E. polycanthus*. If you grow only one form of this species, this should be it.

The plant illustrated was grown from seed collected by Lau in habitat.

Echinocereus pulchellus

On account of its small size, this cactus has always been one of the most sought-after members of the genus, but it is not often offered by dealers. This may be because it is not the easiest of plants to raise, the seedlings being prone to damping off, while the roots of older plants are liable to rot off without warning. Overpotting is certainly to be avoided. In subspecies *sharpii* the body is extremely dwarf and the flower is white, while at the other extreme, subspecies *weinbergii* is a large, vigorous form that reaches 5 inches (13 cm) across.

The plant illustrated was grown from seed collected in the high Sierra Mixteca.

DATA

Form: To 3.9 in (10 cm) long and 1.6 in (4 cm) across, forming small clumps.

Spines: 3–5; usually about 0.2 in (4 mm) long.

Flower: Various shades of pink. To 1.6 in (4 cm) across. May in cultivation.

Flowering time from seed: 3–4 years.

Distribution: Widespread but scattered in the Mexican highlands.

Echinocereus rayonesensis

DATA

Form: Clumping. Stems 4.7–11 in (12–28 cm) long; 1–1.6 in (2.5–4 cm) across.

Spines: Numerous, glassy whitish. Longest centrals to 2 in (5 cm).

Flower: Dark magenta. 1.2–2 in (3–5 cm) across. June–July in cultivation.

Flowering time from seed: 4–5 years.

Distribution: Mexico (Rayones valley in Nuevo León), on limestone slopes.

After its discovery by Alfred Lau this attractive dwarf plant quickly became popular among collectors. Its popularity is well deserved, since it is densely spined and reaches only a relatively small size. Originally thought to correspond to Backeberg's invalid *Echinocereus albatus*, it was eventually described by Nigel Taylor of the Royal Botanic Gardens, Kew, England, as a new species. Although the flowers are a little small for the genus, they usually appear on schedule every year in cultivation.

The plant illustrated is a vegetative propagation from a plant that was collected at Rayones, Lau 1101.

Echinocereus reichenbachii baileyi

Several varieties of *Echinocereus reichenbachii* are currently offered for sale, most of which were originally described as species in their own right. All have dense pectinate (comblike) spination and are highly recommended, particularly var. *fitchii*, which is often still treated as a separate species. Its flowers are especially spectacular, since they have pink petals with contrasting crimson bases. Var. *armatus* is the least attractive and a little tricky to grow—although overwatering any form of this species will lead to its rapid demise.

The plant illustrated below was grown from seed that was collected near Comanche, Oklahoma, HK1148.

DATA

Form: Simple or offsetting sparingly. To 5.9 in (15 cm) high and 2 in (5 cm) across.

Spines: Radials around 14; whitish to brownish; mostly up to 0.5 in (1.2 cm) long. Centrals 1–3; to 0.1 in (3 mm) long.

Flower: Light purple. 2.4 in (6 cm) or more across. June–July in cultivation.

Flowering time from seed: 4–5 years.

Distribution: United States (Oklahoma, e.g., Wichita Mountains, and in adjacent Childress County, Texas).

93

Echinocereus rigidissimus rubispinus

Form: Usually simple. To 11.8 in (30 cm) or more long and 1.6–4.3 in (4–11 cm) across.

Spines: Short; densely comblike; usually yellowish or pinkish.

Flower: Pink. 2.4–3.5 in (6–9 cm) across. Produced in June in habitat and in cultivation.

Flowering time from seed: 4–6 years.

Distribution: Northwest Mexico and southwestern United States (southeast Arizona and southwest New Mexico).

Regarded for a long time as a form of the superficially similar *Echinocereus pectinatus*, *E. rigidissimus* is now firmly reestablished as a species in its own right. The subspecies *rubispinus*, first collected by Alfred Lau (Lau 088) in 1972 in the Sierra Oscura in Chihuahua, Mexico, is a particularly attractive plant (see illustration). With its dense ruby-red spination and spectacularly large, sumptuous flowers, it quickly became a firm favorite and is the form most often seen in collections today. Cultivation presents no problems, provided that overwatering is avoided. Mealy bugs hiding beneath the dense spination can be a problem, however, and can cause fatal damage before they are noticed.

Echinocereus russanthus

DATA

Form: Stems 5.9–9.8 in (15–25 cm) high and 1.6–2 in (4–5 cm) across; branching at the base.

Spines: Radials 30–45; to about 0.5 in (1.2 cm) long. Centrals 7–12; mostly to 1 in (2.5 cm) long.

Flower: Brownish. 1–1.2 in (2.5–3 cm) long; not opening widely. Produced as early as late March in cultivation, but more usually April or May.

Flowering time from seed: 3–4 years.

Distribution: Mexico (Chihuahua); United States (Big Bend region, west Texas).

In European collections this is one of the earliest-flowering cacti. The flowers, although relatively small, are usually produced in great numbers, and the unusual shade of brown has an idiosyncratic attractiveness. In subspecies *weedinii* the spination is always an attractive golden yellow. For many years *Echinocereus russanthus* was listed as a form of *E. chloranthus*, which in turn has now been subsumed (according to some sources) within *E. viridiflorus*. Cultivation is easy enough, but do not overpot.

The plant illustrated was grown from seed that was collected in the Santa Clara Canyon, Chihuahua, Mexico, Lau 1076.

Echinocereus sanpedroensis

Form: Stems to 7.8 in (20 cm) long; 0.6–2 in (1.5–2.5 cm) or more across, forming large clumps.

Spines: Radials 10–11; to 0.4 in (1 cm) long. Centrals 1–4; to 0.8 in (2 cm) long.

Flower: Scarlet, orange, or pink. 2.8–4.7 in (7–12 cm) long and 1.6–3.2 in (4–8 cm) across. Appears May–July in cultivation.

Flowering time from seed: 4–5 years.

Distribution: Mexico (Sonora and Chihuahua).

This day-flowering, recently described plant was seen in collections for many years as a form of *Echinocereus scheerii*. The latter, however, is a more slender-stemmed, sprawling species whose pink flowers open at night and more or less close up during the day. *Echinocereus salmdykianus* is a similar plant, but has more widely opening, pure orange flowers. All three species are worth acquiring if you can spare the room to grow them in pans big enough to enable the stems to clump and reach their full size.

The plant illustrated was grown from seed that was collected along the road from Choix to San Vicente, Sinaloa, Lau 1520.

Echinocereus stoloniferus tayopensis

This is the form that is most often seen in cultivation, being a stouter, less densely spined plant than the type. It is unusual in the genus because of its yellow flowers, which are much larger and more showy than in another yellow-flowered species, *Echinocereus subinermis*. When potting on, allow some space around the plant for the underground stolons to reach the surface.

The plant illustrated below was grown from seed that was collected in the Sierra Obscura, Chihuahua, Lau 1142.

DATA

Form: Stems to 5.9 in (15 cm) long and 3 in (7.5 cm) across, forming clumps via underground stolons.

Spines: Radials 10–13; to 0.6 in (1.5 cm) long. Centrals 1–5, to 1 in (2.5 cm) long.

Flower: Yellow. 2.4–3 in (6–7.5 cm) across. July–August in cultivation.

Flowering time from seed: 5–6 years.

Distribution: Mexico (eastern Sonora and western Chihuahua, in the drainage of the Río Yaqui, westward to near Temósachic; and in southern Durango in the basin of the Río San Ignacio).

Echinocereus stramineus

DATA

Form: Forming mounds to 6.6 ft (2 m) or more across with hundreds of heads. Stems to 17.7 in (45 cm) long and 3.2 in (8 cm) across.

Spines: Glassy whitish. Radials 7–14; to 1.2 in (3 cm) long. Centrals 2–4; 2–2.8 in (5–7 cm) long.

Flower: Pink. Up to 4.9 in (12.5 cm) across. June–July in cultivation; April in habitat.

Flowering time from seed: 6–7 years or more.

Distribution: Southwest United States; central north Mexico.

In habitat some clumps of this attractive species are spectacularly spiny, and even in cultivation in Europe the spination is impressive. Unfortunately, its flowering qualities are less so—the flowers, although individually of great size and beauty, tend to appear with reluctance. Some people never manage to flower their plant, while others may flower it one year and again only after a gap of several years.

The plant illustrated above was grown from seed that was collected near Saltillo, Coahuila, PM 056.

Echinocereus subinermis ochoterenae

This is a much more vigorous plant than the less spiny var. *subinermis*. The latter, although often clumping when old, is usually simple. It also has fewer ribs, giving it a very different appearance. A particularly spiny form of *Echinocereus subinermis* from La Bufa, Chihuahua, has been named as var. *aculeatus*, but has not been universally accepted, although it is well worth growing.

The plant illustrated below was grown from seed that was collected on the northern slopes of the Cerro Culagua, Sinaloa, Lau 771.

DATA

Form: Clumping. Stems to 3.9 in (10 cm) long and 1.6–2.8 in (4–7 cm) across; light green.

Spines: Radials 9; to 0.4 in (1 cm) long. Centrals 4; to 0.8 in (2 cm) long; brownish to blackish, fading to gray.

Flower: Yellow. To 2.2 in (5.6 cm) across. June–July in cultivation.

Flowering time from seed: 4–5 years.

Distribution: Mexico (southern Sinaloa), on bare copper-rich rocks.

Echinocereus triglochidiatus

Form: Clumping. Stems to 11.8 in (30 cm) long and 3 in (7.5 cm) across.

Spines: Radials 3–5. Centrals 0–1; to 2.8 in (7 cm) long. Three-angled, grayish.

Flower: Red. 1.2–3.5 in (3–9 cm) long, lasting more than a week. April–May in habitat; May–June in cultivation.

Flowering time from seed: 5–6 years.

Distribution: Southwest United States; northern Mexico.

There has been much confusion between this plant and *Echinocereus coccineus*, which at one time was known as *E. triglochidiatus melanacanthus*. Both species are extremely variable, and even now it is uncertain that we fully understand where one species ends and another begins. *Echinocereus triglochidiatus* in its strict sense is the relatively fleshy, open-spined, and very free-flowering plant depicted above. In subspecies *mojavensis* forma *inermis* the plant bodies are a little smaller than usual and are spineless (although fully spined plants also occur in the wild population). These are among the hardiest of cacti, requiring no winter heating.

The plant illustrated was grown from seed collected near Placitas, New Mexico.

Echinocereus viereckii morricallii

In habitat the spineless stems of this cactus sprawl across shady cliffs in woodland. It is worth growing for its flowers alone, which are simply stunning, and in cultivation are produced in profusion. To get the best from your plant, however, you will need to grow it in a large pan. In the hot desert lowlands, several other fatter-stemmed, spinier forms of *Echinocereus viereckii* occur, one of which, subspecies *huastecensis*, has particularly long spines and is well worth seeking out.

The plant illustrated was grown from seed collected south of Monterrey, HK376.

DATA

Form: Stems sprawling, richly branched; to 19.6 in (50 cm) long and 0.8–1.2 in (2–3 cm) across; light green.

Spines: Usually absent, but some forms retain small spines even when mature.

Flower: Brilliant magenta. 2.8–4.3 in (7–11 cm) across. June in cultivation.

Flowering time from seed: 5–6 years.

Distribution: Mexico (southwest Tamaulipas and adjacent areas of Nuevo León).

Echinocereus viridiflorus

DATA

Form: Often forms small clumps. Stems 1–4.9 in (2.5–12.5 cm) long and 1–1.5 in (2.5–3.8 cm) or more across.

Spines: Numerous. All spines variable in coloration, often red. Radials to 0.2 in (4.5 mm) long.

Flower: Green, scented strongly of lemons. Borne relatively low down. 1.2 in (3 cm) across. March–April in habitat and in cultivation.

Flowering time from seed: 2–3 years.

Distribution: United States (southwestern South Dakota and southeastern Wyoming to western Oklahoma and Texas).

This is one of the smallest members of the genus, especially subspecies *davisii*. Usually no more than 0.8 inches (2 cm) long, this subspecies does best when grafted and is often listed as a separate species. In the attractive subspecies *correllii* the stems are more cylindrical and the spines have horizontal bands of greenish yellow and whitish color. *Echinocereus viridiflorus* is one of the most cold-resistant cacti of all and will easily withstand temperatures many degrees below freezing.

The plant illustrated was grown from seed collected from Castle Rock, Douglas, Colorado, HK1446.

Echinocereus websterianus

This species is a little easier to grow than its close relative, *Echinocereus scopulorum* from mainland Sonora. Neither species is particularly common in cultivation, but genuine *E. websterianus* is now seen more often since seed collected in habitat by Alfred Lau became available. Before that time, plants of very doubtful identity masqueraded under this name, but they usually had flowers that were much too large to be the genuine species. As with all the densely spined members of the genus, take particular care not to overwater your plant.

The plant illustrated was grown from seed collected from habitat, Lau 098.

DATA

Form: Clumping. Stems to 23.6 in (60 cm) high and 3.2 in (8 cm) across.

Spines: Numerous, golden yellow, and relatively short, densely covering the plant.

Flower: Pink. 1.6–2 in (4–5 cm) across. June–July in cultivation.

Flowering time from seed: 5–6 years.

Distribution: Mexico (endemic to the island of San Pedro Nolasco in the Gulf of California).

Echinopsis ancistrophora

DATA

Form: Body flattened. Dark green. To 3.2 in (8 cm) or more across.

Spines: Radials 3–7. Centrals 1–4. All fairly short and not covering the plant.

Flower: White. 2–6.3 in (5–16 cm) long. May in cultivation; December in habitat.

Flowering time from seed: 3–4 years.

Distribution: Argentina (Tucumán and Salta).

This plant is collected from the wild in large numbers in Argentina for inclusion in Christmas nativity scenes. Fortunately, it is fairly common in the area, growing mainly in thorn woodland and also in open grassy, rocky places, but never in the driest spots. There is great variation from one habitat to another in the size of the flower and body of the plant. The form with the smallest flowers was named *Echinopsis kratochviliana* by Backeberg.

The plant illustrated above was seen growing in the lower end of the Quebrada del Toro, Salta.

Echinopsis leucantha

This is by far the most widespread member of the genus in Argentina, and its variability from one habitat to another has led to a number of additional but superfluous names, such as *Echinopsis melanopotamica* and *E. shaferi*. In cultivation the flowers are freely produced just below the crown of the plant, but they last only one or two days. In recent years, many forms of this plant have been offered from seed collected in habitat, the black-spined examples being particularly notable. The most spectacular form is probably HT90-311 from Valle Castelli, in which the black, twisted central spines reach a length of 4.7 inches (12 cm).

The plant illustrated was growing among palms near Cruz del Eje, Córdoba.

DATA

Form: Spherical to columnar. From 4 in to 6.6 ft (10 cm to 2 m) high and 4–7 in (10–18 cm) across.

Spines: Very variable, pale brown or grayish to black. Centrals usually to about 2.4 in (6 cm) long.

Flower: White, sometimes flushed pink. To 8.7 in (22 cm) long. May–July in cultivation; November–January in habitat.

Flowering time from seed: 5–6 years.

Distribution: Argentina (widespread in the northwestern provinces, south to the Río Negro and Río Colorado).

Echinopsis mamillosa

Form: Simple, hemispherical. To more than 5.9 in (15 cm) across.

Spines: All yellowish brown. Radials 11–16; to 0.5 in (1.2 cm) long. Centrals 4–6; to 1 in (2.5 cm) long.

Flower: White or pink. To 7 in (18 cm) long and 3.5 in (9 cm) across. June–July in cultivation; December in habitat.

Flowering time from seed: 5–6 years.

Distribution: Argentina (Salta, near Santa Victoria and Iruya).

This normally white-flowered species is very common in southern Bolivia, occurring right up to the outskirts of the city of Tarija. Farther north, around Culpina, white- and pink-flowered forms occur together. The most superb flower of all—var. *kermesina*—can be found farther south in Argentina. Rausch's var. *flexilis* occurs nearby on steep hillsides near Iruya, but it has a smaller body with longer, denser spination and smaller flowers that can be white, pink, or magenta.

The plant illustrated, growing near Iruya, is the pink-flowered form of var. kermesina.

Echinopsis obrepanda calorubra

This species is worth growing for its superb flowers, which in older plants are produced in large numbers. It is often still listed as *Echinopsis calorubra*, but is also often regarded as a form of the very variable and widespread *E. obrepanda*. When treated as a species, it has several varieties, such as *mizquensis* and *pojoensis*, both of which were originally described as species and are often still listed as such. These are more miniature plants with smaller but still very striking flowers, perhaps more suitable for anyone with limited space.

The plant illustrated was grown from seed collected north of Totora, PM159.

DATA

Form: Simple or clumping. Somewhat flattened. To 5.5 in (14 cm) across and 2.4–2.8 in (6–7 cm) high.

Spines: Very open. Radials 9–13. Centrals 1; to 1 in (2.5 cm) long.

Flower: Red or magenta. To 6 in (15 cm) long. May–June in cultivation; November–December in habitat.

Flowering time from seed: 5–6 years.

Distribution: Bolivia (Comarapa-Totora and around Aiquile).

Echinopsis oxygona

Form: Bodies to 9.8 in (25 cm) broad and high, forming large clumps.

Spines: Radials 5–15; to 0.6 in (1.5 cm) long. Centrals 2–5; to 0.8 in (2 cm) long.

Flower: Pink. About 8.7 in (22 cm) long. June–July in cultivation; December in habitat.

Flowering time from seed: 5–6 years.

Distribution: Southern Brazil; Uruguay; northeastern Argentina.

This species, often listed as *Echinopsis multiplex*, is best propagated from offsets. Plenty of material is now available derived from plants that were originally collected in habitat. The plant itself is undistinguished but the flowers, which last for two days and nights, are gorgeous. Some people regard this plant as a synonym of the white-flowered *E. eyriesii*, but Friedrich Ritter argues for their continued separation on a number of grounds, not least the very different seeds.

The plant illustrated is a vegetative propagation from a plant collected on the Cerro de Ouro, Rio Grande do Sul, Brazil.

Echinopsis randallii

Form: Simple. To 3.3 ft (1 m) high and 11.8 in (30 cm) across.

Spines: Radials and centrals mixed, 25–32. To 2 in (5 cm) long; reddish brown.

Flower: Purple. 2.8 in (7 cm) across. June in cultivation; October–December in habitat.

Flowering time from seed: 8–9 years.

Distribution: Bolivia (Paicho valley).

Also seen listed in the genera *Trichocereus* and *Helianthocereus*, this is a very handsome plant by virtue of its long and dense spination, which is an attractive shade of reddish brown. The striking purple flowers are not always reliably produced, and a plant may miss the odd year once it has started flowering, while some plants never seem to flower at all in cultivation.

The plant illustrated below was grown from seed that was collected near Paicho, Tarija, Bolivia, RBC363.

Epiphyllum floribundum

Form: Stems flat and soft, with serrated margins. To 19.6 in (50 cm) long and 1.2–2 in (3–5 cm) across.

Spines: Very short, bristly.

Flower: Creamy white to pale yellow. To 4.7 in (12 cm) long and 3.9 in (10 cm) across. During summer in cultivation.

Flowering time from seed: 4–5 years.

Distribution: Peru (Yanomamo, northeast of Iquitos).

Most people who grow these so-called orchid cacti tend to opt for one of the plethora of hybrids with their large, extraordinarily flamboyant blooms. Since they are usually produced by crossing with other genera, to call them *Epiphyllum* is botanically incorrect. Pure-bred species have seldom been available until relatively recently, and this is one of the best. It was discovered in moist Amazonian rainforest by Dr Mildred Matthias. They thrive under the staging, away from the intense glare of direct sunlight, and should be planted in a peat-free compost such as coir mixed with composted bark.

The plant illustrated here is a vegetative propagation from the type collection.

Epithelantha micromeris

DATA

Form: Flattened-spherical. To 0.8 in (2 cm) across; sometimes forming large clumps.

Spines: Very short and dense; usually white, sometimes reddish or blackish.

Flower: Tiny, pinkish, only to 0.2 in (6 mm) across, in spring and summer.

Flowering time from seed: 4–5 years.

Distribution: Southwestern United States to northern Mexico.

In habitat single-headed plants of this diminutive species lurk in cracks in the rocks on arid mountainsides. Seed-raised plants are reasonably easy to grow on their own roots and are self-fertile, so you will always have a continuous supply of seed even from a single plant. Some people add crushed limestone to the compost, but this is not strictly necessary. *Epithelantha bokei* is an even more beautiful miniature with an extremely dense snow-white spination. Sadly, neither species is offered very often by dealers, but if you manage to obtain one, take care not to overwater it.

The plant illustrated above was grown from seed that was collected in Dog Canyon, New Mexico.

Eriosyce aurata

DATA

Form: Simple. To 19.6 in (50 cm) or more high and broad.

Spines: Too variable to describe. Often golden yellow and covering the plant.

Flower: Red, urn-shaped. To 1.4 in (3.5 cm) across. June in cultivation, November–December in habitat.

Flowering time from seed: 15–20 years.

Distribution: Chile (widespread in the north-central desert regions, particularly up the inland valleys).

In recent years all the plants formerly included in *Neoporteria* and *Pyrrhocactus* have been lumped into *Eriosyce*. This approach has not been followed here, and the plant illustrated is an *Eriosyce* in its narrower sense, as originally conceived. In habitat some forms exhibit a splendid long, dense, golden spination—but this aspect is very variable, and some forms are much less attractive. Unfortunately, this species is extremely difficult to keep alive in cultivation, since it is very intolerant of root disturbance, with the result that repotting is often fatal. Cultivated plants seldom, if ever, flower.

The plant illustrated was photographed north of Punitaqui.

Escobaria sneedii

DATA

Form: Stems to 2.4 in (6 cm) long and 0.4–0.8 in (1–2 cm) across, clumping to form colonies of 50 or more heads.

Spines: Radials numerous; 0.1–0.15 in (4–5 mm) long. Centrals 5–7; 0.2–0.3 in (6–8 mm) long; white; tipped darker.

Flower: Purplish pink. 0.6 in (1.5 cm) long. June–July in cultivation.

Flowering time from seed: 4–5 years.

Distribution: United States (Dona Ana County, New Mexico, and El Paso County, Texas).

The dense clumps of whitish heads make this a particularly attractive member of the genus. It should be grown relatively hard, because it will quickly lose its roots if overwatered. The roots will benefit from being restricted inside the smallest pot that looks reasonable. *Escobaria leei* is similar but more slender, and is regarded by some people as a form of *E. sneedii*. Both plants can be propagated easily by detaching offsets and rooting them up.

The plant illustrated is a vegetative propagation of a plant collected in Slaughter Canyon, New Mexico.

Escobaria tuberculosa

DATA

Form: Very variable. Stems 2–7 in (5–18 cm) high and 1–2.8 in (2.5–7 cm) across, usually forming clumps.

Spines: Radials 20–30; 0.1–0.6 in (4–15 mm) long. Centrals 5–9; thicker and longer.

Flower: Pink. 1 in (2.5 cm) wide. June–July in cultivation.

Flowering time from seed: 3–4 years.

Distribution: United States (western Texas and southern New Mexico) to northern Mexico.

Often listed as *Escobaria strobiliformis*, this is probably the most common member of the genus in cultivation. The mode of growth is very variable, from tall, cylindrical plants that offset only sparingly to plants with large clumps of small, almost globular heads. A number of other species, such as *E. dasyacantha*, *E. chihuahuensis*, *E. orcuttii*, *E. organensis*, and *E. villardii* are broadly similar in appearance and have similar flowers.

The plant illustrated was grown from seed collected in southern Texas.

Espostoa huanucoensis

Sometimes listed as a form of *Espostoa lanata*, this attractive plant is becoming more common in collections as seed arrives from South America. Finding the plants is not difficult, since on the arid slopes surrounding the town of Huánuco they occur in their massed thousands, their white wool glistening in the sun. Their proximity to the town is evident from the illustration below. A number of plants formerly included in *Thrixanthocereus* have now been transferred to *Espostoa*, the most attractive and collectable being the superb white-spined *E. senilis*.

DATA

Form: Clumping. Stems to 6.6 ft (2 m) long; 2.4–4 in (6–10 cm) across.

Spines: 30–40. Radials and centrals intermixed; mostly 0.2–0.4 in (0.5–1 cm) long; golden yellow to reddish yellow; mixed with large numbers of white hairs 0.8–1.6 in (2–4 cm) long.

Flower: Whitish. 2 in (5 cm) long.

Flowering time from seed: 20 years or more, but flowers are rare in cultivation.

Distribution: Peru (Huánuco).

Espostoa lanata

DATA

Form: Treelike with a
trunk; woolly. To 13.2 ft
(4 m) high.

Spines: Radials numerous;
needlelike; yellowish.
Centrals usually 2;
0.8–1.6 in (2–4 cm) long.

Flower: Pinkish white.
2 in (5 cm) long.

**Flowering time from
seed:** 20 years or more.

Distribution: Southern
Ecuador to northern Peru.

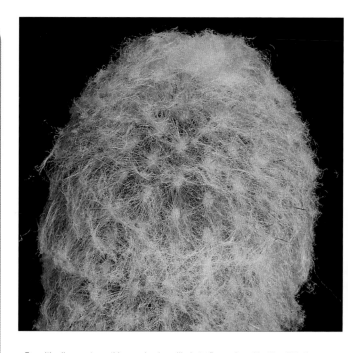

As with all espostoas, this species is unlikely to flower in cultivation. This is no
great loss, however, since the flowers are rather dull, they appear at night, and
they barely protrude from the cephalium that develops along one side of the mature
plant. Espostoas are grown for the beauty of their stems, which in this species are
relatively broad and fairly well covered in whitish cream wool. This has always been
a traditional mass-produced favorite, often available at garden centers. Being slow-
growing, it will not rapidly outgrow its welcome.

The plant illustrated is a typical commercial seedling without provenance.

Espostoa melanostele

This is a taller, more upright plant than *Espostoa nana*, which is closely related but has much shorter stems that tend to lean over (see page 118). *Espostoa melanostele* is characteristic of the coastal valleys near Lima where it often occurs in its thousands in unbelievably arid conditions, as in Tinajas Canyon (see below). Such an ability to survive on very little water might indicate a certain touchiness in respect of watering in cultivation. In fact, it is a very easy plant to keep going and needs no special treatment, although it is worth making an effort to keep the lovely white wool as clean as possible.

DATA

Form: Stems upright, branching from the base. To 6.6 ft (2 m) high and 3.9 in (10 cm) across.

Spines: Numerous; bristly. Yellow, intermixed with abundant white hairs. Mostly only to 0.2 in (0.5 cm) long, but they are mixed with other stouter spines that grow to 1.6 in (4 cm) or more long.

Flower: White. 2 in (5 cm) long.

Flowering time from seed: 20 years or more.

Distribution: Peru (Rio Písco to Rio Saña).

Espostoa nana

Form: Sprawling clumps.
Stems to about 5 ft
(1.5 m) high.

Spines: Yellow. Radials 30
or so; 0.3 in (0.75 cm)
long. Centrals 1; to 2 in
(5 cm) long.

Flower: White. 2 in
(5 cm) long.

**Flowering time from
seed:** 15 years or more.

Distribution: Peru
(near Caraz).

Both in cultivation and in habitat this is a far more elegant plant than *Espostoa lanata*: it is more densely covered in wool that is of a much purer shade of white. It is closely related to the previous species, and since both are slightly sensitive to frost, they should be kept well above freezing in winter. They should also be handled with care when repotting, because the spines project inconspicuously through the nice soft wool and are needle-sharp.

The plant illustrated above was one of thousands seen growing in the Santa valley near Caraz, PM 074.

Espostoopsis dybowskii

This attractive woolly plant has at times been included in *Cephalocereus*, *Gerocephalus*, and, most familiarly, in *Austrocephalocereus*, where it is often still listed in commercial catalogs. Whether it is destined to remain permanently in its present genus is anyone's guess. In cultivation it is a strong and rapid grower, but it must be kept well above freezing in winter. Like many columnar plants, it is grown for its looks rather than its flowers, which are unlikely to appear under greenhouse conditions.

The plant illustrated below was grown from seed that was collected near Flamengo, Bahia, AH430.

DATA

Form: To 13.2 ft (4 m) high; branched from the base.

Spines: Radials short but numerous, concealed beneath abundant white hair. Centrals 2–3; to 1.2 in (3 cm) long; yellowish.

Flower: White; bell-shaped. 1.6 in (4 cm) long.

Flowering time from seed: 15–20 years.

Distribution: Brazil (Bahia, Itumirin).

Eulychnia acida

Form: To about 23 ft (7 m) high, forming a tree with a woody trunk that grows to 3.3 ft (1 m) long.

Spines: Centrals and radials mixed. To 7.8 in (20 cm) long.

Flower: White or pinkish; top-shaped. 2 in (5 cm) broad. Mostly October– January in habitat.

Flowering time from seed: 15–20 years.

Distribution: Chile (from Illapel and Choapa to almost as far north as Vallenar).

In habitat the spines of some plants can be among the longest known in the cactus family, but in cultivation they tend to be shorter. The plants are also more slender than those in habitat. Being slow-growing, they do not reach a great size, even when planted in a bed with full root-run. Similarly, the flowers are not normally seen under greenhouse conditions. The large green fruits are edible and have a sweetly acidic taste.

The plant illustrated was photographed in flower near Vallenar.

Eulychnia saint-pieana

In this rather small member of the genus the areoles are covered in white felt, giving the stems a very attractive appearance. If you grow only one *Eulychnia*, this must be it. Seedlings up to about 10 years old are particularly handsome, but older plants often start to look a little dowdy. Growth is pretty slow, making this plant suitable for a small greenhouse. Despite coming from a frost-free area, this species is relatively hardy, and will easily resist temperatures at or just below freezing.

The plant illustrated was grown from seed collected near Esmeralda, PM 207.

DATA

Form: Branching, bushlike. 6.6–13.2 ft (2–4 m) high.

Spines: Radials 8–12; 0.2–0.8 in (0.5–2 cm) long. Centrals 1–2; 2–3.9 in (5–10 cm) long.

Flower: White. 2–2.9 in (5–7.5 cm) across. Mostly October– January in habitat.

Flowering time from seed: 15–20 years.

Distribution: Chile (north of Chañaral).

Ferocactus chrysacanthus

DATA

Form: Usually simple. Spherical to cylindrical. To 3.3 ft (1 m) high and 11.8 in (30 cm) across.

Spines: Radials usually 4–8; white. Centrals up to 10; to 2 in (5 cm) long; usually yellow, sometimes pink.

Flower: Yellow. 2 in (5 cm) across. June in habitat, September–October in cultivation.

Flowering time from seed: 15–20 years.

Distribution: Mexico (Baja California; Cedros and San Benito Islands).

With its dense golden (sometimes pink) spination, this is one of the most handsome members of the genus, perhaps rivaled only by certain forms of *Ferocactus gracilis*. However, *F. chrysacanthus* is particularly slow-growing, and it takes many years for a seedling to attain flowering size. Even then, it reaches only about 4.7 inches (12 cm) across and 3.9 inches (10 cm) high. Flowering is not guaranteed, and very old plants that are considerably larger than this will often have failed to come up with a single bud.

The plant illustrated above was grown from seed that was collected on Cedros Island, Lau 010.

Ferocactus echidne

Although perhaps not the most handsome member of the genus, the deep, acute ribs are quite distinctive and this species has the merit of being one of the easiest ferocacti to flower in cultivation. Growth is relatively rapid, and large clumps soon form, although this tends to depend on the origin of the seed—some forms are less inclined to offset than others. As with many ferocacti, black sooty mold from the extrafloral nectaries on the areoles can be a big problem, and will need to be washed off regularly.

The plant illustrated was grown from seed collected near Río Jalpán, Querétaro.

DATA

Form: Clumping. Heads to 3.3 ft (1 m) long and 11.8 in (30 cm) across.

Spines: Radials 7; 0.8 in (2 cm) long. Centrals about 7; 0.8–2.4 in (2–6 cm) long.

Flower: Yellow. 1.2 in (3 cm) across. May–June in cultivation.

Flowering time from seed: 6–8 years.

Distribution: Widespread in east-central Mexico.

Ferocactus emoryi rectispinus

Form: Simple. To 6.6 ft (2 m) high and 18.7 in (45 cm) across.

Spines: Radials 8–12; to 2.4 in (6 cm) long. Centrals 1; 1.6–9.8 in (4–25 cm) long; straight or curved over at the tip; not hooked.

Flower: Yellow. 2.4 in (6 cm) long. July–August in habitat.

Flowering time from seed: 15 or so years.

Distribution: Mexico (Baja California).

Enthusiasts for long-spined cacti eagerly seek out this plant, always hoping to find one with an even longer central spine. The plant body is an attractive grayish green. This, together with the length of the spines, compensates for the frequent absence of flowers in greenhouse conditions, although some forms are more free-flowering than others. Growth is a little slow, but faster than in *Ferocactus emoryi emoryi*. The latter has shorter central spines and, in young plants, very prominent tubercles on the ribs.

The plant illustrated above was grown from seed that was collected on the Cerro Colorado, Baja California.

Ferocactus flavovirens

This is one of two similar species that form low, broad mounds composed of large numbers of heads—the other being *Ferocactus robustus*. Both species are common around Tehuacán in Puebla, Mexico. Whereas the latter species seems reluctant to flower in cultivation—even at 30 or more years from seed— *F. flavovirens* flowers freely from about half that age. Despite growing together in habitat, in cultivation *F. flavovirens* seems slightly more frost-sensitive than *F. robustus* and should be kept a few degrees above freezing in winter.

The plant illustrated was grown from seed collected near Tehuacán.

DATA

Form: To 15.8 in (40 cm) high by 7.8 in (20 cm) across; clumping to form mounds 6.6 ft (2 m) broad.

Spines: Radials 14; to 0.8 in (2 cm) long. Centrals 4; the lowermost one being 1.6–3.2 in (4–8 cm) long.

Flower: Brick red. 1.2 in (3.5 cm) across. July– August in cultivation.

Flowering time from seed: About 15 years.

Distribution: Mexico (southeast Puebla to northern Oaxaca).

Ferocactus fordii

Form: Usually simple. Heads to 4.7 in (12 cm) across; 5.9 in (15 cm) tall.

Spines: Radials about 15. Centrals usually 4; to 1.6 in (4 cm) long; one usually flattened and hooked.

Flower: Purple. 1.6 in (4 cm) across. June–July in cultivation.

Flowering time from seed: 5–7 years.

Distribution: Mexico (west coast of Baja California).

This is one of the smallest members of the genus. It will flower freely from quite an early age, which makes it a relatively sought-after species. Seedlings are not always freely available, however, and you may have to make an effort to seek one out. Like most of the cacti from Baja California, this plant is remarkably cold-hardy, and will withstand temperatures near freezing, despite coming from a frost-free environment. In its natural homeland it is severely threatened by habitat destruction.

The plant illustrated above was grown from seed that was collected near San Quintín, Baja California.

Ferocactus glaucescens

In habitat this species, with its distinctive bluish green stems, grows in rocky areas under oaks and pines. In cultivation growth is relatively rapid, and plants can be expected to start blooming within a reasonable timescale, after which they should produce a few flowers every year. Unfortunately, the sooty mold so typical of greenhouse-grown ferocacti can be particularly unsightly on the pale bluish surface typical of this attractive species.

The plant illustrated was grown from seed collected in the Valle de las Fantasmas, west of Río Verde, San Luis Potosí.

DATA

Form: Simple or forming large mounds. Heads to 27.4 in (70 cm) high and 19.6 in (50 cm) across.

Spines: Radials 6–7. Centrals 1. All yellowish; to 1.2 in (3 cm) long.

Flower: Yellow. 0.8 in (2 cm) long. June–July in cultivation.

Flowering time from seed: 12–15 years.

Distribution: Mexico (Hidalgo, Querétaro, and San Luis Potosí).

Ferocactus gracilis

DATA

Form: Simple. To 9.9 ft (3 m) high and 11.8 in (30 cm) across.

Spines: Radials 10; 1–1.6 in (2.5–4 cm) long. Centrals 7–13; one flattened, one hooked; to 2 in (5 cm) long.

Flower: Yellow. 1.6 in (4 cm) long. June–July in cultivation and in habitat.

Flowering time from seed: 20 years or more.

Distribution: Mexico, (central northern Baja California).

The spination of this plant is variable. What also varies is the likelihood of it producing flowers in cultivation. Some forms have a somewhat open covering of thin pinkish spines. In others (see illustration above), the spines are much broader, are of a vivid bright pinkish red color, and occur so densely that they more or less conceal the plant body beneath. Similarly, while some forms may, with a little luck, flower at about 20 years from seed, others will never flower in greenhouse conditions no matter how big they get.

The plant illustrated above was grown from seed that was collected south of Cataviña, Baja California.

Ferocactus hamatacanthus

In some ways this is similar to the previous species in that some forms are much more handsome and densely spined than others. For example, DJF1019.37 from Val Verde County, Texas, is far more densely spined than the plant illustrated. If you like your plants well clothed, it's probably best not to buy this species by mail order—you should at least specify to the nursery owner that you want a heavily spined specimen. Most plants flower freely and have large attractive blooms, but a few forms tend to be a little shy in this respect. In subspecies *sinuatus* the flower is plain yellow and the lowermost central spine is very flattened.

The plant illustrated was photographed near Huizache, San Luis Potosí.

DATA

Form: Usually simple, sometimes clumping. To 23.6 in (60 cm) high and 11.8 in (30 cm) across.

Spines: Very variable. Radials 8–12; 0.4–2.8 in (1–7 cm) long. Centrals 1–4; to 4.7 in (12 cm) long; at least one hooked.

Flower: Yellow with a red throat. To 2.8 in (7 cm) long. July–August in cultivation and in habitat.

Flowering time from seed: 7–8 years.

Distribution: United States (southeast New Mexico, western and southern Texas); Mexico (central north, southward to San Luis Potosí).

Ferocactus histrix

Form: Simple. To about 3.3 ft (1 m) high and 31.5 in (80 cm) broad.

Spines: Radials 7–12. Centrals 3–4; to 2.4 in (6 cm) long.

Flower: Yellow. 1 in (2.5 cm) long. June–July in cultivation.

Flowering time from seed: 8–12 years.

Distribution: Widespread in central Mexico, e.g., common in some spots near San Luis Potosí city.

This is a plant that has often been grown in large numbers for supply to garden centers. It is very easygoing, presenting no problems other than the usual unsightly staining by black mold. However, because of the open spination, a great deal of the epidermis is exposed to the sun, so burning can be a problem under glass if there is not enough shade and ventilation. Older plants flower well, although the flowers are not very large.

The plant illustrated above was grown from seed that was collected near San Luis de La Paz, Guanajuato.

Ferocactus peninsulae

Being fairly slow from seed, this species will not quickly outgrow a smallish greenhouse, but it has the advantage of eventually producing its gorgeous flowers within an acceptable timescale—and every year once they have started. The spines are extremely strong, and the hook on the lowermost central is incredibly sharp and able to draw blood in surprising quantities from an unwary hand—so be careful. Like all the cacti from Baja California, this plant is surprisingly hardy, easily withstanding temperatures close to freezing.

The plant illustrated was grown from seed collected between Mulegé and Santa Rosalía, Baja California.

DATA

Form: Simple. To about 8 ft (2.5 m) high and 15.8 in (40 cm) across.

Spines: Radials about 11; to 1.2 in (3 cm) long; white. Centrals 6; to 2.4 in (6 cm) long; ruby red; hooked.

Flower: From red to yellow, with orange to red mid-veins. About 2 in (5 cm) across. August–October in habitat and in cultivation.

Flowering time from seed: About 20 years.

Distribution: Mexico (central and eastern Baja California).

Ferocactus pilosus

DATA

Form: Clumping. Individual stems to 9.9 ft (3 m) high and about 2 ft (60 cm) across.

Spines: Radials about 5–9, often mixed with hairs. Centrals 4–7; cruciform, not hooked, red; to 1.6 in (4 cm) long.

Flower: Orange. 0.8–1.2 in (2–3 cm) across. July–September in habitat.

Flowering time from seed: 20 years or more.

Distribution: Northern central Mexico.

This plant will be valued for its neat red spination rather than for its small orange flowers, which appear only reluctantly in greenhouse conditions, even on very old plants. As with many cacti, the spination is variable, and plants grown from seed from some localities are far more attractive than from others, so it pays to see a plant before you buy it. This species is still often seen listed as *Ferocactus stainesii* var. *pilosus*. In some parts of Mexico hundreds of plants are dug up from the desert and planted in rows along the central reservations of new roads.

The plant illustrated was photographed near Huizache, San Luis Potosí.

Ferocactus viridescens

This species rivals *Ferocactus fordii* in its willingness to flower at a small size and a young age under greenhouse conditions, even in cool climates. The flowers are less spectacular than in *F. fordii*, but are nevertheless well worth looking out for each year. In terms of spination *F. viridescens* probably has the edge, being slightly the more attractive of the two when out of flower. The ribs are slightly tuberculate, but in var. *littoralis* they are not, and the central spines are not flattened.

The plant illustrated below was grown from seed that was collected near Chola Vista in California.

DATA

Form: Simple or offsetting. Heads to 11.8 in (30 cm) high and broad.

Spines: Radials 9–20; to 0.8 in (2 cm) long. Centrals 4; to 4.3 in (11 cm) long, the largest flattened.

Flower: Yellowish green. 1.6 in (4 cm) across. Spring in habitat, June–July in cultivation.

Flowering time from seed: 6–8 years.

Distribution: United States (California) to Mexico (northern Baja California).

Frailea phaeodisca

DATA

Form: Simple or clumping. Heads 0.6–1.2 in (1.5–3 cm) across.

Spines: 6–9. Bristly, very short, pressed closely against the plant body.

Flower: Yellow. 1.2 in (3 cm) across.

Flowering time from seed: 2–3 years.

Distribution: Paraguay (Tacuarembó).

Fraileas are something of an enigma. Some people do not have any success in growing them and are forced to give up, mainly because most of the plants die. In addition, the flowers of many species seldom, if ever, open. Then suddenly, on a particular afternoon, almost every species will have its cheerful yellow flowers on full display. Some of the smaller and more attractive species (for example, *Frailea cataphracta* and *F. mammifera*), are relatively short-lived anyway, while the slender, more cylindrical ones (such as *F. gracillima*) quickly grow too lax and tall, and topple over. The species offered here is one of the easier ones to grow.

The plant illustrated is a commercial seedling without provenance.

Glandulicactus uncinatus

DATA

Form: Simple. Bluish green. To 7.8 in (20 cm) high and 3.9 in (10 cm) across.

Spines: Radials 7–8; 1–2 in (2.5–5 cm) long. Centrals to 4; one to over 3.5 in (9 cm) long; hooked.

Flower: Brownish. To 1 in (2.5 cm) long. May in cultivation.

Flowering time from seed: 5–6 years.

Distribution: Mexico (Chihuahua to San Luis Potosí); United States (Texas).

In the last few years this species has been placed in *Ancistrocactus*, *Ferocactus*, *Hamatocactus*, *Pediocactus*, and, most recently, *Sclerocactus*. For various reasons the author prefers to revert to Backeberg's *Glandulicactus*. In the most northerly forms (var. *uncinatus*) the central spines are up to 5.9 inches (15 cm) long and there is an orange tint to the flower. Farther south in San Luis Potosí, the plants have spines that reach only about 1.2 inches (3 cm), and the flower is the color of dark chocolate. The long hooked spines make this species a nightmare to handle and to set out among other plants (especially others with hooked spines), and it can be tricky to keep alive, quickly succumbing to rot if the compost is allowed to hang wet.

The plant illustrated above was grown from seed that was collected in the Franklin Mountains, Texas.

Gymnocalycium ambatoense

Form: Flattened-globular. Simple or sometimes clumping. Heads to 5.9 in (15 cm) across; 2–3.9 in (5–10 cm) high.

Spines: 10–12; 0.8–1.2 in (2–3 cm) long; usually wavy; pale brown.

Flower: White with a pinkish stripe in the center. 1.2–1.6 in (3–4 cm) across. June–July in cultivation, December–January in habitat.

Flowering time from seed: 4–5 years.

Distribution. Argentina (Catamarca, Sierra Ambato, among grass, small ferns, and mosses).

Named for the mountain range in which it grows, this species will be valued for its attractive, rather wavy spination rather than for its flower, which is much the same as most other white-flowered members of the genus. Growth is pretty slow, so this is a good one for anyone with restricted space. The Sierra Ambato is home to several other attractive species of cacti, and even today new discoveries are being made in the more remote areas into which few (if any) roads penetrate.

The plant illustrated was grown from seed collected in the Sierra Ambato.

Gymnocalycium andreae

DATA

Form: Dark green. Heads to 2 in (5 cm) across.

Spines: Thin. Radials 5–7. Centrals 1–3; to 1.2 in (3 cm) or more long.

Flower: Yellow, occasionally white. To 1.8 in (4.5 cm) across. May–June in cultivation, November–December in habitat.

Flowering time from seed: 3–4 years.

Distribution: Argentina (Córdoba).

This species clumps strongly and may eventually fill a 6-inch (15-cm) pan (or larger). The yellow flower is relatively unusual in the genus and is produced in abundance. Various forms have been named, the most distinctive of which, the white-flowered subspecies *carolinense,* has recently been elevated to species status. In var. *longispinum* the spines are up to 1.6 inches (4 cm) long, while in var. *fechseri* the offsets are narrowly cylindrical. In subspecies *maznetteri* the plants are mainly simple and the flowers white to pale pink. *Gymnocalycium andreae* is susceptible to damage by red spider mites, so watch out for early signs of their presence.

The plant illustrated above is a vegetative propagation from a plant that was collected in the Sierra Grande.

Gymnocalycium baldianum

DATA

Form: Simple or clumping. Dark green. Heads to 2.8 in (7 cm) across.

Spines: 5–7, usually just radials; 0.2–0.4 in (0.5–1 cm long).

Flower: Usually red, sometimes white. 1.2–1.6 in (3–4 cm) across. May–June in cultivation; November–December in habitat.

Flowering time from seed: 3–4 years.

Distribution: Argentina (Catamarca).

This species is deservedly popular because of its red flower. It is not invariably red, however—in its mountainous habitat populations are known in which plants with various shades of red flowers are mixed with white-flowered ones. The spination also varies, and some recent collections are much more densely and strongly spined than previously known. In some localities this usually solitary plant grows in large clumps. When not in flower it can be hard to spot, since it often nestles down among a dense growth of grasses, ferns, and mosses in places that—in the rainy season at least—are damp and lush. The white-flowered *Gymnocalycium amerhauseri* seems to be simply a form from an outlying population.

The plant illustrated is in habitat near Singuil, Catamarca.

Gymnocalycium bruchii brigittae

DATA

Form: Clumping strongly. Heads usually 1.2–2 in (3–5 cm) across.

Spines: Just 8 radials; about 0.2 in (0.4 cm) long.

Flower: Bright pink. 1.2 in (3 cm) across. May–June in cultivation; December in habitat.

Flowering time from seed: 2–3 years.

Distribution: Argentina (Córdoba).

Named for Brigitte Piltz, wife of Jörg Piltz (a well-known German cactus collector and specialist in *Gymnocalycium*), this is one of the most distinctive and attractive of a number of named forms of *G. bruchii*. Most of them have white or very pale pink flowers (or sometimes yellow) and occasionally rather dense whitish spination. In var. *brigittae* the spination is much shorter and more sparse, almost fully exposing the bluish green body beneath.

The plant illustrated above is a vegetative propagation from a plant that was collected near Taninga, San Luis, Piltz 214.

Gymnocalycium capillaense

DATA

Form: Somewhat flattened
Clumping. Heads to 2.4 in
(6 cm) across.

Spines: Just 5 radials;
to 0.4 in (1.2 cm) long;
yellowish white; thin.

Flower: White, often with
a pink flush. To 2.4 in
(6 cm) across. June–July
in cultivation; November–
December in habitat.

**Flowering time from
seed:** 3–4 years.

Distribution: Argentina
(Córdoba).

This easy-to-grow plant is very similar to *Gymnocalycium parvulum*, although
G. capillaense has broader, flatter heads and more open spination. Clumping
starts from an early age, and clumps with dozens of heads are eventually attained
in cultivation, although in habitat groupings of just a few heads tend to be the norm.
Flowering takes place over several weeks and each flower lasts a few days, making
large clusters quite a sight over a long period. Red spider mites can be a problem on
this soft-bodied plant, so watch out for signs of attack.

*The plant illustrated is a vegetative propagation from a plant that was collected at
Capilla del Monte (hence the specific name).*

Gymnocalycium cardenasianum

The spination of this superb plant is very variable. Some of the most spectacular heavily spined forms were found by Friedrich Ritter near El Paicho and named by him as *Gymnocalycium armatum*, a superfluous name for what is a further range extension of his already described *G. cardenasianum*. Although growth from seed is relatively slow, some pretty impressive spines often start to appear at only three to four years old. If you buy seed, however, you cannot be sure of getting really long-spined plants unless they are from a specific locality where this is the norm.

The plant illustrated, grown from seed collected near Carrizal, was one of a batch, all of which had spectacularly long spines from a very young age.

DATA

Form: Simple. To 11 in (28 cm) high and 7.8 in (20 cm) across.

Spines: Radials 3–6; to 2.4 in (6 cm) long. Centrals 0–2; to 3.2 in (8 cm) long.

Flower: Pink to white. To 3.5 in (9 cm) across (usually smaller). June–July in cultivation.

Flowering time from seed: 5–6 years.

Distribution: Southern Bolivia (Dept. Tarija, originally described from Carrizal but now known more widely, e.g., Villa Pacheco, Socpora, San Luis de Palqui and El Paicho).

Gymnocalycium castellanosii

DATA

Form: Simple. To 5.9 in (15 cm) high; 3.9 in (10 cm) across.

Spines: Radials 5–7. Centrals 0–1; to 1 in (2.5 cm) long.

Flower: White, suffused pink. 1.8 in (4.5 cm) across. May in cultivation; October and often again in December in habitat.

Flowering time from seed: 4–6 years.

Distribution: Argentina (Córdoba).

This is a variable plant, and the form illustrated (subspecies *bozsingianum*) was originally described as a species in its own right. Even in plants raised from a single seed pod the spination can look so different that they could be mistaken for several different species. J. Lambert's *Gymnocalycium acorrugatum*, although distinctive enough to be worth growing, is part of the same complex and is regarded by some people as a form of *G. castellanosii*. In habitat this species generally grows in part shade under thorny trees and bushes.

The plant illustrated was grown from seed collected near Chepes Viejo, PM277.

Gymnocalycium catamarcense

For many years this species was incorrectly given the name *Gymnocalycium hybopleurum*. It was only as recently as 1995 that it received a valid name, reflecting the province of Argentina in which it occurs. Several forms have been named over the last few years, all of them distinct in cultivation and worth a place in the greenhouse. The type plant chosen to represent the name came from near Andalgalá, where it forms very large mounds on steep slopes beneath trees. Other forms clump only sparingly, if at all. Growth rates of the various forms also vary widely, the dark-bodied, wild-spined subspecies *schmidianum* being extremely slow.

The plant illustrated below is forma ensispinum *and was photographed on the Cuesta de Chilca, Catamarca.*

DATA

Form: Broadly spherical. To 5.9 in (15 cm) or more across, often forming large mounds.

Spines: Spines mostly 9. To 1.2 in (3 cm) long. Centrals often absent.

Flower: White. To 1.6 in (4 cm) long. May–June in cultivation; November–December in habitat.

Flowering time from seed: 5–6 years.

Distribution: Argentina (Catamarca).

Gymnocalycium fleischerianum

DATA

Form: Usually clumping. Bright grass green. Heads 2–2.8 in (5–7 cm) across.

Spines: To 20; thin and bristly. To 1 in (2.5 cm) long.

Flower: White. To 1.4 in (3.5 cm) across. June–July in cultivation.

Flowering time from seed: 4–5 years.

Distribution: Paraguay, among grass and rocks.

The bright green body color of this rarely seen plant is distinctive, as is the dazzlingly pure white of the flower. Until recently, genuine verified material was hard to come by, but plants propagated by offsets from field-collected material have recently become more widely available. Growth is relatively slow, and it takes a while to build up a reasonable cluster. *Gymnocalycium denudatum* looks a little similar but is darker green and bears flowers up to 2.8 inches (7 cm) across.

The specimen illustrated is a vegetative propagation from a plant collected near Piribebuy, Uruguay, Piltz 453.

Gymnocalycium gibbosum

DATA

Form: Dark green to blackish, usually simple. To about 23.6 in (60 cm) high; 4.7 in (12 cm) broad.

Spines: Radials usually 7–10; to 1.4 in (3.5 cm) long. Centrals 0–3; of similar length.

Flower: White. To 2.4 in (6 cm) across. June–July in cultivation; October–December in habitat.

Flowering time from seed: 5–6 years.

Distribution: Argentina (from San Luis to Río Chubut and Río Negro).

This species varies greatly over its huge range, one of the largest of any South American cactus. The most spectacular form is subspecies *ferox*, which has a pretty impressive array of spines. In var. *chubutense* the body is generally flattened and rather sparsely spined. Measuring just 1.6 to 2.4 inches (4–6 cm) across, the recently described (1997) *Gymnocalycium berchtii* from Los Chañares in San Luis is closely related and similar to the larger and even more recently described (1999) *G. poeschlii* from near La Toma in San Luis. These two, along with *G. striglianum* and *G. borthii*, form a group of mostly black-bodied plants closely related to *G. gibbosum*.

The plant illustrated was grown from seed collected at Puerto Madryn, Chubut, PM378. The locality has almost certainly now been built over.

Gymnocalycium horridispinum

Form: Bright green; simple or clumping. Heads to 3.2 in (8 cm) across and 7.8 in (20 cm) high.

Spines: Radials 10–12; 0.8–1 in (2–2.5 cm) long. Centrals 4; 1.2–1.6 in (3–4 cm) long.

Flower: Usually bright pink. 2.4 in (6 cm) across. May in cultivation; November–December in habitat.

Flowering time from seed: 4–5 years.

Distribution: Argentina (Córdoba).

The description and distribution (left) fit the original *Gymnocalycium horridispinum*, which was only recently rediscovered in habitat after many years of fruitless searching. In the meantime, *G. achirasense*, which is undoubtedly a form of *G. horridispinum*, was described from San Luis. Subsequently both of them, along with a host of newly named forms, were demoted to subspecies of *G. monvillei*. This seems to be incorrect, because in at least one locality they occur together without interbreeding. This leaves all the new names without any valid combination with *G. horridispinum*, which is a pity, since all the *horridispinum/achirasense* forms are well worth growing for their spination and often spectacularly large flowers.

The plant illustrated below was grown from seed that was collected in the Sierra de las Arboles, GN384-1286.

Gymnocalycium mazanense

DATA

Form: Broadly spherical; simple. To 5.9 in (15 cm) or more across.

Spines: Radials 7 or more; to 2 in (5 cm) long. Centrals usually 0.

Flower: Pinkish white. 1.2 in (3 cm) across. May in cultivation; in habitat October and usually again in December.

Flowering time from seed: 5–6 years.

Distribution: Argentina (Mazán).

Attempts have been made recently to attach the old and poorly typified name *Gymnocalycium hossei* to this species. The author prefers to use Backeberg's unambiguous name derived from the Sierra Mazan in which this heavily spined plant occurs, growing under small bushes and in open rocky places. This is one of the slower-growing species, but given time it will plod its way into being one of the most spectacularly spined members of the genus. A close relative, although not as impressive, is *G. guanchinense* (or *G. rhodantherum*, another old name that has recently been revived).

The plant illustrated was grown from seed that was collected on the Cuesta de la Cebila, La Rioja, PM285.

Gymnocalycium monvillei

DATA

Form: Usually clumping. Heads to 12.6 in (32 cm) across and 11.8–35.4 in (30–90 cm) high.

Spines: Radials 7–13; to 1.6 in (4 cm) long; pale yellow. Centrals usually 1 in older plants.

Flower: White to bright pink. To 3.2 in (8 cm) wide. May in cultivation; November–December in habitat.

Flowering time from seed: 5–6 years.

Distribution: Argentina (Córdoba, in the Sierra Chica and Sierra Grande and in the mountains in the south of Santiago del Estero).

For many years known as *Gymnocalycium multiflorum*, the name *G. monvillei* now seems firmly attached to this plant. Its former reputation for being sparing with its flowers now seems ridiculous, given the abundance of blooms seen every year on present-day material, mostly derived from habitat-collected seed. In subspecies *brachyanthum* the flowers are only 1.6 to 2 inches (4–5 cm) long, but are usually of a flamboyant shade of pink. In the more recently described and prolifically clumping var. *steineri* the long twisted spination is particularly spectacular.

The plant illustrated was photographed in the Sierra de Córdoba.

Gymnocalycium mostii

This species often grows alongside *Gymnocalycium monvillei*, sometimes in places that ooze with water in the rainy season. In cultivation *G. mostii* usually clumps after a few years, although growth is generally slow, and it takes a few years to form a good-sized mound. In the closely related *G. valnicekianum* the spines are more slender and cover the plant more densely. Both species appreciate generous amounts of water in the growing season. The handsome and very slow-growing plant once known as *G. mostii* var. *ferocior* has been transferred to *G. castellanosii*.

The plant illustrated was photographed on a hillside south of Lan Granja.

DATA

Form: Simple or clumping. Body to 3.5 in (9 cm) or more high; 4.7 in (12 cm) across.

Spines: Radials 15; 1–1.2 in (2.5–3 cm) long. Centrals up to 4.

Flower: White with red throat. 2 in (5 cm) across. June in cultivation; November–December in habitat.

Flowering time from seed: 4–5 years.

Distribution: Argentina (Córdoba).

Gymnocalycium neuhuberi

DATA

Form: Simple. To about 2 in (5 cm) high and 2.8 in (7 cm) across.

Spines: Radials 9; to 0.8 in (2 cm) long. Centrals 4; a little longer than radials.

Flower: Bright pink. To 1.4 in (3.5 cm) across. May–June in cultivation; November–December in habitat.

Flowering time from seed: 3–4 years.

Distribution: Argentina (San Luis, in the southern reaches of the Sierra de San Luis).

With its vivid pink flower this is one of the major discoveries of recent years. It was described in 1992 and is named for Gert J. A. Neuhuber, the well-known Austrian *Gymnocalycium* specialist who discovered this distinctive new species during his 1988 expedition to Argentina. Although it is superficially similar to *G. horridispinum* and *G. monvillei*, it is in a different seed group and so only very distantly related. The winter temperatures in its mountainous habitat can drop to 5°F (–15°C), so there need be no worries about providing much heat in cultivation.

The plant illustrated above was grown from seed that was collected from alongside Route 3, San Luis.

Gymnocalycium nigriareolatum

This species, as illustrated here, grows in hundreds on shady, mossy banks on the Cuesta de Portezuelo outside Catamarca, Argentina. On flatter ground beneath thorn trees to the north of the city you can find large multiheaded clumps of var. *densispinum*, looking confusingly similar to *Gymnocalycium valnicekianum* from distant Córdoba. The Sierra de Ancasti is home to forma *carmineum*—probably the best of the bunch with its beautiful carmine-red flower. All are easy to cultivate, although var. *densispinum* and var. *carmineum* are not yet seen often in collections.

DATA

Form: Simple or clumping. Body velvety green; to 5.9 in (15 cm) broad; 3.9 in (10 cm) high.

Spines: Radials 7–8; to 1.2 in (3 cm). Centrals usually 0.

Flower: White with a pink throat. 1.6 in (4 cm) broad. May in cultivation, November–December in habitat.

Flowering time from seed: 4–5 years.

Distribution: Argentina (Catamarca).

Gymnocalycium ochoterenai vatteri

DATA

Form: Simple. Olive green to grayish green. To 1.6 in (4 cm) high; 3.5 in (9 cm) across.

Spines: 1–5. To about 0.6 in (1.7 cm) long.

Flower: White. 1.6 in (4 cm) across. June–July in cultivation; November–December in habitat.

Flowering time from seed: 3–4 years.

Distribution: Argentina (Córdoba, Sierra Grande, near Nono).

Formerly listed as *Gymnocalycium vatteri*, this is probably the best known and neatest-looking of the forms of *G. ochoterenai*, itself an attractively flattened and much larger plant. The more recently described subspecies *herbsthoferianum* is a much taller short-cylindrical plant from Lujan in San Luis. It grows up to 3.9 inches (10 cm) high and is quite densely spined. In habitat all these plants usually grow in dense shade beneath bushes. They are therefore at risk of burning if kept too close to unshaded glass during hot weather in cultivation.

The plant illustrated was photographed right beside the road near Nono.

Gymnocalycium parvulum

This is an old name that is now being widely attached to the plant grown in collections for many years as *Gymnocalycium calochlorum*. It bears a strong resemblance to a large-bodied *G. bruchii*—both species clump strongly, but the flowers in *G. parvulum* are much longer. In habitat the heads are often sunk in the ground among grass and can be difficult to spot until they swell up after rain and start to come into bloom. Propagation from offsets is easy, and the lowermost ones will probably already have rooted themselves down within the clump.

The plant illustrated below is a vegetative propagation from a plant that was collected near Nono.

DATA

Form: Clumping. Heads to 2.4 in (6 cm) across; 1.6 in (4 cm) high.

Spines: Radials 9; thin; to 0.4 in (0.9 cm) long. Centrals 0.

Flower: Usually white, sometimes pink. To 2.4 in (6 cm) long. June–July in cultivation; December in habitat.

Flowering time from seed: 3–4 years.

Distribution: Argentina (Córdoba).

153

Gymnocalycium saglione

DATA

Form: Simple. To 31.5 in (80 cm) high and 11.8–15.8 in (30–40 cm) across.

Spines: Radials 8–15; to 1.6 in (4 cm) long. Centrals usually 1.

Flower: White or pinkish. 1.4 in (3.5 cm) across. July in cultivation; October–December in habitat.

Flowering time from seed: 7–9 years.

Distribution: Argentina (widespread in Salta, Tucumán, Catamarca, and La Rioja; a disjunct northern population in Jujuy).

This is by far the largest-growing member of the genus. In cultivation very handsome, free-flowering specimens can be grown from seed in about 10 years. The spination is a little variable, and plants from some localities grow much larger than others. The urn-shaped flowers, although not large, are most unusual and attractive. In plants from the northern population in Jujuy, now known as subspecies *tilcarense*, the flowers lack a tube, and this inspired Backeberg to create a separate genus, *Brachycalycium*, for them.

The plant illustrated is subspecies tilcarense, *grown from seed that was collected at Tilcara, Jujuy, PM335.*

Gymnocalycium schickendantzii delaetii

This is a widely distributed species. Dense populations are rare—scattered plants, usually hidden in deep shade beneath bushes and small trees, are the norm. Spine length varies greatly, and some very handsome forms with long, heavy spines have been offered for sale in recent years. The subspecies illustrated here, *delaetii*, is now sometimes regarded as a separate but closely related species. It has a broader, flatter body with a more open spination, exposing more of the very distinctively greenish blue epidermis, and it occurs in a completely separate disjunct population.

The plant illustrated below was grown from seed that was collected near El Carrizal, Salta, HU1142.

DATA

Form: Usually simple. To 5.9 in (15 cm) high; 7.1 in (18 cm) across.

Spines: Variable. Radials 6–7; to 1.2 in (3 cm) long. Usually no centrals.

Flower: Pink; broad. About 1.6 in (4 cm) across. June–July in cultivation; mostly December in habitat.

Flowering time from seed: 4–5 years.

Distribution: Argentina (Salta).

Gymnocalycium spegazzinii

DATA

Form: Usually simple. To
7.8 in (20 cm) across;
7.1 in (18 cm) high.

Spines: Radials 5–7; to
2.2 in (5.5 cm) long.
Centrals usually 0.

Flower: Whitish to pinkish.
To 2 in (5 cm) across.
June in cultivation;
November–December
in habitat.

**Flowering time from
seed:** 5–6 years.

Distribution: Argentina
(from the Quebrada del
Toro in Salta to Capillitas
in Catamarca).

Over its wide area of distribution the spination of this handsome species varies greatly. Some collectors acquire a range of plants in order to represent the species fully. The most elegant forms are those in which the spines are relatively long and curve downward, following the contours of the plant. This gives a very neat appearance that, for the author at least, makes this species the finest "gymno" of all. In cultivation growth is relatively slow but trouble-free. Some people now regard *Gymnocalycium cardenasianum* as simply a northern subspecies of *G. spegazzinii*.

The plant illustrated was photographed in the Quebrada del Toro, Salta.

Gymnocalycium stellatum

Usually growing in dense shade under trees and bushes, this plant is closely related to several others that have similar habits, including *Gymnocalycium bodenbenderianum* and *G. ochoterenai*. For a good many years plants of *G. stellatum* were sold under the name *G. quehlianum*, a situation that arose because of confusion about the identity of the latter plant (now regarded as a quite different and distinctive species). One thing remains constant—these are all excellent plants for anyone with little room to spare in their greenhouse, since they remain fairly small and are neat and attractive. Several varieties of *G. stellatum* have been named, but they differ little from the type seen here.

The plant illustrated below was grown from seed that was collected at Capilla del Monte, Córdoba, LB1118.

Form: Usually flattened; sometimes clumping. Body grayish or brownish green; to 3.9 in (10 cm) across.

Spines: 3–8; shortish.

Flowers: White. To 2 in (5 cm) across. July in cultivation; November–December in habitat.

Flowering time from seed: 3–4 years.

Distribution: Argentina (Córdoba, La Rioja, and Catamarca).

Gymnocalycium tillianum

DATA

Form: Simple or sparingly offsetting. Body to 3.9 in (10 cm) high; 5.9 in (15 cm) across.

Spines: Radials 7. Centrals 0–1. All about 1.2 in (3 cm) long.

Flower: Red. 1–1.2 in (2.5–3 cm) across. May–June in cultivation; mainly December in habitat.

Flowering time from seed: 4–5 years.

Distribution: Argentina (Catamarca, Sierra Ambato).

Some people are now attaching Backeberg's name *Gymnocalycium oenanthemum* to this red-flowered plant from the Sierra Ambato. However, since it lacked any specific habitat, and red-flowered forms of *G. nigriarolatum* are now known, it seems safer to use Rausch's well-documented *G. tillianum*. Another name that has been used for a long time, *G. carminanthum*, undoubtedly represents the same species as Rausch's earlier name. Whatever you choose to write on the label, this is a lovely plant, a good strong grower, and worth having for its vivid red flower alone.

The plant illustrated above was grown from seed that was collected near Los Ángeles, Catamarca, ZJ115.

Gymnocalycium uruguayense

The so-called *Gymnocalycium uruguayense* complex involves a very variable set of prolifically clumping plants, some of which have received their own names, such as *G. artigas*, *G. netrelianum*, *G. leeanum*, *G. guerkeanum*, and *G. hyptiacanthum*. Since each of them more or less grades into the next one, and plants a mere stone's throw apart can look very different, it is not really possible to maintain these as valid species. The one really outstanding form that is well worth acquiring is var. *roseiflorum* with a beautiful pink flower—far more rewarding than the usual rather dingy greenish yellow blooms seen on all the other forms. Alas, it is not very freely available at present.

The plant illustrated is a vegetative propagation from a plant collected from Punta Ballena, Maldonado, Uruguay, Schlosser 138.

DATA

Form: Clumping. Heads flattened-globular. To 2.8 in (7 cm) across.

Spines: Usually about 10; thin; all radials. To 0.8 in (2 cm) long.

Flower: Yellow. About 1.6 in (4 cm) long. June in cultivation.

Flowering time from seed: 3–4 years.

Distribution: Widespread in Uruguay and neighboring southern Brazil.

Gymnocalycium zegarrae millaresii

DATA

Form: Simple. 2.4–3.2 in (6–8 cm) high. 4.7–5.5.in (12–14 cm) across.

Spines: Radials 7–9. Centrals 1–2. All 0.8–1.6 in (2–4 cm) long.

Flower: Pinkish. 4 cm (1.6 in) across. June–July in cultivation; October–December in habitat.

Flowering time from seed: 5–6 years.

Distribution: Bolivia (Millares, on quartzite rocks).

This species and its forms have often been included with *Gymnocalycium pflanzii* a generally clumping plant with far fewer ribs and larger, less urn-shaped flowers. *Gymnocalycium zegarrae* is one of the largest-growing members of the genus, exceeded in size only by *G. saglione*. Given a large enough pot, growth in cultivation is fairly rapid, and after 20 years you can have a plant 5.9 inches (15 cm) across that will reward your patient care with a ring of its small but very attractive flowers every year.

The plant illustrated was grown from seed collected at Millares, PM172.

Haageocereus acranthus

This is one of the largest-growing members of the genus, and its fairly fierce but neat spination earns it a place in any collection. Unfortunately, in common with most members of its genus, it seems reluctant to flower in a greenhouse, but it is a vigorous plant that presents no problems in cultivation. One advantage is that it seems to be more cold-resistant than the golden-spined members of the genus (see page 162). Under current thinking, this species encompasses a number of others, including *Haageocereus achaetus*, *H. clavispinus*, *H. deflexispinus*, and *H. zonatus*.

The plant illustrated was photographed in Tinajas Canyon, south of Lima.

DATA

Form: Clumping. Stems to 6.6 ft (2 m) or more high; 3.2 in (8 cm) across.

Spines: Radials 20–30; yellowish; to 0.4 in (1 cm). Centrals several; to 1.6 in (4 cm).

Flower: Greenish white. 2.4–3.2 in (6–8 cm) long.

Flowering time from seed: 15 years or more.

Distribution: Valleys of central Peru to the north and south of Lima.

Haageocereus multangularis

DATA

Form: Clumping. Stem to about 5 ft (1.5 m) tall; 1.6–2.4 in (4–6 cm) across.

Spines: Densely covering the stems; golden; very variable in spine number and length.

Flower: Wine red. 2.4 in (6 cm) long; 1.6 in (4 cm) across. Mostly October–December in habitat.

Flowering time from seed: 15 years or more.

Distribution: Over a wide area of mainly coastal Peru and inland up the valleys.

This is a very old name that some people dismiss as of uncertain application, preferring to use the much more recent name *Haageocereus pseudomelanostele*. However, this plant is so common near Lima that it is inconceivable that it would not have been described very early on. In addition, the original illlustration seems a good match for the plant shown below, for which at least 15 extra names have been coined over the years, covering the great variation in spination seen in habitat. It is very reluctant to flower in a temperate climate and can also be a little cold-sensitive, so keep it a few degrees above freezing. If you want a *Haageoceus* that will flower, try *H. decumbens*, in which white blooms appear freely in cultivation, but whose sprawling stems need plenty of space.

The plant illustrated was photographed in Tinajas Canyon, south of Lima.

Harrisia martinii

DATA

Form: Stems leaning. To over 6.6 ft (2 m) long; 0.8–1 in (2–2.5 cm) across.

Spines: Radials 5–7; short. Centrals 1; 0.8–1.2 in (2–3 cm) long.

Flower: White. 7.8 in (20 cm) long. July in cultivation.

Flowering time from seed: 6–7 years.

Distribution: Argentina (in the Chaco).

This species was formerly listed in *Eriocereus*, a genus that is now dismissed as superfluous by most authorities on cacti. In habitat the plants grow among trees and shrubs on which they can lean for support, but under greenhouse conditions you will probably need to stake your plant to keep it from falling over. The flowers, which appear at night, are sweetly scented. Even larger nocturnal white flowers can be seen on the long, slender stems of *Selenicereus*. Both genera need plenty of space in which to sprawl and flower, but they are cold-sensitive and should be maintained well above freezing in winter.

The plant illustrated is a vegetative propagation of a plant collected by Roberto Kiesling at Ingeniero Juárez, Formosa, Argentina.

Hatiora salicornioides

DATA

Form: Shoots pencil-thin, forming erect shrubs to 15.8 in (40 cm) high.

Spines: None.

Flower: Yellow; bell-shaped. To 0.6 in (1.3 cm) across. May–July in cultivation.

Flowering time from seed: 4–5 years.

Distribution: Brazil (Rio de Janeiro and Minas Gerais).

Like most of the epiphytic cacti, this plant is normally propagated from cuttings rather than from seed. Cuttings root relatively easily and soon start branching to form new plants. Full sun should be avoided, otherwise the stems shrivel and go red; semishade under the staging will give better results. Formerly included in *Rhipsalis*, this is easily one of the most free-flowering of the epiphytic cacti, as well as having one of the most attractive flowers.

The plant illustrated is a vegetative propagation from a plant collected near Sau el Rei, Minas Gerais.

Hildewintera aureispina

Quite recently *Hildewintera* has been included in *Cleistocactus* as *C. winteri*, yet it seems adequately distinct and is treated as such here. In cultivation it is definitely a plant to be grown in a hanging pot, because the stems soon become long and can be seen at their best only when allowed to hang free. Although often propagated from cuttings, which root well, it also comes easily from seed and will quickly grow into a handsome specimen.

The plant illustrated is a commercial specimen of unknown provenance.

DATA

Form: Clumping strongly. Stems pendant; to about 5 ft (1.5 m) long; 1 in (2.5 cm) across.

Spines: Densely covering the stems. Radials about 30. Centrals about 20. All to about 0.4 in (1 cm) long.

Flowers: Orange; curved. 1.6–2.4 in (4–6 cm) long; 2 in (5 cm) across. May–June in cultivation.

Flowering time from seed: 5–6 years.

Distribution: Bolivia (Florida Province, near Fauces Yapacani).

Lepismium cruciforme

Form: Branched. Stems green; 3–winged. To about 23.6 in (60 cm) long.

Spines: None.

Flower: Small, whitish pink. May–June in cultivation.

Flowering time from seed: 5–6 years.

Distribution: Brazil; Argentina; Paraguay.

This is one of the larger-growing members of the genus and, like all epiphytic cacti with unarmed stems, is probably best grown under the staging in partial shade. Some species of *Lepismium* are reluctant to flower in cultivation, but this species usually produces its blooms very freely over a long period. Epiphytic cacti such as this are best grown in a nonmineral medium, such as a mixture of coir and peat-free compost (composted bark).

The specimen illustrated is a vegetative propagation from a plant collected near Monte Alegre, Rio Grande do Sul, Brazil, AH394.

Leuchtenbergia principis

In its Mexican habitat this unusual plant tends to grow as scattered, hard-to-spot individuals rather than as the large populations typical of most cacti. The long, downwardly pointed, triangular, blue-green tubercles give it a unique appearance, helped by the long raffialike spines that in habitat resemble a clump of dead, bleached grass. Cultivation presents few problems, although growth is fairly slow, but flowering can be unpredictable. The buds often form but are then aborted, and some plants only manage to open fully mature flowers every few years.

The plant illustrated below was grown from seed that was collected at Huizache Junction, San Luis Potosí.

DATA

Form: Usually simple. To 27.6 in (70 cm) high.

Spines: Thin and papery. Radials to 14; 2 in (5 cm) long. Centrals 1–2; to 3.9 in (10 cm) long.

Flower: Yellow. To 3.2 in (8 cm) broad. July–August in cultivation.

Flowering time from seed: 8–10 years.

Distribution: Central to northern Mexico.

Lobivia aurea

DATA

Form: High, simple, or clumping. Heads to 4.7 in (12 cm) across and 3.9 in (10 cm) high.

Spines: Radials 8–16; to 0.4 in (1 cm) long. Centrals up to 4; to 1.2 in (3 cm) long.

Flower: Yellow. 2.8–3.5 in (7–9 cm) long. June–July in cultivation; November–January in habitat.

Flowering time from seed: 3–4 years.

Distribution: Argentina (Córdoba, San Luis).

This widespread plant is very variable, and numerous varieties can easily be acquired. In var. *callochrysea* from the Quebrada de los Conchas in Salta the body is up to 7.8 inches (20 cm) tall and the flower is a stunning 4.3 inches (11 cm across, with a sumptuous satiny sheen. In var. *depressicostata*, common in the woods around the city of Catamarca (see illustration), large many-headed clumps are formed and the flower is bright lemon yellow. Just drive a short way from here, up on to the Cuesta de Portezuelo, and you will find var. *dobeana* with its vivid red flower. The most handsome form, noted for its strong, fierce spination and stems up to 15.8 inches (40 cm) high is var. *fallax* from the Sierra de Malanzán. Also worth getting are var. *albiflora* (which has a white flower) and var. *shaferi* (which has small stems, densely clumping, and central spines to 2 inches/5 cm long).

Lobivia bruchii

Form: Sometimes clumping. Heads flattened-globular; to 19.6 in (50 cm) across.

Spines: Radials 9–14. Centrals to 4; 0.2–0.8 in (0.5–2 cm) long.

Flower: Red, sometimes with a purplish sheen. 2 in (5 cm) across. June in cultivation; November–December in habitat.

Flowering time from seed: 6–10 years.

Distribution: Argentina (Tucumán, near Tafí del Valle).

As the road across the Abra de Infernillo winds down into the small town of Tafí, you will see this plant, as illustrated, in large numbers on the grassy hillsides and even on the road verges near the town itself. At one time placed in *Soehrensia*, and still seen there in some plant catalogs, these days it is most often seen in *Lobivia*, although its correct placement, along with all other lobivias, is in *Echinopsis*. In common with all the species formerly placed in *Soehrensia*, *L. bruchii* has to be older and larger than most lobivias before it will produce flowers. They are well worth waiting for, however, and are plentiful once the plant is old enough.

Lobivia caineana

DATA

Form: Simple; bright glossy green. To 7.8 in (20 cm) high; 3.5 in (9 cm) broad.

Spines: Up to 18; to 2.8 in (7 cm) long but usually much shorter.

Flower: Pink. To 2.8 in (7 cm) across. May–June in cultivation; November–December in habitat.

Flowering time from seed: 5–6 years.

Distribution: Bolivia (along the Río Caine at Calahuta, Capinota, La Viña, etc.).

With its very glossy, fresh grass-green epidermis the appearance of this plant is unique, and it could be mistaken for no other member of the genus. It grows much taller than most and eventually has rather a cereoid habit, although it is relatively slow-growing from seed. A white-flowered form, the so-called var. *albiflora*, is also known, although plants are seldom seen in cultivation. As can be seen here, the flowers are borne very high on the crown of the plant.

The plant illustrated above is a vegetative propagation from a plant that was collected at La Viña on the Río Caine.

Lobivia cardenasiana

This species resembles a miniature *Echinopsis obrepanda*, but it takes up far less room in the greenhouse. This makes it popular with those who are pressed for space, especially since most plants—both in habitat and in cultivation—tend to remain much smaller than the 3.9-inch (10-cm) maximum diameter given here. Plants obtained from nurseries always seem to produce magenta flowers, presumably because seed has been collected less often from the red-flowered population found farther east toward Cajas.

The plant illustrated was photographed in late December near the Condor Pass.

Form: Relatively flat; simple. To 3.9 in (10 cm) across.

Spines: Radials 12–14. Centrals 2–3. All spines up to 1.2 in (3 cm) long.

Flower: Magenta or red. To 3.9 in (10 cm) long. June in cultivation; November–December in habitat.

Flowering time from seed: 3–4 years.

Distribution: Bolivia (east of Tarija).

Lobivia chrysochete

Form: Simple. Flattened-globular; to 9.8 in (25 cm) across.

Spines: Radials and centrals hard to tell apart, totaling about 30. To 3.2 in (8 cm) long.

Flower: Orange to red. About 1.6 in (4 cm) across. May–June in cultivation; November–December in habitat.

Flowering time from seed: 5–7 years.

Distribution: Argentina (Jujuy) and southern Bolivia.

The large, rather flattened spheres of this plant are reasonably common among grass and boulders in the far north of Argentina, especially in the mountains on either side of the road that runs from Humahuaca to the Bolivian border. Several varieties have been named. Var. *subtilis* from Santa Ana is a miniature form only 3.5 inches (9 cm) across, with more or less hooked central spines. In var. *minutiflora* the plant body can grow to 15.8 inches (40 cm) across, while the diameter of the flower is only about 0.8 inches (2 cm). These giants grow at very high altitudes, among snow in winter, at a few spots along the road from Yavi to Santa Victoria, where the plant illustrated was photographed, flowering just before Christmas.

Lobivia cinnabarina

Along the road between Sucre and Tarabuco this plant sometimes occurs in the thousands, growing among grass that can look almost like a lawn in the wet season. It is often seen in close association with even larger numbers of *Parodia tuberculata*. Several varieties of *Lobivia cinnabarina* have been named, the most distinctive being var. *grandiflora* from around Padilla and Presto, which has a superb flower up to 3.9 inches (10 cm) across. In var. *draxleriana* (originally described as a species, and often still listed as such) the plant looks distinctively neater and more attractive, and also stays smaller. It grows near Aiquile.

The plant illustrated was grown from seed collected near Tarabuco.

DATA

Form: Simple or forming small clumps. Body to 5.9 in (15 cm) across.

Spines: 12–16, 1 of which is a central spine. To 0.8 in (2 cm) long.

Flower: Red. 2.4–3.2 in (6–8 cm) across. May–June in cultivation, November–December in habitat.

Flowering time from seed: 4–5 years.

Distribution: Bolivia (around Sucre and eastward to Zudañez).

Lobivia crassicaulis

Form: Clumping. Heads
to 3.9 in (10 cm) broad;
5.9 in (15 cm) high.

Spines: Radials up to 10;
to 0.3 in (0.7 cm) long.
Centrals 1–4; stouter; to
1 in (2.5 cm) long.

Flower: Red with a black
throat; not opening widely.
2.4–3.2 in (6–8 cm) long.
June in cultivation;
December in habitat.

**Flowering time from
seed:** 4–5 years.

Distribution: Argentina
(Catamarca, near
Andalgalá).

Also often seen listed as *Lobivia andalgalensis* or *L. grandiflora crassicaulis*, this is
a plant that is well worth growing just for the showy deep-red flowers with
their shiny black throats. As with all lobivias, they open in the morning and generally
start closing just after midday. This once led to a race against time along very poor
dirt roads as the author hurried toward a particular rocky outcrop between Singuil
and Andalgalá, in order to take the above photograph before the flowers closed up. It
was touch and go, and the flowers have just started to shut, but you should see
them slightly more open on your plants in cultivation.

Lobivia ferox longispina

For anyone who is a connoisseur of savagely spined cacti this is a "must," although the length and density of the spination varies from one locality to another, as does the eventual shape and maximum size of the adult plant. The color of the flowers ranges from white through yellow and orange to pink or red, and they have a very powerful and sweet perfume, quite unlike that of the normal white-flowered (occasionally pink) *Lobivia ferox ferox*. Growth from seed is quite rapid, but older specimens have a strong tendency to go brown low down around the sides.

The plant illustrated below was grown from seed that was collected at Cieneguillas, Bolivia, PM184.

Form: Usually simple. To 9.8 in (25 cm) high and broad.

Spines: Radials 10–12; to 2.4 in (6 cm) long. Centrals 3–4; to 5.9 in (15 cm) long; brown to blackish.

Flower: White, yellow, pink, bronze, or red. To 8 cm (3.2 in) across. June in cultivation; November–December in habitat.

Flowering time from seed: 5–6 years.

Distribution: Scattered in numerous localities from southern Boliva to northern Argentina.

Lobivia formosa

DATA

Form: Usually simple. To about 8 ft (2.5 m) high; 19.6 in (50 cm) across.

Spines: Up to 20. To 3.2 in (8 cm) long.

Flower: Yellow. 2.8 in (7 cm) long. June–July in cultivation, November–December in habitat.

Flowering time from seed: 15–20 years.

Distribution: Argentina (from Mendoza to Catamarca).

Often still obstinately clinging on its its old placement in the genus *Soehrensia*, this is the largest-growing species of *Lobivia*. The chances of your plant flowering may depend on where the seed originated. Most seed comes from habitat and, if collected from very large-growing plants, you will probably not see any flowers. The author has seen very large greenhouse-grown plants more than 50 years old that have never flowered, while plants in his own collection have produced blooms at about 15 years of age. Try obtaining var. *kieslingii* from the Sierra de Quilmes in Tucumán. It is a red-flowered dwarf form that is better treated as a separate species, as originally described. The same applies to the even smaller var. *rosarioana* from the Sierra Famatina. It is 3.9 inches (10 cm) across and is easy to flower at 5 to 6 years from seed.

The plant illustrated was photographed at Capillitas, Catamarca.

Lobivia grandiflora

DATA

Form: Clumping. Stems 5.9–15.8 in (15–40 cm) high; 2.4–3.9 in (6–10 cm) thick.

Spines: Yellowish. About 15; to 0.4 in (1 cm) long.

Flower: Red. 8–10 cm (3.2–3.9 in) long. June–July in cultivation; mainly December in habitat.

Flowering time from seed: 5–6 years.

Distribution: Argentina (Catamarca).

You will need to grow this clumping species in a pan. It is worth giving it the extra space because the flowers are superb, although certain plants appear reluctant to produce any while others put on a wonderful display every year. Several varieties have been named, really differing only in small details of size and spination. The most distinctive form is probably var. *longispina*, from Agua de las Palomas, with one to four central spines up to 1.6 inches (4 cm) long. The most space-saving form, and probably the best for a smaller greenhouse, is var. *pumila* from Agua Blanca, with almost globular heads that cluster tightly together to form a compact mound.

The plant illustrated is a vegetative propagation (WR526a) of a plant collected near Catamarca city, where Lobivia grandiflora *is common in the nearby hills.*

Lobivia haematantha

Form: Simple or sparingly clumping. Heads 2–3.9 in (5–10 cm) high and 2.4–2.8 in (6–7 cm) broad.

Spines: Radials 5–6; 0.4 in (1 cm) long. Centrals 3–4; to 2 in (5 cm) long.

Flower: Red with a white throat. 2–2.8 in (5–7 cm) across. May in cultivation; December–January in habitat.

Flowering time from seed: 4–5 years.

Distribution: Argentina (Salta).

In cultivation this is a rather slow-growing plant that will take a long time to reach a reasonable size, making it perfect for the smaller greenhouse in which room is tight. Several varieties have been named, one of which is described more fully on the page opposite. Of the others, var. *hualfinensis,* which has a central spine up to 3.2 inches (8 cm) long and a fiery orange flower, is definitely the best. Not far behind it comes var. *amblayensis* whose short, dark spination contrasts nicely with its yellow or orange flowers, which can reach up to 3.9 inches (10 cm) across. Both varieties were originally described as species and are still often listed as such in plant and seed catalogs.

The plant illustrated is a vegetative propagation of WR165 collected from Cachi.

Lobivia haematantha kuehnrichii

n cultivation this variety tends to stay quite small, although some forms cluster
readily, while others remain solitary. It has a large taproot and therefore needs a
eep pot. The variation in flower color is a great attraction, and some really subtle
ades often turn up in large batches of seedlings. The most similar form is the even
maller and very dark-bodied var. *chorrillosensis* from Chorrillos in the Quebrada del
ro, where it grows on slopes above the road leading up to Puerta Tastil. At some
stance from these—at Abra Blanca near Cafayate—grows var. *viridis*, which has
fresh green body and red flowers 1.6 to 2 inches (4–5 cm) across.

he plant illustrated was grown from seed collected at Piedra del Molino.

DATA

Form: Often clumping.
Heads 1.6–2.4 in
(4–6 cm) across and high,
but usually smaller.

Spines: Radials 9–12.
Centrals 1–4; up to
2.4 in (6 cm) long.

Flower: Yellow, orange,
or red. To 2.8 in (7 cm)
across. May–June in
cultivation, November–
January in habitat.

**Flowering time from
seed:** 2–3 years.

Distribution: Argentina
(Salta, Cachipampa, from
La Poma to Tintin and
Piedra del Molino).

Lobivia hertrichiana

DATA

Form: Clumping strongly. Heads 1.6–3.9 in (4–10 cm) high; 1.6–3.2 in (4–8 cm) across.

Spines: Radials 8–20; 0.6–0.8 in (1.5–2 cm) long. Centrals 1–2; to 2.4 in (6 cm) long.

Flower: Red, sometimes with a white throat. To 2.4 in (6 cm) across. June–August in cultivation; October–December in habitat.

Flowering time from seed: 3–4 years.

Distribution: Peru (mainly in the Urubamba valley).

It is a pity that so many collectors turn up their nose at this plant, regarding it as too "common" to bother with. It deserves more attention, for the flowers are really gorgeous and on large clumps are produced over many weeks, while the spines in some forms are impressively long. Ritter's *Lobivia minuta* from Pisac and Rausch's long-spined *L. echinata* from Ollantaytambo are simply forms lying within a broad range of natural variation. In fact, from a single seed pod collected at Pisac, the author germinated just two seedlings, one of which turned into a typical *hertrichiana* and the other a typical *minuta*.

The plant illustrated above was photographed in deep shade under bushes on the old Inca terraces at Pisac, PM068.

Lobivia huascha rubusta

With its plump, neatly compact upright stems and dense spination *Lobivia huascha rubusta* is probably the best form of this variable species. Unfortunately, if you don't have plenty of room in your greenhouse, then you are probably not going to be able to grow this plant to its best advantage. It will need a pretty large pan in order to thrive and display its magnificent blooms. If you can spare the space, then do so, since the flowers are spectacular and last several days, unlike in most lobivias. The red-flowered var. *rubriflora* from near Andalgalá is slightly smaller-growing and has rather untidy, sprawling stems, but the flowers are wonderful. Near Famatina there is a population of var. *huascha,* which has flowers in shades of red, orange, yellow, white, pink, and violet.

The plant illustrated was grown from seed collected at Hualfín, PM360.

DATA

Form: To about 5 ft (1.5 m) high and 3.5 in (9 cm) thick; forming clumps.

Spines: Radials about 13; to 1 in (2.5 cm) long. Centrals 1–4; to 2.4 in (6 cm) long.

Flower: Yellow. 3.2–3.9 in (8–10 cm) across. June in cultivation; mainly December in habitat.

Flowering time from seed: 8–12 years.

Distribution: Argentina, (Catamarca, Hualfín).

Lobivia jajoiana

DATA

Form: Simple. To 2.4 in (6 cm) high and broad.

Spines: Radials 9–11; 0.4–0.8 in (1–2 cm) long. Centrals 1–3; to 1.2 in (3 cm) long; somewhat hooked.

Flower: Tomato red. 2.4 in (6 cm) across. May in cultivation; December–January in habitat.

Flowering time from seed: 4–5 years.

Distribution: Argentina (Jujuy, Quebrada de Humahuaca, Quebrada de Purmamarca).

This is a relatively slow-growing plant with a large taproot. It tends to be attractive to red spider mites, so keep a lookout for incipient scarring. The typical form has tomato-red flowers, but several other forms have been named. In var. *nigrostoma* from near Tilcara the flowers are yellow, orange, or red and up to 3.2 inches (8 cm) across. In var. *paucicostata* (often offered for sale as *Lobivia glauca*) from high in the Quebrada de Purmamarca, the plant body is very glaucous and the rib count is low. Near Punta Corral grows var. *aurata* with only short radial spines, no centrals, and a lovely golden yellow flower.

The plant illustrated was photographed in the Quebrada de Purmamarca.

Lobivia lateritia

The author was fortunate enough to come upon a population of this species at Puente San Pedro (see photograph below). Hundreds of plants were in flower in spectacular range of colors, making a nonsense of the original description of the ower as red (the color of the red earth known as laterite, hence the plant's name.) cultivation plants with a similar range of flower colors have been raised from seed ent from habitat by various collectors over the years. However, a single seed pod ollected by the author at the above-mentioned locality produced just white-owered plants. In the darker-spined var. *rubriflora* only red flowers are produced, hile in var. *cotagaitensis* and in var. *kupperiana* (which has long, dark spines) the owers are always yellow.

DATA

Form: Simple. To about 19.6 in (50 cm) high and 3.9 in (10 cm) thick.

Spines: Radials 15–17; to 0.6 in (1.5 cm) long. Centrals 2–3; to 1.2 in (3 cm) long.

Flower: White, pink, yellow, orange, or red. 2 in (5 cm) long. May–June in cultivation; December in habitat.

Flowering time from seed: 5–6 years.

Distribution: Bolivia (south of Camargo).

Lobivia marsoneri

DATA

Form: Simple (clumping when damaged). In habitat partly buried in the ground. To 3.2 in (8 cm) across.

Spines: Radials about 10. Centrals 2–5; to 2.8 in (7 cm) long, mostly much shorter; partly hooked.

Flower: Yellow to red, often with a violet sheen, sometimes silvery white. 2.4–2.8 in (6–7 cm) across. May–June in cultivation; December–January in habitat.

Flowering time from seed: 4–5 years.

Distribution: Argentina (Jujuy, along the Quebrada de Humahuaca).

This cactus often occurs in thousands in certain places on the stony hills on either side of the main north–south road from Humahuaca northward to the Bolivian border. Stepping just off the road and coming across hundreds of plants in full flower is an experience to be remembered. The flowers are much loved by bees, which start making their pollen-collecting visits before the flowers are properly open, and they have to force their way in past the slightly parted petals. In cultivation this can be a tricky plant, prone to losing its roots for no apparent reason. Maybe we just keep it too hot under glass, and cook it.

The plant illustrated above was growing right beside the road to the north of Humahuaca, PM371.

Lobivia maximiliana

The type plant as described here has relatively short but striking flowers, and the individual plant bodies are squat. In var. *caespitosa* (below) the flowers are much longer—to 3.5 inches (9 cm)—and the heads, at least in cultivation, are much narrower and more elongated. The flowers in var. *charazanensis* are yellow and to 2 inches (5 cm) long, while in var. *violacea* from Altamachi they are violet and 1.8 inches (4.5 cm) long. One of the most free-flowering forms is var. *miniatiflora* from between Inquisivi and Quime. It has lovely red flowers 2.4 inches (6 cm) long and 1.6 inches (4 cm) across. All forms of *Lobivia maximiliana* in cultivation are prone to attack by red spider mites, but var. *miniatiflora* is more resistant than most.

The plant illustrated below is a vegetative propagation from a plant that was collected from Ayopaya, Lau 310.

DATA

Form: Clumping to form large mounds. Heads to 3.9 in (10 cm) across.

Spines: Radials 7–15. Centrals 1–3; to 2.4 in (6 cm) long; golden brown to yellow.

Flower: Orange with a yellow center. 0.8–1.2 in (2–3 cm) long; 0.8 in (2 cm) across. May–June in cultivation; mostly November–January in habitat.

Flowering time from seed: 4–5 years.

Distribution: Northern Bolivia and southern Peru, mainly around Lake Titicaca.

Lobivia pampana

DATA

Form: Usually clumping. Heads to 3.9 in (10 cm) across.

Spines: 7–20. To 2.8 in (7 cm) long.

Flower: Orange, often with a fiery iridescence. To 2.8 in (7 cm) across. May–June in cultivation; November–December in habitat.

Flowering time from seed: 3–5 years.

Distribution: Southern Peru.

With flowers that appear to glow with an inner fire, this is one of the author's favorite lobivias, although it tends to be prone to attack by red spider mites. In cultivation the individual heads quickly become relatively cylindrical, while in habitat they are usually much broader and flatter, forming compact flat-topped clumps. Rausch's var. *borealis* from farther north near Oyón in the Churin valley is an unusual plant with a strange pink flower, much smaller than in the type. It remains rather rare in cultivation and has defied several recent efforts to rediscover it in the wild.

The plant illustrated above was grown from seed that was collected about 20 miles (33 km) north of Arequipa, PM468.

Lobivia pentlandii

The flowers and spination in this species are both so variable that numerous names have been coined, the most common being *Lobivia boliviensis* (which has long, really wild spination), *L. carminantha*, *L. leucorhodon*, *L. omasuyana*, *L. raphidacantha*, *L. titicacensis*, *L. varians* (another long-spined one), and *L. wegheiana*. All these names, plus a few more, for just one plant! In habitat the heads tend to be much flatter than in cultivation under glass, where they usually become abnormally elongated and cylindrical—but even this varies according to where in habitat the seed originated. No matter what the origin of the seed or the name on the plant, one thing you can be sure of is plenty of flowers.

The plant illustrated was grown from seed collected at Viacha, Bolivia, PM148. Plants from this seed batch also flowered orange yellow, while seedlings of PM144 from nearby Oruro flowered pink, yellow, orange, and salmon, but not red.

DATA

Form: Clumping. Heads to 4.7 in (12 cm) across.

Spines: Radials 9–12; to 0.6 in (1.5 cm) long. Centrals 1–2; to 3.9 in (10 cm) long.

Flower: Yellow, salmon, pink, violet, orange, or red; sometimes almost pure white. 1.6–2 in (4–5 cm) across. May in cultivation; October–December in habitat.

Flowering time from seed: 3–4 years.

Distribution: Highlands of southern Peru and northern Bolivia.

Lobivia thionantha

Form: Simple. To 19.6 in (50 cm) or more high; 5.9 in (15 cm) across.

Spines: Radials around 10. Centrals 1–4; 0.4–1.2 in (1–3 cm) long.

Flower: Yellow. 2 in (5 cm) across. June in cultivation, October–December in habitat.

Distribution: Argentina (Salta, Catamarca, and Tucumán).

Formerly included in the genus *Acanthocalycium*, this is a distinctive species with a number of different forms, apart from the typical form illustrated here. In var. *catamarcensis* from the Sierra de Quilmes the spines are up to 2 inches (5 cm) long and the flowers a more orange shade of yellow. An attractive bluish tint to the body is the most notable characteristic of var. *glaucum,* which grows between Belén and Hualfín. The most attractive form is probably var. *chionanthum.* It has lovely snow-white flowers and occurs in thousands on rocky slopes and gravely plains from Cachi to La Poma. Unfortunately, unlike all the other forms, it is a little tricky in cultivation and tends to lose its roots easily.

The plant illustrated was photographed near Amaicha del Valle, Tucumán.

Lobivia tiegeliana pusilla

Whereas *Lobivia tigeliana* itself usually has single heads and red flowers, var. *pusilla* (orginally described as *L. pusilla* and still often sold as such) offsets so prolifically that it rapidly forms mounds made up of dozens of heads. These then produce an eye-catchingly colorful array of blooms over several weeks. In the equally multiheaded var. *flaviflorus* the flowers are a lively shade of lemon yellow. If your plant gets too big, it is easy to break it up and start again, and you are sure to find that many of the offsets will already have self-rooted.

The plant illustrated was grown from seed collected near La Ventolera, Tarija.

DATA

Form: Flattened-globular; forming large clumps. Heads to 1.6 in (4 cm) across.

Spines: Radials 20; to 0.2 in (0.5 cm) long. Centrals 0–1; slightly longer.

Flower: Pink to red. 1.6 in (4 cm) across. May–June in cultivation; November–December in habitat.

Flowering time from seed: 2–3 years.

Distribution: Southern. Bolivia (Orozas and Concepción).

Lobivia wrightiana winteriana

DATA

Form: Simple. 1.6–2.8 in (4–7 cm) across; 2.8–3.5 in (7–9 cm) high.

Spines: Radials 6–14; to 0.3 in (0.7 cm) long. Centrals 0–3, to 2.4 in (6 cm) long.

Flower: Pinkish violet. 3.2 in (8 cm) across. May–June in cultivation; November–December in habitat.

Flowering tiime from seed: 3–4 years.

Distribution: Southern Peru (Huancavelica, Villa Azul).

Whereas in the type form of *Lobivia wrightiana* the pale pink flowers are a little nondescript, the intense shade of pink seen in in this variety is really stunning and possibly unique among the cacti. The *L. wrightiana* type form also clumps heavily as it gets older, while the variety (often seen for sale still as *L. winteriana*) tends to remain solitary. On all the thousands of seed-raised plants seen by the author the central spines have normally been much shorter than the maximum of 2.4 inches (6 cm) given above left—they are often 0.4 inches (1 cm) or less.

The plant illustrated is a vegetative propagation from a plant raised from seed collected in habitat by the original discoverer, Friedrich Ritter, FR1312

Lophophora williamsii

Because it contains the hallucinogenic drug mescaline, in some countries it is forbidden to own a plant of this species, popularly known as the peyote cactus. The heads are very soft-fleshed and arise from a large taproot, so a deep pot will be needed in cultivation. This is an easy plant to grow and it comes readily, albeit slowly, from seed. You will obtain a steady supply of seed from your own plant, since the flowers are self-fertile, and fruits are produced regularly throughout the summer. A second species, *Lophophora diffusa*, is similar but has a slightly larger white flower and greener body, and is a little more cold-sensitive in winter.

The plant illustrated was photographed at Huizache Junction, San Luis Potosí.

DATA

Form: Clumping strongly. Individual heads flattened-globular. Bluish green. To 2 in (5 cm) across.

Spines: Absent; replaced by dense felty tufts of hair.

Flower: Pink. About 0.5 in (1.25 cm) across. Produced over a long period in cultivation and in habitat.

Flowering time from seed: 5–7 years.

Distribution: United States (Texas) and Mexico (from the northeast south as far as Querétaro).

Loxanthocereus ferrugineus

DATA

Form: Branching from the base. Stems upright; to 31.5 in (80 cm) high; 1.6–2 in (4–5 cm) across.

Spines: Radials numerous; thin and interlacing. Centrals 1–4; to 0.8 in (2 cm) long.

Flower: Red. 3.9 in (10 cm) long. June–July in cultivation; December in habitat.

Flowering time from seed: 10 years or more.

Distribution: Peru (Nazca valley).

The name attached to the plant illustrated, photographed between Nazca and Puquio, is tentative, since it clearly has much longer central spines than the Rauh and Backeberg description of *Loxanthocereus ferrugineus*, although the locality is the same. The preferred name could be *L. clavispinus*, described from the same area, but a smaller plant than the one illustrated. That aside, the illustration gives an idea of what a *Loxanthocereus* looks like in flower, although some of the species most often seen in cultivation have sprawling rather than upright stems. The plants in this genus have recently been transferred to *Cleistocactus*, a move that does not appear to be entirely warranted, and it is likely that the name *Loxanthocereus* will continue to appear in lists and on plant labels for some time to come.

Maihuenia patagonica

Large mounds of this unusual plant are a common sight in certain parts of Patagonia, mainly in the Andean foothills, but it is more rare in cultivation, though quite a lot of seed has been brought back in recent years from various cactus-hunting expeditions. Unfortunately, seed is not always easy to germinate, and many resulting plants are extremely slow-growing under glass, with growth usually grinding to a halt as soon as the summer heat sets in. Some people swear that they get far better results outdoors in summer, although this cactus is perfectly hardy if kept out all year, provided it is protected from too much rain in winter.

The plant illustrated below was photographed beside Laguna Blanca in Neuquén Province, Argentina.

DATA

Form: Segments to 2.4 in (6 cm) long and 0.6 in (1.5 cm) across; forming dense cushions to 3.3 ft (1 m) across and 11.8 in (30 cm) high.

Spines: 3, to 1.6 in (4 cm) long, accompanied by tufts of short-cylindrical leaves.

Flower: White to pink to yellow. To 1.6 in (4 cm) across. November–January in habitat.

Flowering time from seed: 15 years or more.

Distribution: Argentina (Patagonia).

Maihueniopsis archiconoidea

DATA

Form: Segments 0.7 in (1.7 cm) long and 0.6 in (1.5 cm) thick; forming flattened clumps atop a long neck arising from a large tuberous root.

Spines: 3–5. About 0.2 in (0.5 cm) long; plus a flattened central spine.

Flower: Yellow. 1.2 in (3.5 cm) across. June in cultivation; November– December in habitat.

Flowering time from seed: 10–12 years.

Distribution: Chile (upper Tránsito valley).

When Friedrich Ritter described this plant he had never seen the flower, and so it was with great interest that the author awaited the opening of the first buds on his own plant (PM231), grown from seed collected at the probable type locality. As can be seen, the flowers are yellow and very similar to those on *Maihueniopsis minuta* (see page 198). The plant illustrated has flowered every summer for the past five years. Until recently very rare in collections, this dwarf cactus is becoming more widely seen, partly because of a large number of propagations made from plants grown from seed collected by the author in habitat in February 1987.

Maihueniopsis darwinii

As with all the *Opuntia* group, propagation of this plant is mainly by rooting the segments rather than from seed. *Maihuueniopsis darwinii* is an extremely variable plant, if the plethora of very different forms currently dismissed as "just another *darwinii*" really belong here and are not, in fact, good species that currently lack a name. Some of them flower every year in cultivation, while others never flower at all, even at great age and size, which does help confirm the doubts.

The plant illustrated is a reasonably typical example of the species, photographed at Puerto Madryn in Chubut province. In cultivation this form tends to sprawl wth age. LB 347 from Cerros del Rosario, San Luis, remains more upright, as does the best form of all, FK91-59-341/2 from Playa Union in Chubut. Both of these are listed by specialist dealers.

DATA

Form: Segments to 2 in (5 cm) long and 1.2 in (3 cm) broad; forming clumps.

Spines: 1–3. Flattened. To 1.2 in (3.5 cm) long.

Flower: Yellow to orange. 1.6–2 in (4–5 cm) across. May–June in cultivation; November–January in habitat.

Flowering time from seed: 5–6 years.

Distribution: Widespread in Patagonia, Argentina.

195

Maihueniopsis glomerata

DATA

Form: Segments to 1.4 in (3.5 cm) long and 0.6 in (1.5 cm) broad; forming large mounds, sometimes with thousands of tiny heads.

Spines: Very variable; sometimes absent or just 1 short spine, sometimes up to 4 principal spines that are up to 2 in (5 cm) long and always flattened.

Flower: Yellow. 1.2–1.6 in (3–4 cm) across. May–June in cultivation; December–January in habitat.

Flowering time from seed: 8–10 years.

Distribution: Argentina (Mendoza).

Just how far north in Argentina this plant extends depends on how wide your concept is of this species. For some people it reaches as far north as Jujuy, while others prefer to restrict their concept of the species to plants from Mendoza, from where this species was originally described. Even here, the variability from one population to another is considerable, and covers most aspects of the plant—from segment size to spine length, number, and color, as well as flower size and shade of yellow. Whatever their origin, they are all handsome and free-flowering plants in cultivation, so it is worth acquiring plants from each named locality whenever they are offered by specialist dealers.

The plant illustrated below was photographed on the high pass between Iturbe and Iruya, Jujuy and is a distinctive form now often known as Maihueniopsis hypogaea.

Maihueniopsis mandragora

DATA

Form: Segments ovoid; to 0.8 in (2 cm) long; forming small clumps.

Spines: 1–3. Very short and thin.

Flower: Yellow. 1.4 in (3.5 cm) across. June in cultivation; December–January in habitat.

Flowering time from seed: 6–7 years.

Distribution: Northern Argentina (Salta, in the upper reaches of the Quebrada del Toro).

n habitat the small stems are often partly covered by soil, and the first you see of the plant may be its yellow flower appearing above the ground. In cultivation rowth is slow, and flowering is not very reliable. Some specimens are better in this espect than others, although the conditions you give it, especially the amount of un, will also come into the equation. This is the perfect cactus for anyone with estricted space, since it will happily keep on adding a few new segments every ear, even when confined in a relatively small pot. In fact, keeping it underpotted eems to help promote flowering.

he plant illustrated above is a vegetative propagation from a collection that was ade at Puerta Tastil, Salta, FK167-576.

Maihueniopsis minuta

DATA

Form: Segments to 0.5 in (1.2 cm) long and 0.3 in (0.8 cm) thick; forming flat clumps.

Spines: Absent or very small.

Flower: Yellow. To 1.2 in (3.5 cm) across. May–June in cultivation; November–December in habitat.

Flowering time from seed: 8–10 years.

Distribution: Argentina (Los Andes).

This relatively small plant is perfect for greenhouse cultivation, since it flowers freely and, if grown slowly, will never need a very large pot. In most respects it is similar to *Maihueniopsis archiconoidea* (see page 194), and it may be that they are nothing more than forms of the same species from different sides of the Andes. As with all these Andean mini-opuntias, it is very hardy and can withstand temperatures well below freezing for long periods. Propagation is normally by detaching the segments, which will usually root down quite quickly even when not much bigger than an oversized pea.

The plant illustrated is a vegetative propagation from a collection that was made in the Sierra de Pie de Palo, Mendoza, Rausch 65245.

Maihueniopsis nigrispina

ow mats of this very dark-looking species are a characteristic sight alongside
■ many of the rough dirt roads that wend their way through the bleak Andean
)lands of northernmost Argentina. In the month coming up to Christmas they are
nsiderably brightened up by crowds of their vivid reddish flowers. Fortunately,
ese are produced in equal abundance in cultivation, making this relatively
minutive species one of the best of the small opuntias for greenhouse culture.
is now becoming more freely available, mostly as vegetative propagations from
eld-collected material.

he plant illustrated was photographed in flower near Abra Pampa, Jujuy.

DATA

Form: Segments elongate-
oval. 0.8–1.2 in (2–3 cm)
long; forming dense,
low bushes to 7.8 in
(20 cm) high.

Spines: 3–5. To 1.6 in
(4 cm) long.

Flower: Purplish red.
To 1 in (2.5 cm) long.
June–July in cultivation;
December–January
in habitat.

**Flowering time from
  seed:** 4–5 years.

Distribution: Argentina
(Jujuy and Salta).

Mammillaria albata

DATA

Form: Clumping. Individual heads to 3.2 in (8 cm) high and broad.

Spines: Radials 23–29; 0.1–0.6 in (0.3–1.5 cm) long; white. Centrals 2–4, 0.2–0.3 in (0.4–0.8 cm) long; white with a brown or blackish tip, or completely black.

Flower: Magenta. About 0.6 in (1.5 cm) across. June–July in cultivation.

Flowering time from seed: 4–5 years.

Distribution: Mexico (San Luis Potosí; fairly widespread).

The above description takes in varieties *sanciro* (black centrals) and *longispina* (long white spines). These are now known to grade into the original type species and into each other over the whole range of the plant, which is now seen to be far more widespread than suspected by its describer, Werner Reppenhagen. In cultivation clumps of this species are about as handsome as a cactus gets, but you do need to use a relatively large pan to get the best results. In recent treatments *Mammillaria albata* has been treated as a subspecies of *M. geminispina*, reviving the far older but rather dubious name of *leucocentra*, rather than using *albata*.

The plant illustrated above was grown from seed that was collected at Arroyo Cannizal, San Luis Potosí.

Mammillaria albicans

n flower this plant is a real stunner, and a "must" for anyone interested in beautiful cacti. The dense white spination is very ornamental at any time of year. As with all namms" from Baja California, however, take care not to overwater it, otherwise ss of roots is virtually guaranteed. It has a fairly sparse, weak root system, so a nall pot is recommended, but adding limestone to the soil does not seem to be ssential, despite the fact that this species grows only on limestone in habitat. *Mammillaria slevinii* from the islands of San Josef and San Francisco is very milar, being rather more slender and less likely to clump, and is now considered s a form of *M. albicans*.

he plant illustrated below was grown from seed collected at Dolores on the ainland of Baja California, Lau 1374.

DATA

Form: Clumping. Stems to 7.8 in (20 cm) high and 2.4 in (6 cm) across.

Spines: Radials 14–21; 0.2–0.3 in (0.5–0.8 cm) long; white. Centrals 4–8; yellowish white, tipped brown; sometimes hooked; of similar length.

Flower: White with a pink midstripe. About 1.2 in (3 cm) across. May–June in cultivation.

Flowering time from seed: 3–4 years.

Distribution: Mexico (Baja California, on Santa Cruz and San Diego Islands and on the mainland west of La Paz).

Mammillaria albicoma

Form: Clumping. Heads 1.6–2 in (4–5 cm) across; rather dome-shaped.

Spines: Radials 30–40; hairlike; to 0.4 in (1 cm) long. Centrals 0–4; to 0.4 in (1 cm) long.

Flower: Greenish yellow to whitish. 0.6 in (1.5 cm) long. April–May in cultivation.

Flowering time from seed: 3–4 years.

Distribution: Mexico (Tamaulipas, near Jaumave, Miquihuana, etc.).

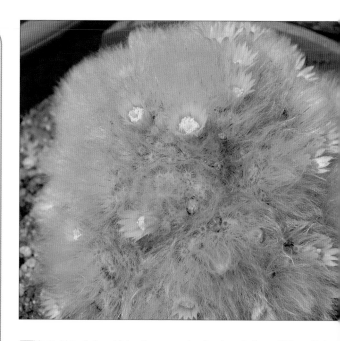

This could easily be mistaken for a more dwarf and woolly form of *Mammillaria bocasana*, but it is a far less common plant in cultivation. It also has central spines that are far less obvious—they are more or less invisible among the dense cloak of white hairs but can be detected by running a fingertip over the plant. It needs more care in terms of watering, since it is much more sensitive to careless overwatering than its larger lookalike. However, because of its small size, it is far more suitable than *M. bocasana* for those who have a small greenhouse but would like to own a handsome woolly plant.

The plant illustrated was grown from seed collected near Jaumave.

Mammillaria albilanata oaxacana

This is now probably the commonest form of *Mammillaria albilanata* in cultivation, although it is often still known by its original name of *M. noureddiniana*. It is certainly one of the finest of the white-spined "mamms" and, like all the forms of *bilanata*, is a very easy plant to grow, so it is highly recommended. As now more broadly conceived, it includes several more of Reppenhagen's names, including *M. lanigera* and *M. monticola*. His *M. igualensis*, which differs mainly in its habit of clumping to form large mounds, is now included within *M. albilanata albilanata*. In subspecies *reppenhagenii* from Colima the spines are darker.

The plant illustrated below was grown from seed that was collected near Totolápan, Oaxaca, ML261.

DATA

Form: Usually simple. To 3.2 in (8 cm) broad; 5.9 in (15 cm) or more high.

Spines: Radials 15–20; to 0.2 in (0.4 cm) long. Centrals 2–4; to 0.1 in (0.3 cm) long. All spines more or less white.

Flower: Deep carmine. To 0.3 in (0.7 cm) long. April–May in cultivation.

Flowering time from seed: 3–4 years.

Distribution: Mexico (Oaxaca and Puebla).

Mammillaria armillata

Form: Clumping. Heads to 11.8 in (30 cm) high and 1.6–2 in (4–5 cm) across.

Spines: Radials 9–15; to 0.5 in (1.2 cm) long. Centrals 1–4; 1 or more hooked, 0.4–0.8 in (1–2 cm) long; brownish to almost black.

Flower: White to pink. To 0.8 in (2 cm) broad. April–May in cultivation.

Flowering time from seed: 3–4 years.

Distribution: Mexico (Baja California, San José del Cabo, Todos Santos, etc.).

In the right compost this is quite a fast-growing plant that will soon begin to offset around the base to form a small, attractive clump. The flowers are perhaps not in the same class as some of the other "mamms" from Baja California, since they are rather dull and, unlike the best of the rest, do not open very widely. Even so, this is a worthwhile addition to any collection. *Mammillaria phitauiana* is very similar, and both species require the smallest pot that will comfortably accommodate their rather sparse root sytems.

The plant illustrated below was grown from seed that was collected at San José del Cabo, Lau 055.

Mammillaria backebergiana

In habitat the long stems of this plant hang from nearly inaccessible cliffs in the great barranca near Ixtapan. In cultivation a tall, old, well-grown plant of this species makes a fine sight in any collection, with its yellowish spination and pale green body. It flowers freely over a relatively long period, and the flowers often open simultaneously in double or even triple rings from a plant apex bearing up to six rings of buds. In subspecies *ernestii* (formerly *Mammillaria ernestii*) from Tonatico in the state of Mexico, the body is darker green and the spination is a little more open.

The plant illustrated below is a vegetative propagation from a plant that was collected at Ixtapan.

DATA

Form: Usually simple. To 11.8 in (30 cm) tall and 2–2.4 in (5–6 cm) across.

Spines: Radials 8–12. Centrals 2–3. All to 0.4 in (1 cm) long; yellowish.

Flower: Purplish red. About 0.5 in (1.2 cm) wide. May–June in cultivation.

Flowering time from seed: 3–4 years.

Distribution: Mexico (state of Mexico, near Ixtapan de Sal; Guerrero).

Mammillaria baumii

Form: Freely offsetting to form large clumps. Heads 1.6–2 in (4–5 cm) across.

Spines: Radials 30–35; hairlike; white; to 0.4 in (1 cm) long. Centrals 5–6; to 0.7 in (1.8 cm) long; pale yellow.

Flower: Yellow. 1.2 in (3 cm) across. May–June in cultivation.

Flowering time from seed: 3–4 years.

Distribution: Mexico (Tamaulipas, near San Vicente and Jaumave; in half shade under bushes).

A large clump of this showy plant covered in its bright yellow flowers is not only a sight to be enjoyed but also a feast for the nose, since the flowers have a powerful scent of lemons. While some plants rapidly offset to form dozens of small heads, others get far larger before beginning to form clumps, which contain just a few, much larger heads. In older books and in lists supplied by more conservative plantsmen this species will be seen listed under *Dolichothele*, which is now generally regarded as a subgenus of *Mammillaria*.

The plant illustrated was grown from seed collected at San Vicente, Lau 1139.

Mammillaria blossfeldiana

Of all the hooked-spined "mamms" from Baja California, this is probably the gem of gems, combining a neat and attractive appearance with a dazzlingly lovely flower. In habitat the plants grow singly, almost buried in granite and gravely soil, but in cultivation they usually form clumps of a dozen or more heads. A taller-growing form, var. *shurliana*, with more cylindrical, usually simple bodies that grow 3.9 inches (10 cm) high is often still listed as a separate species, *Mammillaria shurliana*. Both are worth growing, but you will need to treat them with great care because the slightest hint of too much water will spell death.

The plant illustrated is a typical commercial seedling.

DATA

Form: Simple (in habitat). 1.2–1.6 in (3–4 cm) across and 1.6–2 in (4–5 cm) high.

Spines: Radials about 20; to 0.3 in (0.7 cm) long. Centrals usually 4; to 0.4 in (1 cm) long; hooked; dark brown to black.

Flower: Pinkish with a darker midstripe. 0.8–1.6 in (2–4 cm) across. May–June in cultivation.

Flowering time from seed: 2–3 years.

Distribution: Mexico (Baja California, Punta Prieta and Santa Rosalillita).

Mammillaria bocasana

DATA

Form: Clumping. Individual heads to 2.8 in (7 cm) across; 2 in (5 cm) high.

Spines: Radials 25–30; to 0.8 in (2 cm) long; hair-like. Centrals usually 1; about 0.3 in (0.8 cm) long; hooked; dark brown.

Flower: Cream to pinkish with a darker midstripe. About 0.4 in (1 cm) across. April–June in cultivation.

Flowering time from seed: 2–3 years.

Distribution: Mexico (San Luis Potosí).

Many years ago the author found small clumps of this species in late August, growing in the shade of bushes northwest of the city of San Luis Potosí, Mexico. They bore a few flowers and several ripe fruits. Seedlings raised from a single fruit flowered either pink or yellow and eventually formed mounds far larger than any seen in habitat, as in the above illustration (PM036). The large numbers of plants raised commercially in cultivation tend to be much more densely covered in white wool, being cultivars selectively bred for their appearance. A cristate form of these plants is also sometimes offered, looking rather like a sleeping sheep. A short spined plant is also often seen marketed under the name *Mammillaria schelhasii*.

Mammillaria bocensis

Originally discovered on sandy flats on the coastal plain near Las Bocas in Sonora, this species is now known from a wide area, reaching fairly high up in the mountains. In cultivation older plants begin to clump from the base, but it is a gradual process, since this is one of the slower-growing members of the genus. In var. *rubida* (also seen as *Mammillaria rubida*) from Bacubirito in Sinaloa the body grows to 3.5 inches (9 cm) high and 5.1 inches (13 cm) across; the spination is not so dark and heavy, but the flower is almost identical. The distinctive form that grows around Guamúchil and other localities nearby has been called *M. neoshwarzeana*.

The plant illustrated was grown from seed collected near Pitaya, Sonora.

DATA

Form: Simple or clumping. Heads to about 3.5 in (9 cm) across and high.

Spines: Radials 6–8; to 0.6 in (1.4 cm) long. Centrals 1; to 0.5 in (1.2 cm) long.

Flower: Greenish cream to pinkish. 0.8 in (2 cm) long. May–July in cultivation.

Flowering time from seed: 4–5 years.

Distribution: Mexico (Sonora, Sinaloa, Jalisco, and Nayarit).

Mammillaria bombycina

DATA

Form: Clumping strongly.
Heads 3.2–3.5 in
(8–9 cm) high; 2–2.4 in
(5–6 cm) across.

Spines: Radials 30–40; to
0.4 in (1 cm) long; white.
Centrals 2–4, the lowest
hooked, 0.8 in (2 cm)
long; the rest straight;
to 0.4 in (1 cm).

Flower: Pink. 0.6 in
(1.5 cm) across.
Appearing for many
weeks through the
summer in cultivation.

**Flowering time from
seed:** 2–4 years.

Distribution: Mexico
(Aguascalientes
and Jalisco).

This is a magnificent cactus, and huge clumps with hundreds of heads arranged in a beautifully elegant fashion have been winning "best cactus in show" for years. Yet it was only relatively recently that this popular plant was rediscovered in the wild, and only then after a certain amount of detective work. It is now known to occur in the high winter-cold mountains of the Sierra Fria, so it is not surprising that reasonable amounts of frost are not a problem in cultivation. These days it is not grown as often as it should be, having been replaced in people's hearts by so-called rarer species.

The plant illustrated is a good old "traditional" specimen of the sort that has been grown over many years.

Mammillaria boolii

n cultivation plants eventually become quite cylindrical, but they never fail to
mpress when they are garlanded with rings of their very showy pink flowers.
nfortunately, such a show is not guaranteed to last—this can be a tricky customer,
ble to rot off for no apparent reason, and watering needs to be done with care at
l times. As with all "mamms," make sure that you detach every ripe fruit if you
uffer from damp winters, otherwise you may lose the plant to mildew as the fruit
ts its way into the plant.

he plant illustrated is a typical commercial specimen.

DATA

Form: Usually simple.
To 1.2 in (3.5 cm) tall;
1.2 in (3 cm) across.

Spines: Radials about 20;
to 0.6 in (1.5 cm) long;
white. Centrals 1; to
0.8 in (2 cm) long;
hooked; yellowish.

Flower: Pink with paler
margins. 1.2 in (3 cm)
across. May–June
in cultivation.

**Flowering time from
seed:** 3–4 years.

Distribution: Mexico
(Sonora, San Pedro
and San Carlos Bays).

Mammillaria brandegeei lewisiana

DATA

Form: Simple. To 2.8 in (7 cm) high and 4.3 in (11 cm) across, with a large taproot.

Spines: Radials 10–13. Centrals usually 1; to over 0.8 in (2 cm) long; usually curved and contorted.

Flower: Yellowish green. 0.4 in (1 cm) across. June in cultivation.

Flowering time from seed: 3–4 years.

Distribution: Mexico (Baja California, northern Vizcaíno Desert, near Mezquital Ranch).

Of the three subspecies of the relatively nondescript-looking *Mammillaria brandegeei*, this is the only one worth owning, thanks to its attractive curly spination. In cultivation it is very slow-growing and will never need much space, making it perfect for a small greenhouse. Because of its large taproot, it requires a relatively deep pot and also needs care in watering—it is not the easiest plant to keep growing well, since its native habitat (on granite hills) is very dry.

The plant illustrated above was grown from seed that was collected at the type locality, Lau 029.

Mammillaria candida

A large, snow-white cluster of this slow-growing species is a fine sight but will inevitably be many years old, since this is a fairly slow-growing plant. Some forms never seem to clump, eventually making relatively large single heads. In habitat simple plants a maximum of 2.4 inches (6 cm) across and 1.6 inches (4 cm) high are sometimes all that you see. Offsetting takes place early and in profusion in subspecies *ortizrubiana* (which also has fewer spines, revealing more of the body beneath). In cultivation some care is needed with watering because this species is notoriously intolerant of any prolonged dampness around the roots. In recent works this plant has refound a home in *Mammilloydi*, based on differences in its seeds.

The plant illustrated was grown from seed that was collected many years ago Río Verde, San Luis Potosí, PM025.

DATA

Form: Simple or offsetting. Heads to 7.8 in (20 cm) high and 5.5.in (14 cm) across.

Spines: Radials 50 or more; white; thin; to about 0.4 in (1 cm) long. Centrals 8–12; to 0.3 in (0.7 cm) long; white; tipped brownish.

Flower: Whitish to pinkish with a darker midstripe. 0.6 in (1.5 cm) across. May–June in cultivation.

Flowering time from seed: 3–4 years.

Distribution: Mexico (San Luis Potosí, Nuevo León, Coahuila, Guanajuato, and Tamaulipas).

Mammillaria canelensis

DATA

Form: Simple or clumping. Heads flattened-globular; to 5.1 in (13 cm) across and 4.7 in (12 cm) high.

Spines: Radials 22–25; to 0.6 in (1.5 cm) long; whitish. Centrals 2–4; to 1.2 in (3 cm) long; yellow.

Flowers: Yellowish to pink. 0.6 in (1.5 cm) across. June–July in cultivation.

Flowering time from seed: 4–5 years.

Distribution: Mexico (southwest Chihuahua, in the Sierra Canela; southeast Sonora).

Named for the mountain range in which it grows, this is a close ally of *Mammillaria standleyi*. Although the flower color was originally described as light greenish yellow, plants grown from seed collected from a single site also flower purplish pink. Localities are also known where only pink-flowered plants occur, these having been described as *M. floresii*. Other synonyms include *M. auricantha*, *M. auritricha*, *M. bellacantha*, and *M. montensis*. In cultivation growth is relatively rapid, and watering can be fairly liberal.

The plant illustrated was grown from seed collected from plants growing in humus among rocks near Loreto, Chihuahua, Lau 1256.

Mammillaria carmenae

After being described in 1953, this beautiful species fell into a lengthy period of obscurity until its rediscovery in the wild by Alfred Lau in 1977. With its wonderful spination it became an instant "hit" among collectors, who paid relatively large sums for specimens and even for the small amounts of seed that trickled out. Since then its star has waned somewhat as collectors have concentrated on the next choice "rarity" to appear on the scene. This is a pity because, as is evident from the illustration below (of a typical commercial specimen), *Mammillaria carmenae* is undoubtedly one of the most attractive of all cacti and has the added bonus of being extremely easy to grow.

DATA

Form: Clumping. Heads 2–3.2 in (5–8 cm) long and 2 in (5 cm) across.

Spines: Radials more than 100; 0.2 in (0.5 cm) long; white or pale yellow, often with red-brown tips. Centrals absent.

Flower: White, cream, or pale pink. About 0.4 in (1 cm) across. May–June in cultivation.

Flowering time from seed: 2–3 years.

Distribution: Mexico (Tamaulipas, north of La Reforma).

Mammillaria carnea

DATA

Form: Clumping. Heads to 3.9 in (10 cm) high and 2.4 in (6 cm) across; bright green.

Spines: Mostly just 4 centrals; 0.6–3.5 in (1.5–9 cm) long.

Flower: Pink. To 0.6 in (1.5 cm) across. June–July in cultivation.

Flowering time from seed: 3–4 years.

Distribution: Mexico (Puebla, Oaxaca, and Guerrero).

This cactus can be found in thousands growing on almost bare ground in fairly deep shade in the dry thorny woodland that covers the gently sloping ground around the town of Tehuacán in Puebla. On most plants the spines are short, but the occasional specimen has much longer spination—up to about 3.5 inches (9 cm)—giving the plant a very different and quite spectacular appearance. In cultivation red spider mites can be a problem, so keep an eye open for signs of scarring.

The plant illustrated was grown from seed collected at Tehuacán.

Mammillaria compressa

Between Zimapán and Ixmiquilpán large colonies of this plant—some 3.3 feet (1 m) or more across, with hundreds of heads—lie scattered among small trees and bushes on the stony hillsides. Some plants have spines less than 0.4 inches (1 cm) long, while an adjacent plant may be covered with a dense thatch of spines 2–2.4 inches (5–6 cm) long. This natural variation accounts for two other names now included in this species: *Mammillaria tolimensis* and *M. bernalensis*. In subspecies *centralifera* (originally *M. centralifera*) two central spines are present. *Mammillaria compressa* is not always a very free-flowering species (some people cannot flower it at all), but it does rapidly make an impressively large show plant.

The plant illustrated was grown from seed collected many years ago at Zimapán, Hidalgo, PM002.

DATA

Form: Heads to 3.2 in (8 cm) across and 7.8 in (20 cm) high; clumping.

Spines: Radials 4–6; 0.2–2.8 in (0.5–7 cm) long; white to reddish; tipped darker.

Flower: Dark pink. To 0.6 in (1.5 cm) long. May–June in cultivation and in habitat.

Flowering time from seed: 5–6 years or more.

Distribution: Mexico (Hidalgo, San Luis Potosí, and Querétaro).

Mammillaria crinita wildii

DATA

Form: Freely clumping. Heads to 5.9 in (15 cm) long; 2.4 in (6 cm) across.

Spines: Radials 8–10; to 0.3 in (0.8 cm) long; white, bristly. Centrals 3–4; to 0.4 in (1 cm) long; yellowish; lowermost spine hooked.

Flower: Dingy whitish. 0.5 in (1.2 cm) broad. April–June in cultivation.

Flowering time from seed: 2–3 years.

Distribution: Hidalgo (Metztitlán).

This soft-bodied, strongly offsetting plant, for many years known as *Mammillaria wildii*, was the first cactus ever owned by the author, at 14 years of age, and was acquired from a local florist. Many years later, it is still offered by garden centers and florists, and still often retains its old name. In recent works, however, it has been demoted to a form of *M. crinita*, a plant that in its typical form has a much longer and denser spination, which is distinctive in that it is often pubescent. Both forms require plenty of water during the summer growing season and would benefit from partial shading in really hot weather.

The plant illustrated above is a vegetative propagation from a plant that was collected at Metztitlán.

Mammillaria deherdtiana dodsonii

n full flower this is one of the most stunning of all mammillarias and is a firm favorite with collectors. It is not always the easiest plant to grow, however, since e roots are sometimes prone to rot off. In subspecies *deherdtiana* the central ɔines are much shorter and are often not present until the plant is quite old. It ɔmes from a relatively dry habitat on thin soil overlying rock, which is probably hy it is more difficult to keep alive than subspecies *dodsonii*, which grows in ɔmus among moss and also clusters more readily in cultivation.

he plant illustrated was grown from seed collected on the Cerro de San elipe de Agua, Lau 669.

DATA

Form: Clumping. Heads 1.2 in (3 cm) tall; 1.6 in (4 cm) across.

Spines: Radials 20–21; to 0.7 in (1.8 cm) long. Centrals 3–5; 0.4–0.8 in (1–2 cm) long; brownish red.

Flower: Pink. To 2 in (5 cm) across. May–June in cultivation; March–April in habitat.

Flowering time from seed: 3–4 years.

Distribution: Mexico (Oaxaca, in woodland near Mitla, etc.).

Mammillaria densispina

Form: Simple or clumping. Globular or elongated. To 3.9 in (10 cm) high and broad.

Spines: Radials 20–25; to 0.5 in (1.3 cm) long; white to yellow. Centrals 5–6; 0.4–0.8 in (1–2 cm) long; yellow to brownish red.

Flower: Yellow. 0.4 in (1 cm) across. May–June in cultivation.

Flowering time from seed: 3–4 years.

Distribution: Mexico (San Luis Potosí, Zacatecas, Guanajuato, Querétaro, Aguascalientes, Durango, and Jalisco).

In habitat this lovely species often grows among cushions of moss on rocky outcrops beneath the seasonal shade of oaks. In cultivation it develops fairly slowly into a densely spined yellowish or brownish black ball that eventually elongates. In the form originally described as *Mammillaria buxbaumeriana* (later corrected to *M. buxbaumiana*) growth is more cylindrical right from the start, and clumping is initiated after just a few years from seed.

The the form illustrated below is M. buxbaumiana, *grown from seed collected at Tierra Blanca, near San Luis de La Paz, Guanajuato.*

Mammillaria discolor

DATA

Form: Simple or clumping. Heads to 7.1 in (18 cm) high; 5.1 in (13 cm) across.

Spines: Radials 15–20; to 0.4 in (1 cm) long; white. Centrals 6–8; 0.4 in (1 cm) or more long; blackish red.

Flower: White with a pink midstripe. 0.6 in (1.5 cm) across. May–June in cultivation.

Flowering time from seed: 2–3 years.

Distribution: Mexico (Puebla, Oaxaca, Veracruz, Hidalgo, and Mexico State).

n habitat this species usually occurs as solitary heads growing half-concealed among grass and rocks. In cultivation seed collected from such single-headed ecimens eventually, after many years of fairly slow growth, produces large clumps th 30 or more heads, all of which remain more or less flattened-globular. In bspecies *esperanzaensis* growth is always simple, old plants becoming near-lindrical, measuring some 5.9 inches (15 cm) high by 3.3 inches (8.5 cm) across, t it is doubtful that this form merits any formal recognition.

e plant illustrated was grown from seed that was collected near San ejo, Hidalgo, Mexico.

Mammillaria dixanthocentron

DATA

Form: Simple. To 7.8 in (20 cm) high and 3.2 in (8 cm) across.

Spines: Radials 19–20; to 0.2 in (0.4 cm) long. Centrals usually 2; the uppermost to 0.2 in (0.5 cm); the lowermost curving downward, to 1 in (2.5 cm).

Flower: Small, pink. May–June in cultivation.

Flowering time from seed: 4–5 years.

Distribution: Mexico (Puebla and Oaxaca, mainly in the Tomellín valley).

It is the neat arrangement of slightly curved central spines that gives the original form of this plant (illustrated above) its distinctive and extremely pleasing appearance. In recent years there has been a large amount of exploration in the Tomellín Canyon area, and numerous new forms of this species have been discovered. Some of them have short, straight white or blackish centrals, while others lack them altogether. In var. *rubrispina* the central spines are reddish brown, but this form is really no more or less deserving of recognition than any of the others. Fortunately, all the various forms are relatively easy to cultivate and are highly recommended, although one or two are rather winter-tender and mark badly if allowed to get near to freezing.

The plant illustrated was grown from seed collected south of Teotitlán del Camino, Oaxaca.

Mammillaria elongata

This is a very variable plant in terms of the width and length of the stem and of the number, length, and color of its spines. Dozens of names have been coined, trying to cover what is just a natural degree of variation within a single species. These days the only one of these to survive seems to be subspecies *echinaria*. It describes a form with relatively long stout centrals and all-yellow spination that grows in open desert rather than in the steep-sided canyons where the type plant is found, often hanging from vertical rock walls.

The plant illustrated is a vegetative propagation from material collected near Vizarrón, Querétaro.

DATA

Form: Heads cylindrical. To 1.6 in (4 cm) across; 7.8 in (20 cm) or more long.

Spines: Radials about 20; 0.3 in (0.8 cm) long. Centrals 0–4; to 0.4 in (1 cm) long. Color varies from whitish through pale yellow to rich chocolate brown.

Flower: Pale yellow, sometimes tinged pink. To 0.6 in (1.5 cm) long. April–June in cultivation.

Flowering time from seed: 3–4 years.

Distribution: Mexico (Hidalgo and Querétaro).

Mammillaria fittkaui

Form: Clumping. Heads to 3.9 in (10 cm) high; 2 in (5 cm) across.

Spines: Radials 7–9; white; weak; to 0.3 in (0.7 cm) long. Centrals 4, one of which is hooked; to 0.4 in (1 cm) long; dark brown.

Flower: Whitish with a pink midstripe. 0.4 in (1 cm) across. April–May in cultivation.

Flowering time from seed: 3–4 years.

Distribution: Mexico (Jalisco, near Lake Chapala and in the Barranca de Guadalajara; Guanajuato, south of San Miguel Allende).

This is a relatively recently discovered species, having been described by Glass and Foster in 1971 and named after its finder, Father Fittkau. It has rapidly become very popular in collections, since it is a vigorous, trouble-free plant that keeps on producing its dainty pink flowers for many weeks and quickly forms clumps that fill a small pan with its attractive, glossy green heads.

The plant illustrated was grown from seed that was collected near Jamay, Jalisco, ML295.

Mammillaria flavicentra

Several forms of this easy-to-grow plant are in cultivation, of which by far the most attractive is the plant illustrated below, with its dense, bright, golden yellow spination. Reppenhagen relegated *Mammillaria flavicentra* to a variety of *M. dixanthocentron*, but this has been discredited by later observations in habitat, which indicate that the two species occur together without apparently interbreeding. Although the flower size given here is as originally described, the author has found that none of the flowers on his two plants has measured less than 0.4 inches (1 cm) across.

The plant illustrated was grown from seed collected near Pala, Puebla, ML194.

DATA

Form: Simple, to 7.1 in (18 cm) high and 3.9 in (10 cm) across.

Spines: Radials 22–24; to 0.2 in (0.4 cm) long; glassy. Centrals 4–6; to 0.2 in (0.6 cm) long; yellow.

Flower: Deep magenta. About 0.2 in (0.4 cm) across. May–June in cultivation.

Flowering time from seed: 4–5 years.

Distribution: Mexico (Oaxaca, Tomellín valley).

Mammillaria formosa

DATA

Form: Usually simple, sometimes forming clumps with up to 20 or more heads. Heads 3.9 in (10 cm) or more tall and wide.

Spines: Radials 20–25; to 0.2 in (0.6 cm) long; white. Centrals 4–6; to 0.3 in (0.8 cm) long; flesh-colored, tipped blackish.

Flower: Purplish pink. 0.6 in (1.5 cm) broad. April–June in cultivation.

Flowering time from seed: 4–5 years.

Distribution: Mexico (fairly widespread in the state of San Luis Potosí; also in Tamaulipas, Coahuila, Aguascalientes, Nuevo León, Zacatecas, and Guanajuato).

The amount of white wool in the axils varies greatly from one locality to another in this attractive, neatly spined, almost indestructible species. In the north, in various parts of Coahuila, somewhat heavily spined, very woolly plants have been named *Mammillaria chionocephala*, and rather less woolly ones, *M. ritteriana*. Since these are scarcely different from some forms of *M. formosa* found very close to San Luis Potosí city, they scarcely merit recognition at any level. Although the flower is described as purplish pink, the author has only seen this shade on plants grown from seed collected at the type locality, San Felipe in San Luis Potosí; all other plants seem to have creamish white blooms.

The plant illustrated was grown from seed collected many years ago near Matehuala, SLP, PM053.

Mammillaria fraileana

is the large flowers with their huge, brilliant magenta, spiderlike stigmas that
grab the attention on this otherwise untidily clumping hooked-spined "mamm"
m Baja California. Like a number of its close relatives, it can be a tricky plant
keep going in cultivation. It requires great care in watering and in selecting a
table pot, which should not be too large, since the roots are liable to rot if they
e allowed to hang wet in a large mass of compost. It has recently been demoted
a subspecies of *Mammillaria albicans*, but this is not accepted here.

*e plant illustrated is a vegetative propagation from a plant collected at
n Juan de la Costa, Baja California.*

DATA

Form: Clumping. Stems
cylindrical. To 5.9 in
(15 cm) high and 1.2 in
(3 cm) across.

Spines: Radials 11–12;
to 0.4 in (1 cm) long;
whitish. Centrals 3; to
0.4 in (1 cm); dark brown;
the longest one hooked.

Flower: White with a pink
midstripe. 1.2 in (3 cm)
across. April–May in
cultivation.

**Flowering time from
seed:** 4–5 years.

Distribution: Mexico
(Baja California, on
several islands and the
adjacent mainland).

Mammillaria geminispina

DATA

Form: Clumping. Heads to 7.1 in (18 cm) long; 3.2 in (8 cm) across.

Spines: Radials 16–20; to 0.3 in (0.7 cm) long. Centrals 2–4; 0.3–1.6 in (0.7–4 cm) long.

Flower: Small, pinkish. September in cultivation.

Flowering time from seed: 6–8 years.

Distribution: Mexico (Hidalgo, Querétaro, and San Luis Potosí).

Some of the largest clumps of mammillarias seen on the show bench belong to this species—the hundreds of heads, covered with a dense array of white spines, make a very impressive display. The most spectacular specimens are those with very long spines. Spine length is very variable, so if you buy a plant by post, you could get anything from less than 0.4 inches (1 cm) upward. In cultivation this can be a shy-flowering plant, although the flowers are rather small and add little to what is already a beautiful and culturally forgiving plant.

The plant illustrated was grown from seed collected at Metztitlán, Hidalgo.

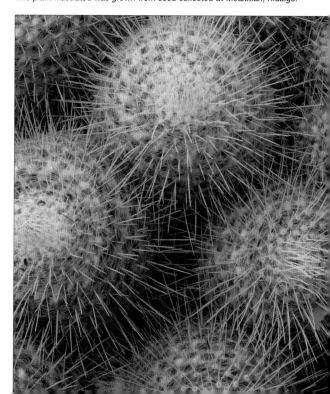

Mammillaria gigantea

This species, which now includes *Mammillaria hamiltonoytea*, will eventually grow into some of the largest single heads seen in this genus. Spine color varies somewhat, and the darker-spined forms—in some the centrals are almost black—are definitely the most attractive. This is a very easy plant to grow, being much less prone to attack by red spider mites than its close ally, *M. petterssonii*.

The plant illustrated was grown from seed collected from plants growing in yellowish clay soil in a spectacular canyon between Huejuquilla and San Juan Capistrano, Jalisco, Lau 1118.

DATA

Form: Simple. To 9.8 in (25 cm) or more across; 7.8 in (20 cm) high.

Spines: Radials 12; to 0.2 in (0.5 cm); whitish. Centrals 4–6; 0.6–0.8 in (1.5–2 cm); yellowish to blackish.

Flower: Greenish yellow. 0.6 in (1.5 cm) broad. May–June in cultivation.

Flowering time from seed: 6–7 years.

Distribution: Mexico (Querétaro, Guanajuato, Durango, San Luis Potosí, and Jalisco).

Mammillaria giselae

DATA

Form: Stems 0.6–1.2 in (1.5–3 cm) broad, forming clumps 2–3.2 in (5–8 cm) across.

Spines: Radials 16–21; 0.2 in (0.5 cm) long. Centrals 0–5; shorter than the radials.

Flower: Pink. About 0.4 in (1 cm) across. March in habitat; April–June in cultivation.

Flowering time from seed: 2–3 years.

Distribution: Mexico (Tamaulipas, Cerro Bufa el Diente).

This attractive little plant was described as recently as 1997 and has rapidly become popular with collectors. Most of the material on offer, as illustrated here, has been propagated from plants originally collected from habitat, where they grow beneath oaks, maples, and pines. Offsets are produced so prolifically and root up so well that large numbers of plants can quickly be built up. Lüthy has reduced this pretty little species to a subspecies of *Mammillaria schiedeana*, without much real justification, and therefore this is not followed here.

Mammillaria glassii

This species occurs in a number of forms, each of which seems to grow on its own isolated outcrop of limestone rock. The very popular var. *ascensionis* has much the largest and most attractive flowers—up to 0.9 inches (2.2 cm) across. In var. *nominis-dulcis* (illustrated below) the heads are to 2 inches (5 cm) broad and the flowers to 0.7 inches (1.8 cm) across. They all form mounds of numerous heads (newest and biggest in var. *siberiensis*) that are covered in flowers during late spring. Growing them is no problem, as long as you limit the amount of compost—the roots are usually wedged into rock crevices in habitat—so use a half-pot or shallow pan.

The plant illustrated is a vegetative propagation from a plant collected near Dulces Nombres, Nuevo León, Lau 1186.

DATA

Form: Clumping. Bodies to 3.9 in (10 cm) across.

Spines: Fine and numerous; glassy whitish.

Flower: Pale pink. To 0.1 in (0.4 cm) across. May–June in cultivation.

Flowering time from seed: 1–3 years.

Distribution: Mexico (Nuevo León, Coahuila, and Tamaulipas).

Mammillaria glochidiata

DATA

Form: Clumping. Heads globular; to 2.4 in (6 cm) across.

Spines: Radials 15–22. Centrals 2–4; to 0.7 in (1.7 cm) long.

Flower: White with a pinkish midstripe. 0.5 in (1.2 cm) across. April–May in cultivation.

Flowering time from seed: 2–3 years.

Distribution: Mexico (Hidalgo, near Gilo and in the Barranca de Tolimán).

The plant illustrated is var. *xiloensis*, which is somewhat spinier and more globular than the type, which quickly becomes cylindrical. Both plants rapidly offset to form attractive clumps that are bright glossy green. In habitat the plants grow in rich black humus in narrow cracks in rocks beneath trees. In cultivation this cactus will appreciate rather more water than some of the other more purely desert types.

The plant illustrated was grown from seed harvested from a plant collected from Gilo, Hidalgo, and pollinated in cultivation.

Mammillaria grahamii

DATA

Form: Often clumping. To 7.8 in (20 cm) long and 3.2 in (8 cm) across, but usually much smaller.

Spines: Radials 18–28; to 0.5 in (1.2 cm) long. Centrals 1–3; usually hooked; to 0.7 in (1.8 cm), sometimes longer.

Flower: Pink. 0.8–1.6 in (2–4 cm) across. April–May in cultivation; July–August in habitat.

Flowering time from seed: 2–3 years.

Distribution: United States (Arizona, New Mexico, and east Texas).

Still often seen in catalogs as *Mammillaria microcarpa* or *M. milleri*, many different forms of this widespread little gem are found in habitat, some of which have been given names. Although most of them have been discarded by the conservative-minded botanists of today, they can still be useful in identifying which type of plant you are likely to get. For example, if you order the form previously known as *M. oliviae,* you should receive a straight-spined plant that remains relatively globular and clumps freely while still young. Whatever you get, treat it with care, since *M. grahamii* is notoriously prone to dying for no obvious reason. It has very weak roots that rot off at the slightest provocation, but especially when someone has been too generous with the watering can.

The plant illustrated was photographed in Arizona.

Mammillaria grusonii

Form: Simple. To 9.8 in (25 cm) across; 11.8 in (30 cm) high.

Spines: Radials 14; to 0.3 in (0.8 cm) long. Centrals 2; to 0.2 in (0.6 cm); reddish at first, fading to white.

Flower: Pale yellow. 1 in (2.5 cm) across. May–June in cultivation.

Flowering time from seed: 5–6 years.

Distribution: Mexico (Coahuila, Sierra Bola; Durango).

The accompanying description covers this species as originally known. In cultivation it eventually forms quite a large solitary head. This takes time, however, since growth is relatively slow and cannot be pushed without the risk of losing the plant. Other former species now included here (but not, of course, by everyone, so look out for these names) include *Mammillaria pachycylindrica*, which differs mainly in being a little more cylindrical and having more spines; and *M. zeyeriana* (illustrated), which has thicker, longer spines, giving it a distinctive appearance. Even more distinctive—spectacularly so—is *M. papasquiarensis*, a magnificently spiny plant with centrals up to 3.9 inches (10 cm) long.

The plant illustrated was grown from seed collected near Viesca, Coahuila.

Mammillaria guelzowiana

When out of flower, this plant could perhaps be mistaken for *Mammillaria bocasana*, but there the resemblance ends. Whereas the latter species has quite small flowers, in *M. guelzowiana* they are the largest and most sumptuously showy in the genus. Sadly, while *M. bocasana* is a tough customer, thriving on neglect for years, *M. guelzowiana* is often distressingly short-lived, all too frequently losing its seemingly very weak roots and dying, despite desperate attempts to save it. Try using a half-pot, thereby minimizing the amount of compost that the sparse root system will have to try to occupy.

The plant illustrated was grown from seed collected near San Francisco de Asis, Lau 640.

DATA

Form: Stems simple or clumping from the base. 1.6–2.4 in (4–6 cm) high and 2.8 in (7 cm) across.

Spines: Radials 60–80; hairlike; 0.6–0.8 in (1.5–2 cm). Centrals 1–6; to 0.4 in (1 cm).

Flower: Bright pink. 1.6–2.4 in (4–6 cm) across. May–June in cultivation.

Flowering time from seed: 3–4 years.

Distribution: Mexico (Durango, in the Nazas valley).

Mammillaria guerreronis

DATA

Form: Stems to 2.4 in (6 cm) wide and about 23.6 in (60 cm) tall, clumping from the base.

Spines: Radials 20–30; white; bristlelike; 0.2–0.4 in (0.5–1 cm) long. Centrals usually 4; to 1 in (2.5 cm) long, the lower one often hooked.

Flower: Purplish. About 0.4 in (1 cm) across. June in cultivation.

Flowering time from seed: 5–6 years.

Distribution: Mexico (Guerrero, Zopilote Canyon).

Perhaps because of the more or less subtropical climate in its canyon home, this species is rather tender in winter. To avoid unsightly marking, you should try to maintain a temperature of at least 10 degrees above freezing. This cactus has a reputation for being a little reluctant to flower, at least in dull climates, but the author has never had any problem and finds that it flowers as well as any other member of the genus.

The plant illustrated was grown from seed collected at Mezcala, Lau 1096.

Mammillaria haageana

DATA

Form: Solitary or clumping from the base. Heads to 6.3 in (16 cm) high and 2.8 in (7 cm) across.

Spines: Radials 15–30; 0.1 in (0.3 cm) long; whitish. Centrals 1–4; to 0.4 in (1 cm) long; red to black.

Flower: Purplish pink. 0.4 in (1 cm) across. April–June in cultivation; slightly earlier in habitat.

Flowering time from seed: 3–4 years.

Distribution: Mexico (Puebla and Oaxaca).

There has been much debate about whether the old name of *Mammillaria elegans* should be applied to this species, as indeed it often still is. However, there are cogent reasons why this name should disappear and be replaced by the one above. Many different forms have been discovered, and some of the most distinctive have valid names of their own. Thus, subspecies *conspicua* (also seen as *M. conspicua*), is a very large, stout plant up to 5.9 inches (15 cm) high and 3.9 inches (10 cm) across, usually remaining solitary. In subspecies *elegans* (also known as *M. collina*) the flowers are a very pale shade of pink and much larger than in the type.

The plant illustrated was grown from seed that was collected along the road from Oaxaca to Tehuacán.

Mammillaria hahniana woodsii

DATA

Form: Simple. To 3.2 in (8 cm) wide; 5.5.in (14 cm) high.

Spines: Radials 25–30; to 0.3 in (0.8 cm) long. Centrals 2–4, 0.2–0.7 in (0.4–1.6 cm); dark.

Flower: Pink. 0.6 in (1.5 cm) across. May–June in cultivation; slightly earlier in habitat.

Flowering time from seed: 4–5 years.

Distribution: Mexico (Guanajuato).

Formerly known as *Mammillaria woodsii*, this plant has now been demoted to a subspecies of *M. hahniana*, as have *M. mendeliana* and *M. bravoae*. The typical *M. hahniana* in the trade is a much broader, flatter plant than subspecies *woodsii*, it usually forms large clumps in age, and is generally much hairier. It comes from the Sierra de Jalapa in Querétaro and from Ocotitlán in Guanajuato. In subspecies *mendeliana* the hairs are absent and the central spines are up to 0.8 inches (2 cm) long, giving a very different appearance, but the flower is the same. The smallest of the bunch is subspecies *bravoae*, which also lacks hairs and is glossy light green. No matter which plant you have, it should give you no problems.

The plant illustrated was grown from seed collected at Río Blanco, Guanajuato.

Mammillaria hertrichiana

Plants of this species in cultivation are generally derived from seed obtained by Alfred Lau (Lau 086), as illustrated here. This seed was collected from plants growing in the Sierra Oscura on the borders of Chihuahua and Sonora. They seem to have been widely accepted as *Mammillaria hertrichiana*, but they are not a very good match for the original plant as described by Craig. *Mammillaria standleyi* from the Sierra de Alamos in Sonora is a close relative. In cultivation Lau 086 is relatively slow-growing and remains solitary for many years before it starts to offset.

DATA

Form: Heads to 5.5.in (14 cm) across and 2 in (5 cm) high, forming clumps to 3.3 ft (1 m) across.

Spines: Radials 12–15; to 0.4 in (1 cm) long. Centrals 4–5, to 1 in (2.5 cm) long.

Flower: Pink. 0.7 in (1.8 cm) across. May–June in cultivation.

Flowering time from seed: 5–6 years.

Distribution: Mexico (Sonora, east of Tesopaco).

Mammillaria heyderi

Form: Simple. Flattened-globular. To 3.9 in (10 cm) broad.

Spines: Radials 15–22; to 0.5 in (1.2 cm) long. Centrals 1–4; to 0.3 in (0.8 cm) long.

Flower: Brownish pink. 0.8–1 in (2–2.5 cm) across. May–June in cultivation.

Flowering time from seed: 3–5 years.

Distribution: United States (Texas, New Mexico) and northern Mexico.

This widespread species exists in various forms, most of which were originally described as species but are now generally considered to be subspecies of *Mammillaria heyderi*. Of these subspecies, perhaps the most attractive is *hemisphaerica*, which has a very flattened habit and attractively fine and neat spination. A distinctly yellow tinge to the flowers is typical of subspecies *macdougalii*, while a smaller number of rather stronger spines is typical of *meiacantha*. Some people find these easy to grow, while others (including the author) find them a little tricky, since the roots tend to die.

The plant illustrated was grown from seed collected near Hipólito, Coahuila.

Mammillaria huitzilopochtli niduliformis

Since the original description of *Mammillaria huitzilopochtli* by David Hunt, numerous forms of this elegant plant have been discovered in the area in and around the Tomellín valley. Some of them appear to be halfway toward being *crucigera*, a much slower-growing plant with no central spines. A more distinctive form with a dense covering of long wavy spines was named as var. *niduliformis*. It was found by Alfred Lau in Arroya Salado, beside the Río Santo Domingo, and has been widely distributed under his numbers 1495 and 1557. On the opposite side of the river he found yet another form without the long wavy spines, which has been distributed as Lau 1500, and has proved to be the trickiest form to cultivate.

The plant illustrated was grown from seed that was collected in Arroyo Salado, Lau 1495.

DATA

Form: Eventually clumping. To 3.2 in (8 cm) or more high and 2.4 in (6 cm) across.

Spines: Radials about 22; very short. Centrals usually 2; brown or black; to 1.2 in (3 cm) long; wavy and flexible.

Flower: Small; pink. February–June in cultivation.

Flowering time from seed: 4–5 years.

Distribution: Mexico (Oaxaca, Tomellín valley).

Mammillaria humboldtii

Form: Clumping. Heads to 2.8 in (7 cm) broad and tall.

Spines: Radials 80 and more; to 0.3 in (0.8 cm) long; white. Centrals 0.

Flower: Magenta. 0.6 in (1.5 cm) broad. May–June in cultivation; December–January in habitat.

Flowering time from seed: 4–5 years.

Distribution: Mexico, Hidalgo (between Ixmiquilpán and Metztitlán).

In habitat the white "snowballs" of this lovely plant grow in accumulations of humus among limestone rocks beneath small oak trees. Unfortunately, in cultivation it has never been particularly common, partly perhaps because seed is not often available and partly because it is not the easiest plant to grow. It needs to be kept both underpotted and underwatered if it is to survive into old age. Two forms appear to be in circulation, one of which clumps freely from early on. The other remains solitary or clumps only sparingly—as in the accompanying photograph of a commercially obtained plant of unknown provenance.

Mammillaria insularis

Although clumps consisting of more than 100 heads have been found in the wild, most plants in cultivation tend to remain solitary, at least for many years from seed: growth is relatively slow and this species does not take kindly to being pushed. This is because the rather soft body arises from a substantial fleshy root that rots away easily if water is given too generously or if the plant is overpotted. Care in cultivation is therefore essential if you are not to lose the enjoyment of seeing the lovely flowers appearing every summer.

The plant illustrated was grown from seed collected on Isla Ventana.

DATA

Form: Often clumping. Heads to 2.4 in (6 cm) high and broad.

Spines: Radials 20–30; 0.2 in (0.5 cm) long; white. Centrals 1, 0.4 in (1 cm) long; hooked; brownish to blackish.

Flower: Pink with white margins. To 1 in (2.5 cm) across. May–June in cultivation.

Flowering time from seed: 3–4 years.

Distribution: Mexico (Baja California, Isla Ventana and other islands; also found more recently from the mainland at Bahía Tortugas and in a few other places).

Mammillaria jaliscana

DATA

Form: Simple or occasionally clumping. Heads to 2.4 in (6 cm) across; 3.2 in (8 cm) high.

Spines: Radials 30 or more; 0.3 in (0.8 cm) long; white. Centrals 4–8; to 0.4 in (0.9 cm) long; reddish brown to yellow; the lowermost hooked.

Flower: Pale pink to bright purplish pink. To 0.4 in (1 cm) across. March–April in cultivation.

Flowering time from seed: 2–4 years.

Distribution: Mexico (Jalisco, Zacatecas, Michoacán, and Durango).

Many years ago this was a rare plant in cultivation, but then Alfred Lau distributed seed from several localities, which produced a variety of attractive plants. Of these the most commonly seen have been Lau 1044 from El Salto, Lau 1048 from nearby Monte Escobedo, and Lau 1050 from San Juan Capistrano. All three seem to remain solitary in cultivation (at least for the author), eventually becoming cylindrical and tatty around the base. At about 10 years from seed it was deemed necessary to cut off their heads and start again by rooting up the ring of offsets that resulted. However, other people report that their plants start clustering naturally after a few years.

The plant illustrated was grown from seed that was collected to the west of Huejucar, Zacatecas.

Mammillaria johnstonii

habitat this plant grows in the crevices of low cliffs just above high-water mark.
As with most cacti, there is a certain amount of variation, and the two named
rieties, var. *guaymensis* (centrals 4–6; to 0.7 inches/1.8 cm long) and var.
ncarlensis (centrals wavy; to 1 inch/2.5 cm long), are now included in the species
scription. In cultivation growth is a little slow but generally free of problems.

*e plant illustrated was grown from seed that was collected at San Cárlos
y, Sonora, Lau 1434.*

Form: Simple. 5.9–7.8 in
(15–20 cm) high; 3.9 in
(10 cm) across.

Spines: Radials 10–15;
to 0.4 in (0.9 cm) long.
Centrals usually 2, to
1 in (2.5 cm) long;
brown to blackish.

Flower: Pink with a
brownish midstripe.
0.8 in (2 cm) broad.
May–June in cultivation.

**Flowering time from
seed:** 4–5 years.

Distribution: Mexico
(Sonora, San Cárlos Bay).

DATA

245

Mammillaria karwinskiana

DATA

Form: Clumping. Heads to 3.9 in (10 cm) high and broad.

Spines: Radials 4–6; 0.2–1.2 in (0.5–3 cm) long. Centrals usually 0.

Flower: Whitish with a reddish midline. 0.6 in (1.5 cm) across. June–July in cultivation.

Flowering time from seed: 4–5 years.

Distribution: Mexico (Oaxaca, Puebla, Morelos, and Michoacán).

Around the large city of Oaxaca, Mexico, it is common to see relatively large clumps of this plant growing in shade beneath bushes. The spine length and th amount of white wool in the axils vary so much that it is hard to accept subspecies *nejapensis* (formerly *Mammillaria nejapensis*) from Nejapa as being anything more than simply another form. In addition, recent collections from the area are almost indistinguishable from typical *karwinskiana* from Oaxaca city. In cultivation the head of older plants generally start to divide dichotomously, resulting in characteristically top-heavy clumps. The abundant striped flowers are very attractive.

The plant illustrated above was grown from seed that was collected near San José Lachiguri, ML383.

Mammillaria klissingiana

This is one of a number of very choice species in which the white spination is so dense that it masks the body color completely, giving a snowball-like effect. Growth from seed is fairly slow, and it takes a good many years before the plant starts to divide, but eventually a very handsome clump will grace your collection. In habitat the plants grow among shrubs and low bushes on steep limestone cliffs.

The plant illustrated was grown from seed collected near Jaumave.

DATA

Form: Clumping. Heads to 6.3 in (16 cm) high; 3.5 in (9 cm) broad.

Spines: Radials 30–35; to 0.3 in (0.7 cm) long; white. Centrals 2–4; shorter; white, tipped brown.

Flower: Pink. 0.3 in (0.8 cm) wide. May–June in cultivation.

Flowering time from seed: 4–5 years.

Distribution: Mexico (Tamaulipas, near Ciudad Victoria, Jaumave, Palmillas, etc.; Nuevo León, Galeana; San Luis Potosí, Sauz Pass).

Mammillaria lasiacantha

DATA

Form: Simple. 1.6–2 in (4–5 cm) broad and tall.

Spines: 40–60; all radials; to 0.2 in (0.5 cm) long; white.

Flower: White with a darker midstripe. 0.5 in (1.2 cm) across. April in cultivation.

Flowering time from seed: 2–3 years.

Distribution: United States (Texas, New Mexico, and Arizona); Mexico (Coahuila, Sonora, and Zacatecas).

Being one of the more miniature members of the genus, this species is ideal for anyone who wants to squeeze plenty of plants into a limited space. Most plants remain solitary, even when many years old, but a minority will eventually form small clusters of attractive white-spined heads. It is not the easiest plant to keep going and needs care with watering. Some people swear by incorporating limestone chippings into the compost to try to mimic the conditions found in the plant's natural limestone habitats.

The plant illustrated is SB500, grown from seed harvested from plants collected near Cuatro Ciénegas, Mexico, and pollinated in cultivation.

Mammillaria laui dasyacantha

This is a relatively new species, described in 1979, along with two other forms: forma *laui,* which is similar to *Mammillaria laui dasyacantha* but has stiffer, slightly yellower spines; and forma *subducta,* which clumps less profusely and has stiff yellowish spines with well-marked centrals. Forma *dasyacantha* is the most vigorous. It rapidly forms large white clumps that by April will be covered in a virtual carpet of flowers. Both these forms have now been promoted to the status of subspecies. Propagation is usually by offsets (derived in the main from original material collected by Alfred Lau, as illustrated here), rather than from seed. A very attractive new form, Lau 1496 from Novillo Canyon, has long white spines and is now becoming more widespread in cultivation.

DATA

Form: Clumping heavily. Heads 1.6–2 in (4–5 cm) tall and wide.

Spines: Very thin and numerous. Radials and centrals all mixed up; white.

Flower: Pink. 0.6 in (1.5 cm) across. April–May in cultivation.

Flowering time from seed: 3–4 years.

Distribution: Mexico (Tamaulipas, La Reja, between Ciudad Victoria and Jaumave).

Mammillaria lenta

DATA

Form: Flattened; clumping.
Heads 1.2–2 in (3–5 cm)
across.

Spines: Radials 30–40;
bristly; white; to 0.2 in
(0.5 cm) long. Centrals 0.

Flower: White. 1 in
(2.5 cm) across.
June–July in cultivation.

**Flowering time from
seed:** 4–5 years.

Distribution: Mexico
(Coahuila, Viesca, Torreón,
Cuatro Ciénegas, Cerro
Bola, etc.).

This has always remained rather a rare plant in cultivation, which is a pity—it is one of the most beautiful members of the genus, and the lovely white flowers are a real bonus. Its scarcity is due partly to a perennial shortage of seed and partly to the difficulty of raising the plants successfully when seed becomes available. The seedlings are slow-growing and prone to die off from a variety of causes, the main one seeming to be a reluctance to grow anywhere other than the sunny rock crevices of its native homeland. For the best results, keep it underpotted and go easy on the water.

The plant illustrated was grown from seed collected near Viesca, Lau 797.

Mammillaria lindsayi

Although originally described with a yellowish flower, plants of this species in cultivation, originating from seed collected in the Barranca de Cobre (Copper Canyon), are purple-flowered and resemble its close relative, *Mammillaria standleyi*. One of these plants, Lau 1134, is illustrated below. Growth is far slower than in some of the other similar "mamms" from the mountains of Chihuahua, but eventually offsets begin to appear and a fair-sized clump will eventually result.

DATA

Form: Heads to 5.9 in (15 cm) high and broad, forming mounds to 3.3 ft (1 m) across.

Spines: Radials 10–14; to 0.3 in (0.8 cm) long. Centrals 2–4; to 0.5 in (1.2 cm); brown to reddish.

Flower: Greenish yellow or purple. To 0.8 in (2 cm) across. May–June in cultivation.

Flowering time from seed: 4–5 years.

Distribution: Mexico (southwest Chihuahua, from Molinas to Sierra Colorado; Sinaloa, Río Fuerte).

Mammillaria longiflora

DATA

Form: Simple. 3.2–3.5 in (8–9 cm) across; 2–2.3 in (5–6 cm) high.

Spines: Radials about 30; about 0.4 in (1 cm) long; white. Centrals 4; one hooked; to 0.5 in (1.3 cm); white, yellow, or reddish brown.

Flower: Pink. To 1.6 in (4 cm) broad. April in cultivation.

Flowering time from seed: 1–2 years.

Distribution: Mexico (Durango, Santiago Papasquiaro, Puerto Coneto, Guanacevi, etc.).

This species is often listed by conservative-minded dealers in *Krainzia*. With its large showy flowers, usually produced in spectacular rings, it has always been a favorite among collectors wanting something special. Unfortunately, this often means replacing plants on a regular basis as they die off, since it is a notoriously short-lived species that is apt to lose its roots and rot off at short notice. Using the smallest pot you can get away with and going easy on the watering may help reduce losses. In subspecies *stampferi*, found in Chihuahua as well as Durango, the flowers are smaller, with much shorter tubes. Plants that manage to survive long enough will eventually form small clumps.

The plant illustrated is a typical commercial product.

Mammillaria longimamma

⁀his is one of the "mamms" that can still be found occasionally listed under *Dolichothele*. Its most distinctive features are its long, 1.2 to 2 inch- (3–5 cm-) ⁚h, bright green, rather soft tubercles, which are always fully on display beneath ⁚ very sparse and open spination. The large flowers are pretty impressive and ⁚ally appear every year, making it worth growing this species for its flowers alone. ⁚mmillaria uberiformis, with shorter, stumpier tubercles and flowers only to ⁚ inches (3.5 cm) across is now normally regarded as just a slightly more ⁚sterly form of this species.

⁚ plant illustrated below was grown from seed that was collected at ⁚nados, Hidalgo, ML002.

DATA

Form: Clumping. Heads to 3.9 in (10 cm) wide and tall.

Spines: Radials 9–10; to 0.8 in (2 cm). Centrals 0–1; to 1 in (2.5 cm).

Flower: Lemon yellow. To 2.4 in (6 cm) across. June in cultivation.

Flowering time from seed: 3–4 years.

Distribution: Mexico (Hidalgo, between Ixmiquilpán and Tasquillo; also Metzquititlán, Venados, etc., and in various localities in Querétaro).

Mammillaria luethyi

Form: Clumping. Heads to 0.6 in (1.5 cm) tall and broad.

Spines: Up to 80; minute; white.

Flower: Magenta. To 0.8 in (2 cm) across. June in cultivation.

Flowering time from seed: 2–3 years.

Distribution: Mexico (Coahuila, Sierra Paila).

Originally coming to notice as a single plant growing in a coffee can in a hotel in Coahuila in 1952, this gem of a species was not discovered in the wild until 1996, when Jonas Lüthy (for whom it is now named), found it growing among limestone slabs in the Sierra Paila. It immediately became one of the most sought-after species of cacti, but plants were slow to come onto the market. Those that are available now have mainly been propagated on grafts from field-collected material, as illustrated here. When grafted, it rapidly forms clumps of small heads, but it will also survive on its own roots, although growth is far slower and more uncertain.

Mammillaria magnifica

DATA

Form: Clumping. Stems to 15.8 in (40 cm) high and 2.8–3.5 in (7–9 cm) across.

Spines: Radials 18–24; to 0.3 in (0.8 cm) long. Centrals 4–6; to 2.2 in (5.5 cm); the lowermost normally hooked.

Flower: Pink. 0.7 in (1.8 cm) long. June in cultivation; slightly earlier in habitat.

Flowering time from seed: 3–4 years.

Distribution: Mexico (Morelos, between Cuautla and Izúcar de Matamoros, Peñón de Amayuca; Puebla).

The original locality of this plant, given by its discoverer, F. Buchenau, was San Juan Bautista in Puebla, Mexico. However, this has turned out to be misleading, and the first people to rediscover the plant in the wild found it growing on steep cliffs in Morelos. More recently, it has indeed been discovered in several localities in Puebla, but not where given by Buchenau. In cultivation growth is relatively rapid, and after a few years you can usually expect to have a handsome clump that will need to be housed in a pan—although some plants are reluctant to clump and remain solitary for many years. Field-collected seed distributed as var. *minor* produced attractive golden-spined plants which then spoiled everything by sprawling in untidy masses once they had started to clump.

The plant illustrated was raised from commercial seed of unknown origin.

Mammillaria magnimamma

DATA

Form: Clumping. Heads 3.9–4.7 in (10–12 cm) broad.

Spines: Radials 3–5; 0.6–1 in (1.5–2.5 cm). Centrals usually 0.

Flower: Cream or purple. To 1 in (2.5 cm) across. July–August in cultivation.

Flowering time from seed: 3–4 years.

Distribution: Mexico (widespread in the Central Highlands west to Durango).

This is a relatively common plant over large areas of Mexico. Spination, body size, tendency to cluster, and flower color all vary considerably over its wide area, and this has led to a number of different names. You will still find most of them in plant and seed lists, although they are all just *Mammillaria magnimamma*. *Mammillaria bucareliensis* is a magenta-flowered, strongly clustering form from Bucarel in Guanajuato. Similar flowers occur on *M. priessnitzii*, a simple form from Jalpán in Querétaro. Both of these will guarantee you a magenta flower, but if you order simply *M. magnimamma* you could get either magenta or cream, so it may pay to buy a plant that you can see in flower.

The plant illustrated was grown from seed collected many years ago just outside San Luis Potosí city, PM034.

Mammillaria marcosii

is is a fairly recent discovery, of which two clones originating from field-
collected material are commonly seen in cultivation. In one of them the spination
dark brownish red (see illustration), while the other has golden yellow spines. In
bitat this small, attractive, freely clumping plant grows in cracks on almost vertical
es of brown volcanic rock. In cultivation it thrives in a variety of different
mposts and has proved to be a very easy plant to grow.

DATA

Form: Clumping. Heads to
2 in (5 cm) tall and wide.

Spines: Radials 16–25;
to 0.5 in (1.2 cm) long.
Centrals 7–14; one
sometimes hooked; to
0.8 in (2 cm) long.

Flower: Cream. 0.4 in
(1 cm) across. May–
June in cultivation.

**Flowering time from
seed:** 2–3 years.

Distribution: Mexico
(Guanajuato, municipio
Atarjea, east of Xichú).

Mammillaria marksiana

Form: Clumping. Heads
to 5.5.in (14 cm) across;
3.2 in (8 cm) high.

Spines: Radials 8–10;
to 0.3 in (0.8 cm) long.
Centrals 1; 0.3 in
(0.8 cm) long.

Flower: Greenish yellow.
0.6 in (1.5 cm) long.
May–June in cultivation.

**Flowering time from
seed:** 4–5 years.

Distribution: Mexico
(Sinaloa and Durango).

The bright grass-green body color is one of the most distinctive features of this
plant, along with the yellow spines, although plants with beautiful rust-red spine
also cropped up in batches of plants grown from seed of Lau 635, collected near
Topia, Durango. The more common yellow-spined plant is illustrated here. By
contrast, seedlings of Lau 621 from Bacuberito, Sinaloa have more glaucous-green
bodies and much shorter, duller, more open spination.

Mammillaria matudae

hen its slender, neatly spined stems are garlanded with several rings of bright purplish pink flowers, this is a striking plant, at least when young. As it s older, unfortunately, it can be a bit of a nuisance—it begins to lean and will entually sprawl over the edge of the pot. Cultivated plants rarely seem to clump. La Laguna in Guerrero the stems hang down from vertical rock faces and can ch a length of about 5 feet (1.5 m). This form was originally described as var. rpentiformis but is no longer recognized as separate.

e plant illustrated was grown from seed collected at La Junta, Lau 1438.

DATA

Form: Simple or clumping. Stems to 7.8 in (20 cm) or more long; 1.2–1.6 in (3–4 cm) across.

Spines: Radials 18–20; very short. Centrals 1; 0.1 in (0.4 cm) long.

Flower: Magenta. 0.5 in (1.2 cm) long. June–July in cultivation.

Flowering time from seed: 2–3 years.

Distribution: Mexico (Michoacán and Guerrero).

Mammillaria melanocentra

DATA

Form: Simple. Bluish green. To 6.3 in (16 cm) high and wide.

Spines: Radials 7–9; to 1 in (2.5 cm) long. Centrals 1–2, to 2.2 in (5.5 cm) long.

Flower: Bright pink.1 in (2.5 cm) across. May–June in cultivation.

Flowering time from seed: 4–5 years.

Distribution: Mexico (Nuevo León, Coahuila, and Durango).

This vigorous plant is one of the larger-flowered members of the "milky-sapped" group of mammillarias, so it is fortunate that it blooms with great abandon for several weeks during April and May. Although normally pink-flowered, a white-flowered variant has recently been described as subspecies *linaresensis* (originally described as *Mammillaria linaresensis*). Other differences are its dark green body and paler spines, which can reach a length of 2 inches (5 cm). In another form, the so-called *M. runyonii* from El Mirador near Monterrey, the flowers are pink (but smaller than in the type) and the spination is more open.

The plant illustrated was grown from seed collected near Rinconada, Nuevo León, Lau 1020.

Mammillaria meyranii

habitat the tall stems of this plant, a close relative of *Mammillaria guerreronis*, can be seen growing high up on cliffs, where they are often inaccessible. In tivation it grows fairly rapidly into a tall, very cylindrical plant that will probably entually offset from the base, although not all plants seem willing to do this. Like st of its relatives, it flowers over a relatively long period, but is considerably more nter-hardy than the tender *M. guerreronis*.

e plant illustrated was grown from seed collected between Valle de Bravo and nta Barbara (ML048).

DATA

Form: Clumping from the base. Stems to 21.7 in (55 cm) long and 2 in (5 cm) broad.

Spines: Radials 17–19; to 0.2 in (0.6 cm) long. Centrals 4–7; 0.6–1 in (1.5–2.5 cm); the longest hooked.

Flower: Purple. 0.7 in (1.8 cm) long. May–June in cultivation.

Flowering time from seed: 3–4 years.

Distribution: Mexico (in the state of Mexico near Santa Barbara, close to the Miguel Aleman hydroelectric plant; and in Michoacán, near San José Purna).

Mammillaria microhelia

DATA

Form: Clumping. Stems to 9.8 in (25 cm) tall; 2.4 in (6 cm) wide.

Spines: Radials to 50; to 0.2 in (0.6 cm) long; white to reddish yellow. Centrals 0–8; to 0.4 in (1.1 cm); red to dark brown.

Flower: Very pale yellow to pink. 0.6 in (1.6 cm) across. April–May in cultivation.

Flowering time from seed: 2–3 years.

Distribution: Mexico (Querétaro, Sierra Zamorano).

This has always been a traditional favorite in collections, largely because of the beautiful contrast between the sunburstlike radial spines (*microhelia* means "little sun") and the dark centrals, giving a neatness of spination that has few rival among the Cactaceae. As with many cacti, older plants can eventually lose some of their glamor, becoming somewhat tatty around the lower parts of the stems. It may then be time to start again by taking a few cuttings and rooting them up.

The plant illustrated above was grown from seed that was collected in the Sierra Zamorano, ML285.

Mammillaria microthele

ssigned by some to a subspecies of *Mammillaria formosa*, this plant is
maintained here in its own right, mainly because of its habit of dividing
hotomously rather than offsetting, as in typical *M. formosa*. Generally speaking,
microthele is a much slower-growing plant than *M. formosa*, although it varies
mewhat in this respect, according to the origin of the plant from which the seeds
re obtained. The slowest-growing forms tend also to be those with the densest
d whitest spination, often offered under the provisional name of var. *superfina*,
illustrated here. This form resents being pushed and will eventually make a
ndsome clump in its own good time.

*e plant illustrated was grown from seed that was collected near Ciudad
l Maíz, San Luis Potosí.*

Form: Flattish, forming
large clumps. Heads to
3.2 in (8 cm) across.

Spines: Radials 20–24;
bristly; white; interlacing.
Centrals slightly thicker;
very short; brown then
gray.

Flower: White. 0.5 in
(1.2 cm) broad. June–
July in cultivation.

**Flowering time from
seed:** 4–5 years.

Distribution: Mexico
(Coahuila, San Luis
Potosí, Tamaulipas,
and Guanajuato).

Mammillaria miegiana

DATA

Form: Simple. To 3.9 in (10 cm) across and 6.3 in (16 cm) high.

Spines: Radials 10–11; to 0.4 in (0.9 cm) long. Centrals 2; about the same length as radials.

Flower: Pink. 1 in (2.5 cm) across. May–June in cultivation.

Flowering time from seed: 4–5 years.

Distribution: Mexico (Sonora, west of Moctezuma).

Named for Charles E. Mieg of Scottsdale, Arizona, in habitat this species grows on rocky hills between grasses and shrubs under palms and oaks. In cultivation growth from seed is relatively slow, but eventually it will make a broad, fairly flattened plant that, given a good number of years, will grow taller than it is broad. As well as being one of the more densely spined of a group of closely related species from the mountains of northwestern Mexico, it is particularly noted for its abundant production of bright pink flowers.

The plant illustrated was grown from seed collected from Moctezuma, Lau 612.

Mammillaria moelleriana

Form: Simple. To 4.3 in (11 cm) high; 3.9 in (10 cm) across.

Spines: Radials 35–40; to 0.4 in (0.9 cm) long. Centrals 8–10; the 2–4 lowermost being hooked; red or yellow; to 1.2 in (3 cm) long.

Flower: Whitish, yellow, or pink. 0.5 in (1.2 cm) across. March–May in cultivation.

Flowering time from seed: 1–3 years.

Distribution: Mexico (Durango to Zacatecas, Sierra Santa María).

In its mountainous habitat this beautiful little plant grows under pines in crevices filled with leaf mold, under small bushes, or in full sun on top of rocky outcrops. In cultivation it grows rapidly into a beautifully ornamental and attractively spined ball that eventually elongates and becomes less attractive. Some of the pink-flowered variants with reddish central spines are particularly pretty. A yellow-spined form is often mistakenly traded as *Mammillaria cowperae*.

The plant illustrated above was grown from seed that was collected at Hornillos near Fresnillo, Zacatecas, Lau 694.

Mammillaria muehlenpfordtii

Form: Slowly clumping. Heads to 7.8 in (20 cm) or more wide and tall.

Spines: Radials 40–50; to 0.2 in (0.6 cm) long. Centrals 4; 0.1–1.4 in (0.4–3.5 cm) long; yellow.

Flower: Purplish. 0.4 in (1 cm) broad. June–July in cultivation.

Flowering time from seed: 5–6 years.

Distribution: Mexico (Querétaro, Guanajuato, and San Luis Potosí).

Years ago this plant was usually traded as *Mammillaria celsiana*, a name that clearly applies to a very different species. The name used here, although rather a mouthful, has gradually become accepted. Plants in cultivation vary mainly in the length of the central spines, which are much shorter in plants from certain localities than from others. In age the heads gradually start to divide dichotomously to form impressively large cluster. This is a really trouble-free species, seldom bothered by red spider mites or other common problems.

The plant illustrated above was grown from seed that was collected near San Luis de la Paz, Guanajuato, ML082.

Mammillaria multidigitata

1 its island habitat this plant grows on open rocky slopes in full, burning sun, so t might be expected to have problems when grown in a damp, cloudy climate. 1 fact, this turns out to be a very tough plant that seems to thrive whatever the nditions. It is not too fussy about compost and rapidly forms a broad clump ade up of dozens of relatively small heads.

he plant illustrated was grown from seed collected from habitat, Lau 099.

DATA

Form: Clumping. Heads to 7.8 in (20 cm) high and 2 in (5 cm) across, but usually much shorter.

Spines: Radials 15–25; to 0.3 in (0.8 cm) long. Centrals usually 4; same length as radials; one sometimes hooked.

Flower: Off-white. 0.6 in (1.5 cm) long. April–May in cultivation.

Flowering time from seed: 2–3 years.

Distribution: Mexico (Baja California, San Pedro Nolasco Island).

Mammillaria mystax

DATA

Form: Usually clumping. Heads to 5.9 in (15 cm) high and 3.9 in (10 cm) across.

Spines: Radials 5–6; to 0.3 in (0.8 cm) long. Centrals 3–4; to 2.8 in (7 cm) long.

Flower: Purplish pink. 0.8 in (2 cm) across. June in cultivation.

Flowering time from seed: 4–5 years.

Distribution: Mexico (Puebla, Oaxaca, Morelos, and Veracruz).

When several rings of its vivid purplish red flowers are open simultaneously on a warm sunny day, this species is a satisfying sight to behold. It is relatively slow-growing and in cultivation tends to remain solitary, although in habitat fairly large clusters are common. The length and number of spines vary greatly, which probably explains why various populations over its wide range have received separate names, these being *Mammillaria casoi*, *M. crispiseta*, *M. erythra*, *M. huajuapensis*, and *M. mixtecensis*. Some are far more attractive than others, the more densely and longer-spined plants being the best.

The plant illustrated was grown from seed that was collected at San Pedro Nopala, Oaxaca, ML185 (as M. casoi).

Mammillaria nana

cultivation this species, sometimes listed as *Mammillaria monancistracantha*, slowly forms a cluster of rather soft heads perched atop a fairly substantial, fleshy otstock. The yellowish flowers appear in rings over a reasonably lengthy period, d are very similar to those of a closely related plant, *M. duwei*. This was originally scribed from San Luis de la Paz in Guanajuato and differs mainly in its very tractive pubescent spination. Because of its overall similarities, it is often listed as subspecies of *M. nana*, but it is certainly more tricky to grow to a good age in ltivation, since it is more prone to losing its roots than the type form.

e plant illustrated was grown from seed collected near Balneario de Lourdes, San is Potosí, Lau 1091.

DATA

Form: Clumping. Heads to 1 in (2.5 cm) across and 1.2 in (3 cm) high.

Spines: Radials about 35; to 0.3 in (0.7 cm) long; very thin. Centrals 1–2; to 0.2 in (0.5 cm) long; tawny brown; lowermost hooked.

Flower: Yellow. 0.6 in (1.5 cm) across. April–May in cultivation.

Flowering time from seed: 1–3 years.

Distribution: Mexico (San Luis Potosí, Guanajuato, and Querétaro).

Mammillaria neopalmeri

Form: Clumping. Heads to 3.5 in (9 cm) high; 2 in (5 cm) across.

Spines: Radials 25–30; about 0.2 in (0.5 cm) long; very fine; white. Centrals mainly 4; to 0.3 in (0.8 cm) long; brownish.

Flower: Creamy white. 0.4 in (1 cm) across. June in cultivation.

Flowering time from seed: 3–4 years.

Distribution: Mexico (Baja California, mainly on San Benito Island; also on Isla Guadalupe).

Large pans of this species are often seen on the show bench, since it is relatively easy to grow it to a good size, and flowering takes place prolifically over several weeks. Fortunately, it is less prone to rotting off at the roots than most of the "mamms" from Baja California, although some care in watering will be needed with large clumps that take a long time to dry out.

The plant illustrated above is a vegetative propagation from a plant that was collected on San Benito Island, Lau 007.

270

Mammillaria nunezii bella

Originally described by Backeberg as *Mammillaria bella*, this plant has now been demoted to a subspecies of *M. nunezii*, which is a slightly more columnar plant. The latter is now also taken to include the much larger *M. hubertmulleri* from Morelos, which reaches 11.8 inches (30 cm) tall and 3.9 inches (10 cm) across. They all form similar-looking plants, although the last-named has much darker central spines. In cultivation subspecies *bella* grows rather slowly into an attractive clump that is ornamented each year with rings of its bright flowers.

The plant illustrated was grown from seed collected south of Taxco, ML028.

DATA

Form: Simple or offsetting. Heads to 5.9 in (15 cm) high; 3.5 in (9 cm) broad.

Spines: Radials to 20; 0.3 in (0.8 cm) long; very thin; centrals to 1.2 in (3 cm) long; slightly thicker; one of them hooked.

Flower: Carmine. 0.7 in (1.8 cm) broad.

Flowering time from seed: 3–4 years.

Distribution: Mexico (Guerrero, near Taxco).

Mammillaria obconella

DATA

Form: Clumping. Stems to 11.8 in (30 cm) or more high and 4.7 in (12 cm) across.

Spines: Radials 0. Centrals usually 4; to 1 in (2.5 cm).

Flower: Carmine red. 0.8 in (2 cm) long, June–July in cultivation.

Flowering time from seed: 3–4 years.

Distribution: Mexico (Hidalgo, Barranca de Metztitlán, etc.).

Often now seen listed as a subspecies of *Mammillaria polythele*, this is a very vigorous and handsome species with distinctive spination, not quite like any of its close relatives. It gradually elongates to form a reasonably sizeable column before eventually offsetting around the base. In habitat, where it grows among rocks and bushes, relatively large multistemmed colonies are gradually built up.

The plant illustrated above was grown from seed that was collected at Venados, Hidalgo, ML004.

Mammillaria orcuttii

fter a somewhat checkered history, the plant depicted here is firmly fixed as
being the genuine *Mammillaria orcuttii*, as described in 1930 by Boedeker. The
nfusion arose because the original locality was given as being in Puebla, but this
s questioned by Boedeker, and in subsequent years plants growing in San Luis
osí were found that matched the original description very well. In cultivation the
nse white wool that fills the axils contrasts nicely with the blue-green body, set
to perfection for a few weeks in June by the rings of bright carmine flowers.

e plant illustrated was grown from seed that was collected many years
o from plants growing beneath oaks right beside the main road from Río Verde
San Luis Potosí, PM030.

DATA

Form: Simple. 2.4–5.9 in
(6–15 cm) across and
3.9–5.9 in (10–15 cm)
high.

Spines: Radials 6–8;
hairlike; white; soon
falling off. Centrals
usually 4; blackish
brown to pitch black;
to 0.2 in (0.6 cm) long.

Flower: Bright carmine.
0.4 in (1 cm) across.
June in cultivation.

**Flowering time from
seed:** 3–4 years.

Distribution: Mexico (San
Luis Potosí, Sierra Alvárez,
Valle de las Fantasmas).

Mammillaria painteri

Form: Clumping. Heads 0.8 in (2 cm) across.

Spines: Radials 20 or more; about 0.2 in (0.5 cm) long; hairlike; white. Centrals 4–5; 0.4 in (1 cm) long; dark brown above; the lowermost one hooked.

Flower: Greenish white. About 0.4 in (1 cm) across. May–June in cultivation.

Flowering time from seed: 2–3 years.

Distribution: Mexico (Querétaro, San Juan del Río).

As with so many other cacti, there is disagreement among the experts about whether this should be regarded as a valid species or regarded merely as a form of *Mammillaria crinita*. Since people who compile lists of plants and seeds for sale tend to be conservative-minded, it is retained as a species here. The plant illustrated was grown from seed collected from Cerro Prieto, between Cadereyta and Infernillo, Querétaro (ML057). It has much larger heads than originally described— up to 2 inches (5 cm) across. However, another seedling from the same batch produced dozens of much smaller heads, much as in the original description, so there is obviously some degree of variation.

Mammillaria parkinsonii

This is one of a number of species that form clumps via gradual division of the heads rather than by forming offsets. In this way large and extremely showy clumps are eventually formed, although it takes a good many years to grow the large mounds sometimes seen winning prizes in shows. However, since it is a very trouble-free plant, you stand a good chance of achieving a sizeable specimen. The length of the central spines varies greatly, with both long-spined and short-spined plants arising from the same seed batch.

The plant illustrated was grown from seed collected near Peña Blanca.

DATA

Form: Clumping. Heads to 5.9 in (15 cm) high and 3.2 in (8 cm) across.

Spines: Radials 30–35; to 0.3 in (0.7 cm) long; white. Centrals 2–4; to 1.2 in (3.5 cm) long; white; tipped dark.

Flower: Brownish pink, with a pale border. 0.6 in (1.5 cm) long. January in habitat; May–June in cultivation.

Flowering time from seed: 4–6 years.

Distribution: Mexico (Querétaro).

Mammillaria pennispinosa

DATA

Form: Clumping. Heads to 1.2 in (3 cm) high and broad.

Spines: Radials 16–20; to 0.3 in (0.8 cm) long. Centrals usually 1; to 0.5 in (1.2 cm) long; hooked.

Flower: White. 0.5 in (1.2 cm) broad. April–May in cultivation.

Flowering time from seed: 2–3 years.

Distribution: Mexico (Coahuila to Durango).

The beautifully feathered spines of this miniature gem are a real attraction, making it a sought-after species. Unfortunately, it is not always available, since it can be tricky to raise from seed in large numbers because of its tendency to lose its roots and die. Careful watering should be the rule at all times. Even old plants are very slow to clump, whereas in the less feathery-spined subspecies *nazasensis* from near the Río Nazas in Durango, clumping commences from a very early age. Because of these and several other differences, this form is often regarded as a separate species, *Mammillaria nazasensis*.

The plant illustrated was of commercial origin.

Mammillaria perbella

This is a distinctive species in which the rather broad heads have distinctly flattened tops. They gradually split dichotomously to form handsome clumps. At least two forms derived from field-collected seed are in cultivation, differing mainly the whiteness of the spines and the density with which they cover the plant. In cultivation growth is a little slow, and you will have to wait many years to get a cent-sized clump.

e plant illustrated below was grown from seed that was collected near zos, Guanajuato, ML087.

DATA

Form: Branching. Heads 2.4–3.2 in (6–8 cm) across.

Spines: Radials 14–18; to 0.1 in (0.3 cm) long; white. Centrals 2; to 0.3 in (0.6 cm) long; whitish; tipped darker.

Flower: Carmine red. 0.4 in (1 cm) across. June–July in cultivation.

Flowering time from seed: 5–6 years.

Distribution: Mexico (Querétaro, mainly between Cadereyta and Vizarrón; Hidalgo, e.g., near Tolimán; Guanajuato).

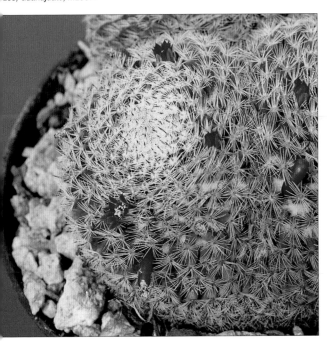

Mammillaria perezdelarosae

DATA

Form: Simple or clumping. Stem to 2.9 in (7.5 cm) high; 1.8 in (4.5 cm) broad.

Spines: Radials about 64; very short; white. Centrals usually 1; to 0.6 in (1.4 cm) long; dark; hooked.

Flower: White, petals bordered pink. 0.5 in (1.3 cm) across. April–June in cultivation.

Flowering time from seed: 1–3 years.

Distribution: Mexico (border area of Jalisco and Aguascalientes states).

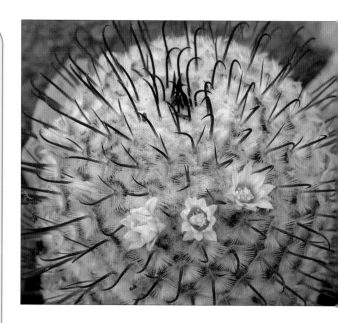

The description of this exquisite little plant in 1985 launched something of a botanical bombshell, and it was not long before both seeds and plants were being offered at highly inflated prices. Since then, material has become more freely available, although difficulty in setting seed on cultivated plants has been a common problem. In the recently described subspecies *andersoniana* the central spines are not hooked. In cultivation growth is very slow and plants tend to stay solitary, in contrast to the closely related *Mammillaria bombycina*, which quickly forms large mounds, and to which *M. perezdelarosae* has been assigned recently (as a subspecies) by David Hunt.

The plant illustrated is a typical commercial specimen.

Mammillaria petterssonii

So many different forms of this species have come into cultivation recently that it is getting difficult to sum up its defining characteristics. Some plants remain simple, while others clump from a young age. Some have red spines, others yellow or black. Some have pink flowers, while other plants, raised from the same batch of wild-collected seed, bloom yellow. Some have long thin spines, yet in others they are short and thick. Just what is a typical *Mammillaria petterssonii*? Some of these plants are sold as separate species, such as *M. obscura* or *M. apozolensis*, but they are dismissed as "just another *petterssonii*" by experts on the genus. Fortunately, they all make handsome, relatively trouble-free plants in cultivation.

The plant illustrated was grown from seed collected at El Salto, Monte Escobedo, Zacatecas, Lau 1045 (as M. apozolensis saltensis*).*

DATA

Form: Simple or clumping. Heads to 7.8 in (20 cm) across and about 7.1 in (18 cm) high.

Spines: Radials 10–12; to 0.6 in (1.5 cm) long. Centrals 1–4; to 1.8 in (4.5 cm) long.

Flower: Purplish pink. 1 in (2.4 cm) long. May–July in cultivation.

Flowering time from seed: 5–6 years.

Distribution: Mexico (Guanajuato, Zacatecas, Querétaro, San Luis Potosí, Aguascalientes, Durango, and Jalisco).

Mammillaria picta

DATA

Form: Simple or clumping. Heads to 1.6 in (4 cm) high and broad.

Spines: Radials 12–14; to 0.3 in (0.8 cm) long. Centrals usually 1; to 0.4 in (1 cm) or more long; dark.

Flower: Creamy white. 0.4 in (1.1 cm) across. April–May in cultivation.

Flowering time from seed: 1–3 years.

Distribution: Mexico (Tamaulipas, near Jaumave and Palmillas; Nuevo León, east of Matehuala).

In habitat this plant generally remains as tiny single heads, but in cultivation the forms currently available seem to clump readily. This is the normal habit in subspecies *viereckii* (formerly *Mammillaria viereckii*) from Nogales in Tamaulipas, which rapidly forms mounds made up of dozens of smallish heads. These have far more spines than the type, giving them a very different appearance. Even the type plant varies somewhat, the plant illustrated being a vegetative propagation of a distinctive form collected near Aramberri, Nuevo León, by Alfred Lau. It has been widely distributed under his field number 1063.

Mammillaria plumosa

This is not a plant to be grown for its flowers, which are small, dingy, and often fail to show up for years on end. Rather, it is the superb feathery spination that has always drawn collectors to this unusual species. Although usually thought of as being white, in some forms the spination has a distinctly creamy tinge. Two growth forms occur, one rapidly offsetting into flat-topped cushions, the other "golfball" form clumping more sparingly and its more elongate heads giving it a clear identity. Since the roots are relatively sparse and weak, use a pan and always water with care.

The plant illustrated is a typical commercial specimen.

DATA

Form: Forming cushions. Heads to 2.8 in (7 cm) across and 3.2 in (8 cm) high.

Spines: Radials to 40; 0.1–0.3 in (3–7 mm) long; white and feathery.

Flower: White with a greenish throat. 0.6 in (1.4 cm) broad. November–January in cultivation.

Flowering time from seed: 10 years or more.

Distribution: Mexico (Nuevo León and Coahuila, especially in Huasteca Canyon).

Mammillaria polyedra

DATA

Form: Clumping. Heads to 11.8 in (30 cm) high and 3.9–4.7 in (10–12 cm) broad.

Spines: Radials usually 4; to 1 in (2.5 cm) long. Centrals 0.

Flower: Pink. 0.8 in (2 cm) across. May–June in cultivation.

Flowering time from seed: 4–5 years.

Distribution: Mexico (Oaxaca).

This is the type of the series Polyedrae, the so-called *Mammillaria polyedra* group, which contains plants such as *M. karwinskiana*, *M. carnea,* and *M. mystax*, all of which are far more often seen in collections than *M. polyedra* itself. This is a pity, because it is an attractive and easy-to-grow species that deserves a place in any collection. It can be spectacularly generous with its flowers, which often appear in several rows and are of a very distinctive and attractive shade of pink.

Its most characteristic features are the flattened sides to the tubercles, which give them a distinctly angled appearance. The plant illustrated was grown from seed collected near Tonalá, ML346.

Mammillaria polythele

number of names that are very familiar in cultivation have been lumped into this variable species. They include *Mammillaria hidalgensis*, *M. kewensis*, *neophaeacantha*, and *M. tetracantha*. In cultivation they all form tallish, cylindrical nts that may eventually fall over under their own weight. Long before this pens, it would be wise to chop off the head and start again from the resulting ets, or acquire a replacement plant. By contrast, the plant illustrated is an active stout form that does not elongate unduly.

s plant was grown from seed collected near San Luis de la Paz, Guanajuato.

DATA

Form: Usually simple. To about 2 ft (60 cm) high; 3.9 in (10 cm) across.

Spines: Radials 0. Centrals 2–4; to 1 in (2.5 cm); reddish, yellowish, or dark brown.

Flower: Carmine. 0.4 in (1 cm) across. June–July in cultivation.

Flowering time from seed: 3–4 years.

Distribution: Mexico (Hidalgo, near Ixmiquilpán and Zimapán, westward to Guanajuato and Querétaro).

283

Mammillaria prolifera

DATA

Form: Offsetting. Heads to 2.4 in (6 cm) high; 1.6 in (4 cm) broad.

Spines: Radials 40; to 0.4 in (1 cm) long. Centrals 5–9; to 0.3 in (0.8 cm); yellow or brown.

Flower: Creamy yellow with a reddish midline. 0.7 in (1.8 cm) long. April–June in cultivation.

Flowering time from seed: 1–3 years.

Distribution: Untied States (Texas); Mexico (Coahuila, Nuevo León, Tamaulipas); West Indies (Cuba and Haiti).

While it is wise to detach fruits from your "mamms" as soon as possible after they ripen, in case they cause the plant to rot, in this prolifically clumping species they can safely be left on. This is partly because they never seem to cause any problems, but mainly because they are so beautifully ornamental, especially when they are accompanied by a mass of flowers. Several subspecies have been described, the most distinctive of which is *zubleri* (often still offered, and probably wisely so, as *Mammillaria zubleri*), a distinctive-looking plant with yellow spines from Ocampo in Tamaulipas.

The plant illustrated above is subspecies texana *and is by far the most common form seen in cultivation. It was grown from seed that was collected in Cameron County, Texas, DJF1022.49.*

Mammillaria rekoi

everal forms of this species exist, varying in body size, spination, and tendency
to cluster. As often happens with cacti, several of the more distinctive forms
e been given specific names. In "normal" *rekoi* (= *Mammillaria mitlensis*) from
a the body generally stays solitary and the spination is yellow. In *M. pullihamata*
n Nejapa the body remains smaller and is more densely covered in long golden
nes. *Mammillaria krasukae* is a dwarf form with long, blackish spines, and is the
nt illustrated—grown from seed collected near Reforma. All these forms have
v been "dumped" into *M. rekoi* with no recognition, along with *M. albrechtiana*
M. sanjuanensis. The most attractive of the recognized forms are subspecies
tacantha (strongly clumping with long, wavy, yellowish spines) and *aeureispina*
mping from the base, with straight golden spines and a rather cylindrical stem).

DATA

Form: Simple or clumping.
Stems to 4.7 in (12 cm)
high; 2.4 in (6 cm) broad.

Spines: Radials 20; to
0.2 in (0.6 cm) long.
Centrals 4; 0.4–0.6 in
(1–1.5 cm); the
lowermost hooked.

Flower: Magenta. 0.6 in
(1.5 cm) long. May–
June in cultivation.

**Flowering time from
seed:** 1–3 years.

Distribution: Mexico
(Oaxaca).

Mammillaria rhodantha

Form: Simple or clumping. Stems to 11.8 in (30 cm) tall: 3.9 in (10 cm) wide.

Spines: Radials 16–20; to 0.4 in (1 cm) long. Centrals 4–7; 0.4–1 in (1–2.5 cm); yellow to red.

Flower: Purplish. 0.6 in (1.6 cm) broad. May–August in cultivation.

Flowering time from seed: 3–4 years.

Distribution: Mexico (states of Mexico, Hidalgo, and Querétaro).

At its most typical this species often has reddish central spines. In subspecies *pringlei* (formerly *Mammillaria pringlei*) they are golden yellow and rather mc twisted and interlacing, giving a very attractive effect. In subspecies *fera-rubra* the are an unusual shade of orange. The subspecies *mccartenii* (formerly *M. verticeal* from Tuxpan in Michoacán is a distinctive variant that in cultivation tends to remai rather shortly globular. In habitat it grows under oaks with orchids and begonias.

The plant illustrated is a typical example of what you might get if you order an unprovenanced plant of this species by mail.

Mammillaria rubrograndis

habitat this species usually grows under pines and oaks and is one of the largest members of the genus. It has a reputation for being shy-flowering, and even when wering commences it may be interrupted for a few years before starting again. Lau 1447, from hills along the road from Siberia to Encantada in Nuevo León, e flowers are almost pure white. They contrast well with the long black central ines, making it a very distinctive plant. The shy-flowering nature of *Mammillaria brograndis* is in stark contrast to the free-flowering *M. melanocentra*, of which rubrograndis* is now often considered a subspecies.

e plant illustrated was grown from seed collected at the type locality, Lau 1220.

DATA

Form: Simple. To 7.1 in (18 cm) across; 3.9 in (10 cm) high.

Spines: Radials 11–13; 0.1–0.5 in (0.4–1.2 cm) long. Centrals 1–4; 0.4–0.8 in (1–2 cm).

Flower: Pink or whitish. To 1.6 in (4 cm) across. February–April in cultivation; January in habitat.

Flowering time from seed: 7–8 years.

Distribution: Mexico (Tamaulipas, asbestos mine between Jaumave and Ciudad Victoria; also at Dulces Nombres).

Mammillaria saboae haudeana

DATA

Form: Clumping. Heads to 1.6 in (4 cm) tall; 0.6 in (1.5 cm) across.

Spines: 18–27; all radials; to 0.2 in (0.6 cm) long.

Flower: Lilac pink. To 1.8 in (4.5 cm) across. April–May in cultivation.

Flowering time from seed: 2–3 years.

Distribution: Mexico (Sonora, in lava fields at Yécora).

Known in cultivation for some time simply as Lau 777, this miniature cactus was eventually described as *Mammillaria haudeana*, before being quickly reduced to the status of form under *M. saboae*. It was then promoted to the higher status of subspecies, where it currently stands. This is easily the most common subspecies of *M. saboae* in collections (the other being the rarely seen subspecies *goldii*). It is also by far the most vigorous, clumping rapidly from its fleshy rootstock and flowering its heads off every spring. Cuttings root rapidly and soon start to clump, so it does not take long to build up a nice stock of this spectacularly flowered plant. *Mammillaria theresae* is similar but larger and takes longer to start clumping.

The plant illustrated is a cutting from material originally collected by Lau.

Mammillaria sartorii

Form: Clumping. Heads to 4.7 in (12 cm) broad and 5.9 in (15 cm) high.

Spines: Radials usually 4; to 0.3 in (0.8 cm) long. Centrals absent, or sometimes 1 or more; of similar length to radials.

Flower: Yellowish to carmine. To 0.8 in (2 cm) long. July–September in cultivation.

Flowering time from seed: 4–5 years.

Distribution: Mexico (Veracruz).

For many years after its original discovery and description this species was not seen again in the wild and it was probably unknown in cultivation. All this changed with its rediscovery in the 1970s, after which material quickly became available, and this plant is now relatively common in collections. It makes an attractive clump and is notable for the large amounts of whitish wool in the axils and its prolific production of (usually) carmine flowers.

The plant illustrated is a vegetative propagation from a plant collected in the Barranca de Tenampa.

Mammillaria scheinvariana

DATA

Form: Simple or clumping. Heads about 2 in (5 cm) across.

Spines: Radials 20–24 (sometimes to 36); to 0.8 in (2 cm) long; white; hairlike. Centrals usually 0, sometimes 1; to about 0.6 in (1.5 cm) long; not hooked.

Flower: Creamy whitish with pink midstripes. About 0.4 in (1 cm) wide. June–July in cultivation.

Flowering time from seed: 2–3 years.

Distribution: Mexico (border area of Hidalgo and Querétaro).

Regarded by some authorities on the genus as no more than a subspecies of *Mammillaria crinita*, this attractive plant is probably unique in the cactus world for having been discovered from a boat. This came about because the species was unfortunate enough to be growing just where the Zimapán dam was about to fill, and the new plant was discovered during a rescue attempt for other cacti that were marooned by the rising waters. It is still scarce in cultivation and most plants, including the one illustrated above, have been propagated vegetatively from material rescued from the dam site.

Mammillaria schiedeana

n recent years this once popular species has been somewhat overshadowed by the rediscovered *Mammillaria carmenae*. This is a pity, since a large clump of *. schiedaena* richly deserves a place in any collection, and commercially produced ants are most attractive (see illustration). In subspecies *dumetorum* (formerly *. dumetorum*) from San Luis Potosí the radial spines are white, fewer in number, nd shorter, exposing more of the dark green body beneath. In both plants growth a little slow, and the roots are very plump and fleshy, so avoid overwatering.

DATA

Form: Clumping. Heads flattish; to 2.3 in (6 cm) across.

Spines: To 75; all radials; to 0.2 in (0.5 cm) long; whitish to golden yellow.

Flower: Whitish 0.6 in (1.5 cm) across. June–August in cultivation; also often in winter and early spring.

Flowering time from seed: 3–4 years.

Distribution: Mexico (Hidalgo, especially around Metztitlán and Puente de Dios; Querétaro).

Mammillaria schumannii

DATA

Form: Usually clumping. Heads 1.6–2.3 in (4–6 cm) tall; 1.2 in (3 cm) wide.

Spines: Radials 9–15; 0.2–0.5 in (0.6–1.2 cm) long. Centrals usually 1; hooked; to 0.6 in (1.5 cm).

Flower: Pink. 1.2–1.6 in (3–4 cm) across. May–June in cultivation.

Flowering time from seed: 2–3 years.

Distribution: Mexico (Baja California, widespread in the Cape area, although being eliminated from some places by construction work).

An illustration of the innately conservative nature of many plantsmen is the fact that this species is even now sometimes listed in the genus *Bartschella*. In cultivation it can be a short-lived plant, owing to its propensity for suddenly collapsing in a heap of goo. This should not happen if you are careful with the watering can, especially early in the year before growth has commenced properly. Some plants clump very early on, while others seem to remain simple, and it is interesting that the clumping forms seem to be much more vigorous and less liable to make an early departure to the compost heap.

The plant illustrated above was grown from seed that was collected at San José del Cabo, Lau 048.

Mammillaria scrippsiana

Having been replaced by more fashionable newcomers in recent years, this easy-to-grow species deserves to make a comeback. It slowly makes attractive clumps of bluish green heads, all of which bear their pink flowers for several weeks through the summer. Several forms exist, of which the one still often listed as *Mammillaria pseudoscrippsiana* is the most distinctive, having smaller, darker green bodies that clump more strongly and bear yellowish white flowers. It comes from near Ahuacatlán in Nayarit.

The plant illustrated was grown from seed collected at Agua Caliente, Pueblo Nuevo, Durango, Lau 1249.

DATA

Form: Clumping. Heads to 2.3 in (6 cm) high and broad.

Spines: Radials 8–10; to 0.3 in (0.8 cm) long. Centrals 8–9; to 0.2 in (0.6 cm).

Flower: Pink. 0.6 in (1.5 cm) across. June–July in cultivation.

Flowering time from seed: 3–4 years.

Distribution: Mexico (widespread in Jalisco and Nayarit, also in Zacatecas and Durango).

Mammillaria senilis

DATA

Form: Clumping. Heads to 5.9 in (15 cm) tall; 2.3 in (6 cm) wide.

Spines: Radials 30–40; 0.8 in (2 cm) long. Centrals 4–6; to 0.8 in (2 cm); the lowermost hooked.

Flower: Red. 2.3–2.8 in (6–7 cm) long. April in cultivation.

Flowering time from seed: 6–10 years.

Distribution: Mexico (Chihuahua and Durango to Jalisco and Nayarit).

Conspicuous white mounds of this species are widespread in the Sierra Madre Occidental at quite high altitudes, where they are often covered by snow in winter. Not surprisingly, in cultivation this is a very cold-hardy plant, but it can be a little slow to flower. It is not unusual to find beautiful old multiheaded plants that have never produced a single bloom, sitting on the bench beside a seedling only a few years old that is covered with flowers. The flowers are pollinated by hummingbirds, and their adaptation for this purpose was one of the main reasons for creating the genus *Mamillopsis* in which this species is still sometimes listed.

The plant illustrated is a typical commercially produced example.

Mammillaria sheldonii

This is a fairly slow-growing species that eventually forms small clumps. Like most of the larger-flowered, hooked-spined members of the genus, it should never be overwatered, otherwise it is likely to rot. In its currently accepted broader sense it now incorporates several other former species, including *Mammillaria inglei* (taller, more robust, wider flowers), *M. inae* (tall-cylindrical, mainly simple, flower smaller), and *M. marnieriana* (short-cylindrical, flower large, pink). The plant pictured is the former *M. alamensis*, a dwarf solitary form, grown from seed collected near Navajoa, Sonora. Despite now being included in *M. sheldonii*, these are all still listed and supplied regularly as species and are different enough to be worth growing in their own right.

DATA

Form: Clumping from the base. Stems 3.2–3.9 in (8–10 cm) tall; 1.6–2 in (4–5 cm) across.

Spines: Radials 10–15; to 0.4 in (0.9 cm) long. Centrals 1–3; to 0.5 in (1.2 cm); dark brown; lowermost hooked.

Flower: Pink; bordered white. 1.2 in (3 cm) across. May–June in cultivation.

Flowering time from seed: 2–3 years.

Distribution: Mexico (Sonora, near Hermosillo, Los Alamos, Guaymas, etc.; Chihuahua).

Mammillaria sinistrohamata

DATA

Form: Clumping. Heads to 2 in (5 cm) across and high.

Spines: Radials 20 or more; to 0.4 in (1 cm) long. Centrals 4; the lowermost to 1.4 cm (0.6 in), hooked; all spines pale yellow.

Flower: Creamish. 0.5 in (1.2 cm) across. May in cultivation.

Flowering time from seed: 2–3 years.

Distribution: Mexico (Zacatecas, near the borders with Durango and Coahuila).

A close relative of *Mammillaria mercadensis*, this lovely species is differentiated mainly by its conspicuously pale spination. In habitat the two species also seem to have a different ecology, with *M. sinistrohamata* growing in predominantly flat areas among grass, while *M. mercadensis* grows on the adjacent hills—on and among rocks. *Mammillaria mercadensis* itself may be the same as *M. jaliscana*, in which case the former name would take priority. In cultivation *M. sinistrohamata* tends to be much slower growing than the others, although it is easy enough to keep going as long as it is not overpotted.

The plant illustrated was grown from seed collected near Río Grande.

Mammillaria sonorensis

n cultivation this species slowly makes small mounds of rather globular, dark green
heads, on which the vivid purplish pink flowers appear over a period of several
eeks. A cream-flowered plant, formerly known as *Mammillaria tesopacensis*
amed for its origin, near Tesopaco in Sonora), is also available. It tends to grow
omewhat larger, with the individual heads reaching up to 7.1 inches (18 cm) high
d 5.1 inches (13 cm) across. Since this plant also had a var. *rubriflora* with a deep
nk flower, it is not surprising that *M. sonorensis* now contains them both.

he plant illustrated was grown from seed collected near Guirocoba.

DATA

Form: Clumping. Heads
to 3.2 in (8 cm) high;
2.3 in (6 cm) broad.

Spines: Radials 8–15;
to 0.8 in (2 cm) long.
Centrals 1–4; 0.2–1.8 in
(0.5–4.5 cm); dark
reddish brown.

Flower: Deep pink or
cream. 0.8 in (2 cm) long.
May–June in cultivation.

**Flowering time from
seed:** 4–5 years.

Distribution: Mexico
(Sonora).

Mammillaria sphacelata

DATA

Form: Clumping. Stems to 7.8 in (20 cm) long; 1.2 in (3 cm) broad.

Spines: Radials 10–15, to 0.3 in (0.8 cm) long. Centrals 1–4; to 0.2 in (0.6 cm).

Flower: Reddish purple. 0.3 in (0.8 cm) broad. May–June in cultivation.

Flowering time from seed: 3–4 years.

Distribution: Mexico (Puebla and Oaxaca).

This is a relatively slow-growing species that gradually forms dense clumps of fingerlike heads, although in cultivation they do not normally reach the maximum length of 7.8 inches (20 cm) seen in habitat. A similar species, *Mammillaria viperina*, with even more slender stems and denser spination, occurs near Zapotitlán de las Salinas and near Calipam. Where the two meet up, they intergrade, so there is a tendency these days to regard the latter as a subspecies of *M. sphacelata*. Both plants can be tricky to keep going, appearing to resent being repotted and always seeming to prefer the smallest pot size that will contain them comfortably.

The plant illustrated above was grown from seed that was collected south of Tehuacán, Puebla, ML018.

Mammillaria sphaerica

With its rather long, plump tubercles and large yellow flowers it will not be surprising to know that this species was once included in the defunct genus *Dolicothele*, now a subgenus of *Mammillaria*. The tubercles are shorter than in *M. longimamma* and the whole plant has a more squat, compact appearance than that species. *Mammillaria sphaerica* is much more free-flowering and is a pretty tough plant, although its large fleshy root needs a pot large enough to hold it comfortably. Clustering takes place early on, so that eventually mounds as large as 19.6 inches (50 cm) across can be formed.

The plant illustrated was grown from seed collected in Starr County, Texas.

DATA

Form: Clumping. Heads to 2 in (5 cm) high and broad.

Spines: Radials 12–14; to 0.4 in (0.9 cm) long. Centrals 1; to 0.2 in (0.6 cm).

Flower: Yellow. 2.3–2.8 in (6–7 cm) across. May–June in cultivation.

Flowering time from seed: 3–4 years.

Distribution: United States (Texas); Mexico (Tamaulipas).

Mammillaria spinosissima

Form: Simple or clumping. Stems to 11.8 in (30 cm) or more tall; 3.9 in (10 cm) across.

Spines: Radials 20–30; to 0.4 in (1 cm) long. Centrals 7–15; to 0.8 in (2 cm).

Flower: Reddish purple. To 0.6 in (1.5 cm) across. May–July in cultivation.

Distribution: Mexico (Morelos, Guerrero, State of Mexico).

In cultivation this species quickly forms an upright cylinder, usually with reddish spines and decorated with several rings of vivid pinkish purple flowers. A popular variant with soft, whitish spination is subspecies *pilcayensis* (formerly *Mammillaria pilcayensis*). In habitat it hangs down from vertical cliffs in the Barranca de Pilcaya in Guerrero, and this habit of falling over is unfortunately repeated in cultivation, with the plant hanging over the side of the pot. The prettiest form is subspecies *tepoxtlana* (formerly *M. crassior*). With its very dense, glassy-whitish spination, it eventually forms clumps of fairly thick, upright stems. This is the form illustrated above—Repp 761—grown from seed set on field-collected plants in cultivation.

Mammillaria tayloriorum

his plant was named in 1975 for Bob and Suzanne Taylor of El Cajon, California. It took a while for it to become widespread in cultivation, but it is now firmly ablished and easy to obtain. Its fairly woolly appearance and attractive pink vers mean that it is unlikely to lose favor over the years, while its ease of ivation ensures that plants remain as long-term residents of the greenhouse. ing to admire it in habitat is a little more problematical—there is nowhere easy a boat to land, and only the most committed of cactophiles have made the trip olasco Island, one of them being Alfred Lau, who collected the seed that resulted e plant illustrated here, Lau 774.

DATA

Form: Clumping. Heads to 9.8 in (25 cm) high; 4.3 in (11 cm) broad.

Spines: Radials 12; to 0.4 in (0.9 cm) long. Centrals 2–3, sometimes to 5; similar to the radials.

Flower: Pinkish with white edges. 0.5 in (1.2 cm) broad. June–July in cultivation.

Flowering time from seed: 4–5 years.

Distribution: Mexico (Sonora, San Pedro Nolasco Island).

Mammillaria tezontle

DATA

Form: Clumping. Heads to 0.4 in (1 cm) tall and 0.6–0.8 in (1.5–2 cm) across.

Spines: Radials 14–20; to 0.2 in (0.5 cm) long. Centrals 1–4; to about 0.1 in (0.4 cm) long; one or more hooked. All spines yellowish white and pubescent.

Flower: Yellowish white. 0.6 in (1.5 cm) across. June in cultivation.

Flowering time from seed: 2–3 years.

Distribution: Mexico (north of the city of San Luis Potosi).

Described as recently as 1995, this species has been reduced to synonymy beneath *Mammillaria crinita* by David Hunt, but it is retained as adequately distinct here. In the wild it is in imminent danger of extinction. It is known only from tiny populations found on one or two remaining outcrops of the rock known as *tezontle*, a form of lava. Unfortunately, this substance is in demand for road building which has led to the destruction of some sites, and at least one locality has been robbed of most of its plants by collectors. Fortunately, some of this illegally removed material has been extensively propagated vegetatively (see illustration), and this endangered miniature is now beginning to appear in collections.

Mammillaria winterae

its typical form this species, which includes Reppenhagen's *Mammillaria* *eudenbergeri*, makes a large single head with very open spination, revealing the ercles beneath. This is the form illustrated here. It was grown from seed collected ar Muralla, Coahuila. By contrast, the appearance of subspecies *aramberri* (often ed by its original name of *M. crassimammillis*) is very different. It has large mbers of fairly small heads that build rapidly into a large clump, and brownish low blooms. It was discovered by Alfred Lau at Aramberri in Nuevo León, hence choice of name at subspecies level.

DATA

Form: Simple. 7.8–11.8 in (20–30 cm) across and high.

Spines: Radials 4; to 1.2 in (3 cm). Centrals 0.

Flower: Yellowish. 1 in (2.5 cm) across. May–June in cultivation.

Flowering time from seed: 3–4 years.

Distribution: Mexico (Nuevo León, near Monterrey; Coahuila, near Saltillo).

Matucana aurantiaca

Form: Simple or clumping. Heads to 5.9 in (15 cm) high and broad.

Spines: Radials and centrals difficult to distinguish; to 34 in number; to 1.8 in (4.5 cm); reddish brown.

Flower: Orange yellow. To 3.5 in (9 cm) long; 2 in (5 cm) across. June–July in cultivation.

Flowering time from seed: 5–6 years.

Distribution: Peru (widespread in the mountains of the departments of Cajamarca and La Libertad and to Huancabamba, department of Piura).

This easy-to-grow species has always been one of the most common members the genus in cultivation and, like several other species, it is still sometimes list under *Submatucana*. In subspecies *currundayensis* the body is less spiny and the flower is pale salmon pink. It comes from the Cerro Currunday near Samne.

The plant illustrated is a vegetative propagation from a plant collected near San Pablo, Cajamarca, Lau 177. In cultivation this is a very strongly clumping form notable for its particularly beautiful flower.

Matucana aureiflora

Whereas most other members of this genus have asymmetrical (zygomorphic) flowers with long tubes, in this species they are shorter, they open widely, and y are of regular shape. In cultivation this species usually remains simple, but very plants can occasionally form substantial clumps. It is a trouble-free plant that ws and flowers well. *Matucana ritteri* has a similar (although darker and glossier en) appearance, but its flowers are 3.5 inches (9 cm) long and bright red.

e plant illustrated is a vegetative propagation from material collected at Baños del a, Lau 104.

Form: Simple or clumping when very old. Body flattened-globular; to 5.1 in (13 cm) across.

Spines: Radials 4–6; 0.3–0.7 in (0.7–1.8 cm) long. Centrals 1–4; 0.5–1 in (1.2–2.5 cm).

Flower: Yellow. 1.2–1.8 in (3–4.5 cm) wide. June–July in cultivation.

Flowering time from seed: 4–5 years.

Distribution: Peru (Baños del Inca near Cajamarca).

305

Matucana comacephala

Form: Simple. 2.8–3.2 in (7–8 cm) broad; to 2.5 ft (75 cm) long.

Spines: Radials 15–20; 0.4–2 in (1–5 cm). Centrals 5–10; 0.4–1.6 in (1–4 cm).

Flower: Pink to carmine. 1.8–2.2 in (4.5–5.5 cm) long. June–July in cultivation.

Flowering time from seed: 4–5 years.

Distribution: Peru (originally found near Rahuapampa, now known in other localities).

With its dense mass of whitish spines, this is probably the most beautiful member of the genus. In cultivation it grows quickly into a short-cylindrical plant, but eventually becomes too tall to be really attractive. In habitat, on steep slopes where the plants can be difficult to reach, they eventually grow columnar. This is one of the most free-flowering members of the genus, its stunning pink blooms appearing in tufts over several weeks in summer.

The plant illustrated was raised from commercial seed.

Matucana haynei hystrix

ften still labeled as *Matucana hystrix*, with its prominent long blackish central
spines this is probably the most handsome form of the very widespread
haynei. The description given here is amplified to incorporate details of
multicolor, which forms part of a single population along the backbone of the
...les. Driving up from Nazca, the plants start to appear only once the road has
...ched an altitude of about 9,900 feet (3,000 m), but after that they become quite
...mmon. In cultivation growth is relatively slow but problem-free. Flowers usually
...ear every year, often several together, rather than the single flower illustrated
...e (on PM450, grown from seed collected between Nazca and Lucanas).

DATA

Form: Usually simple.
Stems to 15.8 in
(40 cm) high; 5.9 in
(15 cm) across.

Spines: Radials numerous;
white; to 0.6 in (1.5 cm)
long. Centrals up to 4; to
2.8 in (7 cm) long; dark
brown to almost black.

Flower: Deep carmine.
To 2.8 in (7 cm) long and
1 in (2.5 cm) across.
July–August in cultivation,
sometimes also in May.

**Flowering time from
seed:** 5–6 years.

Distribution: Peru
(between Nazca and
Lucanas).

Matucana intertexta

DATA

Form: Simple. To 14.1 in (36 cm) high; 7.1 in (18 cm) across.

Spines: Radials 8–12; 0.3–0.8 in (0.8–2 cm) long. Centrals 1–4; 0.8–1.2 in (2–3.5 cm); brown; tipped black.

Flower: Orange. 2.9–4.1 in (7.5–10.5 cm) long. June–July in cultivation.

Flowering time from seed: 4–5 years.

Distribution: Peru (Puente Crisnejas, north of Cajamarca).

This species grows more slowly than *Matucana aurantiaca*, but has beautiful flowers that last for several days and often have bicolored petals. Bicolored flowers are also typical of *M. polzii*, a more recently discovered species that in cultivation covers itself in offsets. When these are present, flowers are seldom see but pick them all off and you should have plenty of stunning blooms every year.

The specimen illustrated is a vegetative propagation from a plant collected from Hacienda Huagal, Lau 175.

Matucana oreodoxa

s with *Matucana aureiflora*, the flowers in *M. oreodoxa* are not long and ▲ zygomorphic, but have a more conventional, circular outline. In cultivation they ▪ear in profusion, often covering the top of the dark glossy green body. This ▪cies normally remains simple, but plants that have been repeatedly propagated ▪m cuttings tend to start clumping heavily, as they do in habitat when the original ▪le head has been eaten off by goats or other animals.

▪ plant illustrated is a vegetative propagation from a plant collected between ▪ari and Llamellin, KK1591.

DATA

Form: Usually simple. Heads 1–3.2 in (2.5–8 cm) across and high.

Spines: Radials 4–12; 0.4 in (1 cm) long. Centrals 1–2; to 1.6 in (4 cm).

Flower: Orange. 1.6–2.4 in (4–6 cm) long. May–June in cultivation.

Flowering time from seed: 4–5 years.

Distribution: Peru (on high hills on both sides of the Rahuapampa gorge).

Matucana paucicostata

DATA

Form: Clumping. Heads to 5.5.in (14 cm) tall; 2.8 in (7 cm) across.

Spines: Radials 4–8; 0.2–1.2 in (0.5–3 cm). Centrals 0–1; to 1.2 in (3.5 cm).

Flower: Red. To 2.4 in (6 cm) long; 1.2 in (3 cm) broad. June–July in cultivation.

Flowering time from seed: 3–4 years.

Distribution: Peru (Huari).

Large clumps of this very easily cultivated species are often found in collections, and when in flower they are a magnificent sight. Seedlings grow well and clu from an early age, although a great many of the plants seen in collections stem fr offsets taken off plants originally collected in the wild by Alfred Lau and Karel Kni Spination and body size vary somewhat, which led Knize to coin a plethora of commercially inspired names, none of which has any botanical significance. Thes include *Matucana caespitosa*, *M. huaricensis*, *M. paucispina*, *M. senile*, *M. senilis*, and *M. turbiniformis*.

The plant illustrated above is M. caespitosa. *It is a vegetative propagation from KK1317 collected at Huari—the type locality of* M. paucicostata!

Matucana weberbaueri flammeus

When this plant was originally discovered it was thought to be the original long-lost *Matucana weberbaueri*. When it produced an orange flower, this proved to [be] false, and it was subsequently named as a variety. The indomitable Alfred Lau [eve]ntually rediscovered *M. weberbaueri* with its canary-yellow flowers and spines. [Ho]wever, it has never become as common in collections as the variety illustrated, [whi]ch does far better in cultivation, being a good vigorous plant with sturdy roots.

[Th]e plant below was grown from seed produced in cultivation on plants collected by [Alf]red Lau at Balsas, Lau 109.

DATA

Form: To 2.8 in (7 cm) high; 5.9 in (15 cm) across.

Spines: About 30. All mixed; to 1.6 in (4 cm) long; yellowish orange.

Flower: Orange. About 2.2 in (5.5 cm) long. June–July in cultivation; November in habitat.

Flowering time from seed: 4–5 years.

Distribution: Peru (Balsas).

311

Melocactus curvispinus

Form: Simple. Stem to 11.8 in (30 cm) high; 10.6 in (27 cm) across.

Spines: Radials 6–11; to about 1.6 in (4 cm) long. Centrals usually 1–4; to 2 in (5 cm) long.

Cephalium: To 7.8 in (20 cm) high; 3.9 in (10 cm) across.

Flower: Pink. About 0.6 in (1.5 cm) across. Appearing over a long period in summer.

Flowering time from seed: 8–10 years.

Distribution: Mexico to Venezuela.

Although it also occurs far inland this is mainly a coastal species and often grows so close to the sea that the plants are splashed with salt spray. In Central America the plants are somewhat smaller than those farther south, which belong to subspecies *caesius* and are illustrated here, photographed near Coro in Venezuela. In parts of Venezuela this cactus is so common that it occurs in thousands, often carpeting the ground locally. Like all members of the genus, it is very sensitive to cold and should be kept at a minimum of 59°F (15°C) in winter. Some of the names now included in a broadened concept of this species include *Melocactus delessertianus*, *M. ruestii*, *M. oaxacensis*, and *M. maxonii*.

Melocactus ernestii

Form: Simple. Stem to about 17.7 in (45 cm) high; 8.6 in (22 cm) across.

Spines: Radials 7–13; 1.8–5.9 in (4.5–15 cm) long. Centrals 4–8; to 3.5 in (9 cm).

Cephalium: To 7.1 in (18 cm) high; 3.2 in (8 cm) across.

Flower: Small; purplish pink. Occur over a long period in summer.

Flowering time from seed: 12–15 years.

Distribution: Brazil (Pernambuco, Sergipe, Bahia, and Minas Gerais).

With its large size and long, fierce spination, varying in color from yellowish red to almost black, this is one of the most impressive members of the genus. It grows on bare rock outcrops, often rooted in lines in cracks where the tiny seedlings have germinated and then thrived in the damp shaded atmosphere. In cultivation, given plenty of warmth, it should eventually form a cephalium and flower.

The plant illustrated was growing on steep rock slabs right beside the road south of Jequié, Bahia, PM130.

Melocactus oreas

DATA

Form: Simple. Stem to
13.8 in (35 cm) across;
7.1 in (18 cm) high.

Spines: Radials 8–11;
1.6–3.2 in (4–8 cm) long.
Centrals 1–4; to 3.2 in
(8 cm) long.

Cephalium: To 4.7 in
(12 cm) high; 3.2 in
(8 cm) across.

Flower: Pink. 0.4 in
(1 cm) across. Produced
throughout the summer.

**Flowering time from
seed:** 12–15 years.

Distribution: Brazil (Bahia.)

This handsome flattened-globular species often grows in hundreds of thousands on smooth, flat, or gently rounded rock outcrops—visible from a distance as gleaming masses as the sun reflects off their spines and glossy bodies. In cultivation growth is strong and relatively rapid, helped along by the fairly vigorous roots. All being well, you should start seeing a cephalium develop after 12 years or so from seed. This is definitely one of the easiest members of the genus to grow well in cultivation, and you need to be unlucky (or have a heating failure on a frosty night) not eventually to get a cephalium and flowers year after year.

The plants illustrated were growing near Milagres, Bahia. This population is also known by the superfluous name Melocactus rubrisaetosus.

Melocactus peruvianus

This smallish member of the genus is extremely common and widespread over large areas of Peru, but only at low or intermediate altitudes, such as valleys. It is common in the valleys to the north and south of the capital, Lima, usually growing with numerous other cacti, such as various species of *Haageocereus, Espostoa,* and *Neoraimondia.* Most of its habitats are extremely arid, and in cultivation it needs less water than other members of the genus otherwise it is liable to lose its roots. It is also, surprisingly enough, more cold-sensitive than some of the Brazilian members of the genus and must be kept warm, at least 59°F (15°C).

The plant illustrated was photographed in the Santa valley near Caraz.

DATA

Form: Simple. Stem to 7.8 in (20 cm) high and broad.

Spines: Radials 6–14; to about 1.6 in (4 cm) long. Centrals 0–1; 0.8–1.6 in (2–4 cm).

Cephalium: Usually fairly flat. To 2 in (5 cm) across; sometimes 7.8 in (20 cm) tall and 3.2 in (8 cm) broad.

Flower: Magenta. About 0.4 in (1 cm) wide. Produced over much of the summer.

Flowering time from seed: 10–12 years.

Distribution: Extreme south of Ecuador; Peru (as far south as Arequipa).

Melocactus salvadorensis

Form: Simple. Stem to 7.8 in (20 cm) high and broad.

Spines: Radials 7–10; to about 1.8 in (4.5 cm) long. Centrals 1–4; to 1.2 in (3 cm).

Cephalium: To 5.9 in (15 cm) high and 3.9 in (10 cm) across.

Flower: Magenta. About 0.4 in (1 cm) across. Produced throughout the summer.

Flowering time from seed: 10 years.

Distribution: Brazil (Bahia).

Unlike the rock-dwelling *Melocactus ernestii* and *M. oreas* (with which it often grows), this species generally occurs on flattish, deep soils, where it sometime hybridizes with the aforementioned species. In cultivation growth is slow but steady and this is one of the best members of the genus to acquire if you want to see a cephalium, which should start to appear after about 10 years or so from seed.

The plant illustrated was photographed near Jequié, PM129.

Micranthocereus auri-azureus

his species will be grown for the beauty of its startlingly bright blue stems rather than for its flowers, which are not always seen in cultivation. Around the small wn of Grão Mogol it is a common plant (see illustration) and can be seen growing nong rocks and bushes in company with the equally blue *Pilosocerus fulvilanatus*. is is a tropical region with constantly high temperatures by day and by night, so inter frosts can be a problem in cultivation. Some people take their plants inside in der to avoid maintaining a higher temperature in the greenhouse than is needed the majority of the nontropical cacti.

DATA

Form: Branching from the base. Stems to about 3.3 ft (1 m) high and 2.8 in (7 cm) across.

Spines: Numerous. Radials and centrals mixed; to 0.6 in (1.3 cm) long; golden yellow.

Flower: Pink or orange pink; nocturnal. To 1 in (2.5 cm) long and 0.4 in (1.1 cm) across; cylindrical. June–July in cultivation.

Flowering time from seed: 8–10 years.

Distribution: Brazil (Minas Gerais, Grão Mogol).

Micranthocereus flaviflorus

Form: Clumping from the base. Stem to 29.5 in (75 cm) high and 1.6 in (4 cm) across.

Spines: Radials numerous; to 0.2 in (0.5 cm). Centrals about 9; to 0.8 in (2 cm).

Flower: Yellowish orange, red, or creamy; tubular. To 0.7 in (1.8 cm) long and 0.2 in (0.6 cm) across. June–July in cultivation.

Flowering time from seed: 7–8 years.

Distribution: Brazil (Bahia, Serra do Curral Feio).

Like all members of the genus, this plant is winter-tender and should be kept above about 59°F (15°C). The bluish green epidermis makes it an attractive species, the more so when it is topped out by a mass of its short but attractive yellow flowers, seen here on a plant of commercial origin. The flowers arise from a woolly and bristly cephalium that develops along the side of the plant as it matures. The plant illustrated is sometimes listed as var. *densiflorus*, originally described as a species in its own right but often now subsumed within *Micranthocereus flaviflorus*.

Mila caespitosa

No fewer than 12 species of *Mila* have been described, but since the kind of differences that supposedly divide them can also be observed in two plants [rai]sed from seeds out of the same pod, it does not seem logical to accept more [tha]n a single variable species. Cultivated plants soon form small clumps, but [flo]wering is unreliable. Some plants never flower, some do so every few years, [wh]ile others produce a crop of buds every year. Unlike *Melocactus peruvianus*, [wi]th which it often grows, this species is surprisingly cold-resistant and can [wit]hstand freezing for short periods.

[Th]e plant illustrated was grown from seed collected in Tinajas Canyon, south [of] Lima, PM479.

DATA

Form: Clumping. Stems to 5.9 in (15 cm) long and 1.2 in (3 cm) broad.

Spines: Radials to about 40. Centrals to 7; to 1.2 in (3 cm). Whitish to brownish.

Flower: Yellow. 1.2 in (3 cm) long. July–August in cultivation.

Flowering time from seed: 5–6 years.

Distribution: Peru (widespread).

Myrtillocactus geometrizans

Form: To 13.2 ft (4 m) high, with a mass of branches above a distinct trunk. Branches 2–3.9 in (5–10 cm) broad.

Spines: Radials usually 5; mostly less than 0.1 in (2 mm) long. Centrals 1; to 2.8 in (7 cm); blackish.

Flower: Greenish white. About 1.2 in (3 cm) across.

Flowering time from seed: 15–20 years.

Distribution: Mexico (San Luis Potosí to Oaxaca).

Large treelike specimens of this species are common in parts of Mexico. They often grow with the equally large *Escontria chiotilla*, a somewhat winter-tende species not dealt with separately here, but which used to be a regular member of the "cactus assortments" offered by flower stores. Seedlings of *Myrtillocactus geometrizans* also used to be popular, but they have recently gone out of fashion (except as grafting stock), partly perhaps because they too are not particularly cold hardy. With their blue-green stems they are quite attractive, but cannot be expecte to flower in cultivation—no great loss in view of their rather uninspiring flowers.

The plant illustrated was photograph near Zimapán, Hidal

Neolloydia conoidea

DATA

Form: Simple or clumping. Stems to 3.9 in (10 cm) high; 2.8 in (7 cm) across.

Spines: Radials about 15; to 0.6 in (1.5 cm); whitish. Centrals 4–5, to 1.2 in (3 cm) long; black.

Flower: Pink. 1.2–2 in (3–5 cm) across. June in cultivation; August in habitat.

Flowering time from seed: 3–4 years.

Distribution: United States (Texas) to Mexico (Coahuila, San Luis Potosí, Tamaulipas, Hidalgo, and Zacatecas).

ver large areas of Mexico this is one of the few species of cacti likely to be encountered on just about any hillside. It also occurs, sometimes in thousands, flat, stony desert, where the sight of such large numbers of plants covered in their owy pink flowers is very impressive. In some populations every plant seems to mp heavily, while in others they remain solitary. A large-flowered population near umave in Tamaulipas was formerly known as *Neolloydia grandiflora*, while a large-died variation from near Matehuala was described as *N. matehualensis*, but it is ubtful that it is distinct. In cultivation *N. conoidea* is a little touchy, needing a light nd with the watering can.

e plant illustrated was photographed near the city of San Luis Potosí.

Neoporteria calderana

DATA

Form: Simple. Green or blackish. 2–3.2 in (5–8 cm) high and broad.

Spines: Radials 8–19; 0.4–1.4 in (1–3.5 cm) long. Centrals 3–5; 0.8–1.6 in (2–4 cm); black.

Flower: Creamy white. 1.4 in (3.5 cm) broad. June in cultivation; November–December in habitat.

Flowering time from seed: 3–4 years.

Distribution: Chile (Caldera to Chañaral).

This is a small, slow-growing species ideal for the collector with limited space. In habitat the plants grow mainly among rocks, often with *Copiapoa calderana*. Several northern forms (including the taller and spinier *Neoporteria intermedia* and the much smaller, rather less spiny *N. pygmaea*, both of which occur to the north of Chañaral) were originally described as species. Cultivated plants will tolerate very low levels of water even in hot weather and do not appear to suffer from red spider attack, even when stressed. They look best when underpotted and grown hard.

The plant illustrated was photographed just north of Caldera.

Neoporteria chilensis

'chidangui is a popular seaside resort in Chile. On the cliffs around the town and on offshore rock stacks, *Neoporteria chilensis* occurs in thousands, but in area all the plants are white-flowered. About 3 miles (5 km) south of town, ulations occur in which the flowers are white with pink outer petals. Another miles (3 km) south of this, almost all of the plants have the stunning pink vers illustrated below (PM438). In cultivation the white-flowered plants tend to more vigorous than the pink-flowered ones, which often exhibit an annoying dency to lose their roots after being repotted.

DATA

Form: Simple. To 3.3 ft (1 m) high and 4.7 in (12 cm) across.

Spines: Radials 16–24, 0.4–0.6 in (1–1.5 cm) long. Centrals 6–8; to 0.8 in (2 cm).

Flower: Pink. 0.8 in (2 cm) across. May–June in cultivation; December in habitat.

Flowering time from seed: 3–4 years.

Distribution: Chile (Pichidangui to Punta Molles).

Neoporteria curvispina

DATA

Form: Simple or clumping. To 9.8 in (25 cm) or more across; 3.9 in (10 cm) high.

Spines: Radials 8–12; 0.8–1.2 in (2–3 cm). Centrals 1–4; slightly longer and thicker.

Flower: Greenish yellow to brick red. 1.6–2.4 in (4–6 cm) across. June in cultivation; November–December in habitat.

Flowering time from seed: 4–5 years.

Distribution: Chile (widespread in the mountains around Santiago and well to the north and south).

Usually growing among grass and bushes, this is quite a common plant around Santiago, which lies in an area of Chile that receives all its rainfall in winter. Th has unfortunate implications for anyone trying to cultivate this species, since it is rather intolerant of being watered through the summer. For best results, start to gi your plants a light watering about a month before the rest of your collection, and stop altogether during the height of summer. Repot as little as possible, since this species seems to resent root disturbance, and many fine old plants are lost becaus they fail to root into the fresh compost.

The plant illustrated was photographed near Caleu, north of Santiago.

Neoporteria echinus floccosa

his species is popular because of its attractively hairy stems. However, this is not
an invariable feature, and virtually hairless plants also occur. The most common
ver color is white, but forms with beautiful pink flowers are found in certain
lities. Despite the incredibly arid nature of its home, this is an extremely easy
nt in cultivation, although it does best if given the smallest pot that looks
sonable. *Neoporteria echinus echinus* (= *N. glaucescens*) is, by contrast, a
priously difficult plant to grow well or even keep alive in the long term.

plant illustrated was grown from seed collected at Blanco Encalada, RMF045.

DATA

Form: Simple. To 11.8 in
(30 cm) long and 2.4 in
(6 cm) across.

Spines: Radials 13; to
0.4 in (1 cm) long.
Centrals 1–2; 0.4–1 in
(1–2.5 cm) long.

Flower: White to pink.
About 1.2 in (3 cm) long.
June in cultivation.

**Flowering time from
seed:** 3–4 years.

Distribution: Chile (coastal
mountains in the province
of Antofagasta).

Neoporteria islayensis

DATA

Form: Simple. 4.9 in–3 ft (10–75 cm) high and 2–4.7 in (5–12 cm) across.

Spines: Radials 6–19, 0.2–0.6 in (0.5–1.5 cm) long. Centrals 1–8, to 3 cm (1.2 in) long.

Flower: Yellow. To 1.2 in (3 cm) across. May–June in cultivation; mostly December in habitat.

Flowering time from seed: 3–4 years.

Distribution: Northern Chile and southern Peru.

Formerly included in the genus *Islaya*, this widespread plant as currently understood encompasses more than a dozen former species. The conditions in habitat are among the driest endured by any cactus, so it is hardly surprising that can be a tricky plant in cultivation, liable to lose its roots for no obvious reason, ev when watering is done with the utmost care. Using the smallest pot that looks reasonable is certainly important. When well grown it can make a very attractive plant—especially those forms that have black spines.

The plant illustrated was one of thousands growing near Chala Viejo (PM452) and probably the form originally described as Islaya copiapoides.

Neoporteria multicolor

This is a beautiful but extremely variable species that grows on very steep hillsides. Near Salamanca the plants have a densely interlacing, rather springy, mainly yellowish spination, sometimes also black. At Quelén the plants are like little snowballs: they are much smaller with very long, soft, wavy white (sometimes black) spines. At Punta Coiron the spination is stout and rigid, generally golden, and the plants can reach nearly 3.3 feet (1 m) in length. This species is closely related to *Neoporteria nidus*, but its much larger flower has usually finished by the time *N. nidus* starts to bloom, thus preventing any interchange of pollen. To keep the spines as dense as possible, grow it very hard, water only sparingly, and confine the roots in the smallest pot possible.

The plant illustrated was grown from seed collected at Quelén, RMF249.

DATA

Form: Simple. 2–3.2 in (5–8 cm) across; to 7.8 in (20 cm) or more long.

Spines: Numerous; too variable to describe.

Flower: Pink. 2.4–3.2 in (6–8 cm) long. April in cultivation; September–October in habitat.

Flowering time from seed: 3–4 years.

Distribution: Chile (east of Salamanca and in the mountains east of Illapel).

Neoporteria napina

DATA

Form: Simple. 0.8–1.6 in (2–4 cm) across; to 1.6 in (4 cm) high.

Spines: Radials mostly 3–9; 0.1 in (3 mm) long; sometimes with 1 central.

Flower: Pale yellow. About 1.2 in (3 cm) long. June–July in cultivation; September–October in habitat.

Flowering time from seed: 3–4 years.

Distribution: Chile (Huasco to Vallenar).

In cultivation plants tend to become somewhat elongated in age, whereas in the wild they are very difficult to spot, since they are flush with the ground or may be partly covered in windblown sand or soil. Below ground there is a large taproot, but in a pot this does not seem to give any problems. It is a pretty straightforward plant to grow, and ideal for anyone with limited space. Going easy on the water and not overpotting is all that is needed to keep this dwarf plant happy for years.

The plant illustrated was grown from seed collected near Huasco, RMF184.

Neoporteria nidus

The use of the older but poorly typified name *Neoporteria senilis* for this species is only possible if *N. multicolor* is considered conspecific, since it is not certain which plant *N. senilis* refers. Because *N. multicolor* is treated separately here, *nidus* is used to describe the attractive cactus that is common around Ovalle, often occurring on rocky hillsides just outside town. It tends to be a dark-looking plant, with a mass of wavy, blackish spines interlacing like a bird's nest, although some seedlings have a more silvery spination. It is fairly easy in cultivation, as long as it is never watered too generously. Grow it hard, and you will be rewarded with the kind of dense spination typical of plants in habitat.

The plant illustrated below was photographed at Recoleta, farther up the valley from Ovalle, PM396.

DATA

Form: Simple. To 4.7 in (12 cm) across and 7.8 in (20 cm) high.

Spines: Radials 15–40; 0.8–2.4 in (2–6 cm) long. Centrals 4–20; 1.2–2.4 in (3–6 cm).

Flower: Carmine. 1.2 in (3 cm) long. April–May in cultivation: November–December in habitat.

Flowering time from seed: 4–5 years.

Distribution: Chile (around Ovalle).

Neoporteria nigrihorrida

DATA

Form: Simple or clumping. Stems to 9.8 in (25 cm) or more high and 3.9 in (10 cm) broad.

Spines: Radials about 16; to 0.6 in (1.5 cm) long. Centrals 6–7; to 1.2 in (3 cm).

Flower: Carmine. 1.6 in (4 cm) long. March–April in cultivation; September–October in habitat.

Flowering time from seed: 4–6 years.

Distribution: Chile (mainly around La Serena, on the coast and inland up the valleys).

Although relatively slow-growing, this close relative of *Neoporteria subgibbosa* wi eventually make a tall, handsome specimen densely covered in black spines that contrast nicely with the generally green body beneath. It is among the first cac to come into flower in the greenhouse in early spring, continuing for several weeks with a succession of bright pink flowers that in habitat are visited mainly by hummingbirds. In most natural populations the plants grow as single heads, but in some locations, for example, near La Paloma reservoir, they form clumps.

The plant illustrated was grown from seed collected near Herradura, RMF192.

Neoporteria paucicostata

ne of the easier members of the genus to grow well in cultivation, this species is tolerant of a variety of treatment methods and seems very reluctant to lose its ts or otherwise act up in the manner typical of some of the more difficult species the genus. Very serious overwatering is the one thing to be avoided. Around poso the body color is mainly green (so-called var. *viridis*), but this is not a nsistent characteristic, even within a small geographical area. In the most rtherly populations the body color tends to be bluish gray.

e plant illustrated was grown from seed collected from a heavily clumping form nd in the hills above Paposo, RMF144.

DATA

Form: Simple or clumping. 2.4–3.2 in (6–8 cm) broad; 5.9–11.8 in (15–30 cm) high; green, blackish, or bluish gray.

Spines: Radials 5–8; 0.6–1.2 in (1.5–3 cm) long. Centrals 1–4; slightly longer.

Flower: White to pink. 2 in (5 cm) broad. June–July in cultivation; mainly December in habitat.

Flowering time from seed: 4–5 years.

Distribution: Chile (Paposo and northward for about 24 miles/40 km).

Neoporteria subgibbosa

DATA

Form: Simple or clumping. Stems to 3.3 ft (1 m) or more long; 3.9 in (10 cm) broad.

Spines: Radials about 24; 0.4–0.8 in (1–2 cm) long. Centrals 1–16; to 1.6 in (4 cm).

Flower: Pink. 1.6 in (4 cm) long. April–May in cultivation; September–November in habitat.

Flowering time from seed: 5–8 years.

Distribution: Chile (from La Serena south to Concepción).

In habitat this plant often occurs in thousands on sea cliffs, but various forms also occur inland, some of which clump strongly. In cultivation it has a largely unwarranted reputation for being difficult to flower, although it is certainly true that one or two of the larger-growing forms tend to be shy in this respect, while others flower profusely every year. Although the flower is usually pink, in RMF 002 from Quintay it is a beautiful, almost pearlescent shade of white. In var. *castanea* (= *Neoporteria castanea*) from Villa Prat the body tends to stay more flattened-globular, and flowers are always prolifically produced in cultivation.

The plant illustrated above was photographed near Puente Confluencia, west of Illapel, PM387.

Neoporteria taltalensis

Despite growing in an area of extreme aridity, with the only moisture for long periods being dense sea mists, this is not a difficult plant in cultivation. To see it its best with a really impressive, dense spination, grow it hard in a small pot and water very sparingly. Unlike many cacti given such uncharitable treatment, it will not become stressed and be more open to red spider attack. Nor will it burn in sunny conditions, or even stop growing. The flowers vary from whitish pink to a vivid rose pink and usually cover the top of the plant in a mass display that is most impressive.

The plant illustrated was grown from seed collected northwest of Chañaral, PM211.

Form: Simple. To 3.2 in (8 cm) broad, 3.9 in (10 cm) high.

Spines: Radials 6–12; to 0.8 in (2 cm) long. Centrals 6–12; to 1.2 in (3 cm); mostly black.

Flower: Pink. 1 in (2.5 cm) across. June–July in cultivation; mainly December in habitat.

Flowering time from seed: 3–4 years.

Distribution: Chile (along the coast north and south of Taltal).

Neoporteria tuberisulcata

Form: Heads simple or offsetting; 1.6–7.8 in (4–20 cm) across; green or black.

Spines: Radials 8–12; to 0.4 in (1.2 cm). Centrals 4–8, to 1.4 in (3.5 cm) or more long.

Flower: Yellowish, often with a reddish midstripe. To 1.6 in (4 cm) broad. June in cultivation; November–December in habitat.

Flowering time from seed: 3–4 years.

Distribution: Central Chile.

This strongly spined plant occurs over a wide area of central Chile, in some place overlapping with *Neoporteria curvispina*, but without normally forming any hybrids. There has been much discussion over the years as to the correct name to use. *Neoporteria horrida* and *N. tuberisulcata* have alternated, but the latter has no apparently won. In cultivation the best plant to grow is probably the clumping form from around Pichidangui (as illustrated above in habitat, PM257). In cultivation this form produces offsets quite prolifically, thereby giving you a second chance to keep the plant going if the main stem dies—alas, not an unusual event in this somewhat tricky species. As in *N. curvispina* it is best to withhold water in the height of the summer, since *N. tuberisulcata* also comes from the winter rainfall zone.

Neoporteria wagenknechtii

is is a densely spined plant that is similar to *Neoporteria nigrihorrida* but has much smaller flowers. In habitat they usually appear in the fall rather than in ly spring as in *N. nigrihorrida*. In cultivation *N. wagenknechtii* can be tricky at es to keep going. It sometimes loses its roots, especially after being repotted in sh compost, but this is a problem that affects several members of the genus. In ent works this plant is listed as a subspecies of *N. subgibbosa* (but in *Eriosyce*) ich seems a little difficult to justify given the different flowering times in habitat.

e plant illustrated below was seen growing beside the Pan-American highway rth of La Serena.

DATA

Form: Simple. To about 11.8 in (30 cm) high and 4.3 in (11 cm) across.

Spines: Radials 10–14; to 1 in (2.5 cm) long. Centrals 3–6; 0.8–1.2 in (2–3 cm) long.

Flower: Pink. 0.9 in (2.2 cm) long. August–September in cultivation; mainly February in habitat.

Flowering time from seed: 3–4 years.

Distribution: Chile (north of La Serena).

Neoraimondia arequipensis

Form: To 33 ft (10 m) high, sometimes with a woody trunk. Stems to 7.8 in (20 cm) or more across; branching.

Spines: Very irregular; flexible. To 9.8 in (25 cm) long.

Flower: Greenish white to pink. About 2 in (5 cm) long.

Distribution: Peru (widespread).

With its small number of very deep ribs this is a distinctive plant—the more s● when it flowers, since the flowers are produced (often two at a time) at the ● of special cylindrical felty shoots. These elongate year after year until they can be long as your finger. Several other species have been described, all now regarded ● *Neoraimondia arequipensis*, but the names are often still used. For example, the plant known as *N. roseiflora* only gets to 6.6 feet (2 m) high and is the best one to grow in cultivation. On the other hand, *N. gigantea* reaches about 26 feet (8 m), a● *N. arequipensis* (used in its restricted sense for the plant from southern Peru) gets a massive 33 feet (10 m). All are rather slow-growing and winter-tender, but very distinctive if you like unusual columnar cacti, although don't expect any flowers.

The plant illustrated was photographed in the Rimac valley near Chosica, making it N. roseiflora *in the restricted sense.*

Neoraimondia herzogiana

his is the largest cactus of the Bolivian Andes, often occurring in great numbers
along favored river valleys. Plenty of seed has arrived in cultivation from habitat
recent years, so plants have been freely available, although they are rather
v-growing, need extra warmth in winter, and cannot be expected to flower in
ivation. In older works this species was generally included in the genus in
ch it was originally described, namely *Neocardenasia*.

*plant illustrated was photographed in habitat and shows the amazing length
he spines on a specimen about 5 ft (1.5 m) high.*

DATA

Form: To about 33 ft
(10 m) high; branching,
with a woody trunk.

Spines: Radials 11–14;
to 0.8 in (2 cm) long.
Centrals scarcely
distinguishable; to
7.1 in (18 cm).

Flower: Pink. 2.4–2.8 in
(6–7 cm) long.

Distribution: Bolivia
(departments of
Cochabamba and
Chuquisaca).

Neowerdermannia vorwerkii

DATA

Form: Simple. To 2.4 in (6 cm) broad; 1.2 in (3 cm) high.

Spines: To 10; to 1.6 in (4 cm) long.

Flower: White with a pink midstripe. About 0.4 in (1 cm) across. June in cultivation.

Flowering time from seed: 4–5 years.

Distribution: Northern Argentina to northern Bolivia.

This is a widespread species of the high Andes that sometimes occurs in hundreds in small grassy and rocky areas between cultivated fields. In habitat often only the top of the stem is visible, the main bulk of the plant being a large underground taproot. In cultivation growth is slow but flowers are reliably produced often several from one areole. The big problem with this species tends to be getting hold of it, since seed is generally in short supply and germination is usually very poor. *Neowerdermannia chilensis*, a slightly larger and more attractive plant from northern Chile, is even more difficult to obtain.

The plant illustrated was grown from seed collected from Comanche, La Paz, Boli

Notocactus buiningii

With its fairly narrow, bluish green ribs this is one of the most distinctive members of the genus. It is deservedly popular, although it is not always the easiest of plants to keep going. Unfortunately, it has a tendency to lose its roots, especially when watering commences again in spring after the long winter rest. Plants grown in coir/bark mixes seem less prone to this problem.

The plant illustrated was grown from seed collected by Buining at the type locality.

DATA

Form: Simple. To 4.7 in (12 cm) high and 7.8 in (20 cm) broad.

Spines: 4; cruciform; to 0.6 in (1.5 cm) long.

Flower: Pale yellow. To 3.2 in (8 cm) across; June in cultivation; October–November in habitat.

Flowering time from seed: 3–4 years.

Distribution: Uruguay (Livramento, near the border with Brazil).

Notocactus claviceps

DATA

Form: Simple. To 3.3 ft
(1 m) high and 5.9 in
(15 cm) across.

Spines: 4–8; rather mixed;
thin and wavy; yellow;
0.8–1.2 in (2–3 cm) long.

Flower: Pale yellow.
1.6–2 in (4–5 cm) across.
July–August in cultivation.

**Flowering time from
seed:** 6–8 years.

Distribution: Brazil (Rio
Grande do Sul, Nova
Palma, etc.).

With its fairly dense, wavy, golden spination and bright green body this is an eyecatching species that is closely related to *Notocactus schumannianus* (= *N. ampliocostatus*). While the latter can be touchy in cultivation, *N. claviceps* seems to be a better grower, although both species (which were formerly included in *Eriocactus*) flower well once they reach maturity. To avoid marking the body, it is best to keep the temperature a few degrees above freezing during winter.

The plant illustrated was grown from seed collected near Júlio de Castilhos.

Notocactus concinnus

DATA

This old favorite is less often seen in collections today, having been ousted by some of the more recent discoveries. This is a pity, since the sumptuously large flowers appear in good numbers, even on small plants, and last several days. As in many members of the genus, the stigma is bright crimson, contrasting nicely with the yellow petals. *Notocactus agnetae*, with flowers only about 2 inches (5 cm) across, is usually now treated as a subspecies. *Notocactus werdermannianus* (including *N. vanvlietii*) is rather similar.

The plant below is N. agnetae, *grown from seed collected near La Vellaja, Uruguay.*

Form: Simple; fairly flattened. To 3.9 in (10 cm) across.

Spines: Radials 10–12; to 0.3 in (0.7 cm) long. Centrals 4; to 1.7 cm (0.6 in); yellowish.

Flower: Pale yellow. To 3.2 in (8 cm) across. May–June in cultivation.

Flowering time from seed: 3–4 years.

Distribution: Southern Brazil; northern Uruguay.

Notocactus graessneri

DATA

Form: Simple. To 3.9 in (10 cm) high and broad.

Spines: Radials about 55. Centrals 5–6. All to 0.8 in (2 cm) long; golden yellow.

Flower: Greenish. 0.8 in (2 cm) across. April–May in cultivation.

Flowering time from seed: 3–4 years.

Distribution: Brazil (Rio Grande do Sul, Jaquirana and Vacaria).

With its golden-spined, globular, bright green body, often with a noticeably slanted apex, this is a distinctive plant which was once included in the separate genus *Brasilicactus*. In var. *albisetus* from Fortaleza the spines are more numerous and are glassy whitish rather than yellow. The small green flowers are appealing if only for their unusual color, which is shared with a small number of other cacti such as *Echinocereus viridiflorus*.

The plant illustrated was grown from seed collected near Jaquirana.

Notocactus haselbergii

lso once included in *Brasilicactus*, this species grows mainly in the forested mountains of the Aparados da Serra, a spectacular landscape thickly covered th a local species of monkey puzzle tree, *Araucaria brasiliensis*. In cultivation *tocactus haselbergii* is a free-flowering plant, but it is somewhat more tender n some and tends to mark in cold winters, so keep it well above freezing. The ght red flowers appear in the center of the plant, and each one lasts for about ee weeks, making them possibly the longest-lived cactus flowers of all.

e plant illustrated was grown from seed collected near Linha Garibaldi.

DATA

Form: Simple. To 7.8 in (20 cm) across and 5.9 in (15 cm) high.

Spines: Radials 18–21; to 0.4 in (1 cm) long. Centrals 3–5; to 0.4 in (1 cm); whitish to straw colored.

Flower: Red. 0.8 in (2 cm) long. April–May in cultivation.

Flowering time from seed: 3–4 years.

Distribution: Brazil (Rio Grande do Sul).

Notocactus herteri

Form: Simple. To 7.8 in (20 cm) high and broad.

Spines: Radials 8–11. Centrals 4–6; to 0.8 in (2 cm) long.

Flower: Lilac. 1.6 in (4 cm) across. July in cultivation.

Flowering time from seed: 4–6 years.

Distribution: Uruguay (dept. Rivera, Cerro Galgo).

One of the largest-growing members of the genus, this bright green species is noted for its striking lilac flowers, which in older plants are produced over a period of several weeks. In forma *pseudoherteri*, which grows between Livramento and Masoller, the flowers are yellow, as in most other members of the genus. Older cultivated plants tend to become brown and ugly around the lower part of the stem, and you may prefer to conceal this beneath a covering of pebbles mixed with coarse grit. Plenty of water is needed in the growing season.

The plant illustrated was grown from seed collected near Livramento, LB765.

Notocactus horstii

arious forms of this plant are in cultivation, most having originally been described
as separate species. In the form illustrated here, forma *purpureus*, the flower is
ght pink and the spines slightly shorter and fewer in number than in the type.
forma *muegelianus* the areoles are noticeably more white and woolly, and the
mon-pink flower is slightly larger. All three forms grow and flower well in
tivation but need adequate water in the growing season.

*e plant illustrated below is a vegetative propagation from a plant that was
llected near Santa María.*

DATA

Form: Usually simple. To
5.5 in (14 cm) broad and
11.8 in (30 cm) high.

Spines: Radials 10–15;
0.4–1.2 in (1–3 cm) long.
Centrals to 4; slightly
longer and thicker.

Flower: Yellowish orange.
To 1.4 in (3.5 cm) across.
July–August in cultivation.

**Flowering time from
seed:** 3–4 years.

Distribution: Brazil
(Rio Grande do Sul,
Serro Geral).

Notocactus leninghausii

Form: Clumping. Stems to 3.3 ft (1 m) long and 3.9 in (10 cm) broad.

Spines: Radials to 15. Centrals 3–4; to 1.6 in (4 cm) long; bristly; golden yellow.

Flower: Yellow. 2 in (5 cm) broad. July–August in cultivation.

Flowering time from seed: 6–8 years.

Distribution: Brazil (Rio Grande do Sul, Montenegro).

Another former member of the now defunct genus *Eriocactus*, in habitat this lovely cactus grows on near-vertical cliffs—anyone wishing to see the plants close up has to go down on a rope. The apex of the stem is set at a distinct slope, and in late summer it is usually covered in a crown of flowers, followed by masses of plump fruits which, if not removed, will eventually spill seeds all over the plant. Clumping takes place from the base, eventually giving rise to spectacular large clumps. It is a hardy species that withstands subzero temperatures surprisingly well

The plant illustrated was grown from seed collected at Arroio de Seca, AH341.

Notocactus linkii

This species is similar to *Notocactus ottonis*, but it has a smaller flower. In some places the two species grow together without apparently forming hybrids, emphasizing their distinct identities. In cultivation *N. linkii* (often also listed as *megapotamicus*) rapidly offsets to form attractive clumps. Eventually the older heads tend to go a little corky around the base. It is easy enough then to split up a clump and start afresh, using the best of the smaller heads, many of which will probably be found to have already rooted into the compost.

The plant illustrated is a vegetative propagation from a plant collected near Cordilheira, AH003.

DATA

Form: Clumping. Body to about 4.7 in (12 cm) across and 2.4 in (6 cm) high.

Spines: Radials about 13; 0.6 in (1.5 cm) long. Centrals 3–4; about the same length as radials.

Flower: Yellow. 1.6 in (4 cm) across. June–July in cultivation.

Flowering time from seed: 3–4 years.

Distribution: Brazil (Rio Grande do Sul).

Notocactus magnificus

Form: Clumping from the base; bluish green. Heads to 23.6 in (60 cm) high and 7.8 in (20 cm) broad.

Spines: 12–15; to 0.8 in (2 cm) long; hair-thin; yellow.

Flower: Pale yellow. 2 in (5 cm) across. July in cultivation.

Flowering time from seed: 6–7 years.

Distribution: Brazil (Rio Grande do Sul, along the Rio Toropi north of San Pedro).

With its striking bluish green body and golden spines this is probably the most handsome member of the genus, although the intensity of the blue varies somewhat and may be almost lacking in some plants. Given plenty of water in summer, growth is fairly rapid; and after a few years from seed, offsets begin to appear around the base of the plant, eventually forming a compact clump.

The specimen illustrated was grown from seed collected near San Pedro where the plants grow on rocks beneath trees close to the river.

Notocactus mammulosus

cultivation this species slowly forms a rather columnar plant which, like many
otocacti, eventually starts to look old and scruffy around the base. This takes
ger to occur in the form known as *Notocactus submammulosus* (illustrated here
abitat near Capilla del Monte, Cordoba, Argentina, PM267). It has fewer spines
n the type, with the central spines being flattened and up to 0.8 inches (2 cm)
g. The whole plant also grows bigger and is noticeably broader from an early
. During the rainy season the rocks on which this species often grows in large
nbers may be saturated with water seepages for quite long periods. In the Sierra
asti there is a population in which many of the plants have stunning red flowers.

DATA

Form: To 4.9 in (10 cm) high; 2.4 in (6 cm) across.

Spines: Radials 10–13; 0.2 in (0.5 cm) long. Centrals 3; to 0.6 in (1.4 cm) long.

Flower: Yellow. 1.6 in (4 cm) long. June in cultivation; November–December in habitat.

Flowering time from seed: 3–4 years.

Distribution: Uruguay; Argentina.

Notocactus neoarechavaletae

DATA

Form: Simple. To 3.9 in (10 cm) high and wide.

Spines: Radials 5–9; 0.4–0.6 in (1–1.5 cm) long. Centrals 1; to 0.8 in (2 cm).

Flower: Yellow. To 2 in (5 cm) broad. June in cultivation.

Flowering time from seed: 4–5 years.

Distribution: Uruguay (Maldonado).

In habitat this species grows on granite rocks among grass. It was formerly placed in the genus *Wigginsia* (also known as *Malacocarpus*), whose members typically have a densely white-woolly crown. It is this crown from which the yellow flowers appear and in which the fruits spend the winter, sunk out of sight. In cultivation growth is relatively slow but does not present any problems.

The plant illustrated was grown from seed collected near Pedras Altas, AH357.

Notocactus ottonis

The degree of variation in this species is considerable, such that in some plants the flower is only 0.8 inches (2 cm) across, while in others it reaches 2.4 inches (cm). In most forms the ribs are rounded, but in some they are very sharp, approaching those of the very similar *Notocactus oxycostatus* (= *N. glaucinus*, *N. incomptus*, and *N. securituberculatus*). All forms clump strongly around the base the original head, which eventually becomes rather tatty, so that starting the plant again from the best of the offsets is often the best option.

The plant illustrated is a vegetative propagation from a plant collected between raja and Seival, Rio Grande do Sul, Brazil, AH051.

DATA

Form: Clumping. Heads to 4.3 in (11 cm) broad and high.

Spines: Radials 7–18. Centrals 0–4; to 1 in (2.5 cm) long.

Flower: Yellow. 0.8–2.4 in (2–6 cm) broad. June in cultivation.

Flowering time from seed: 3–4 years.

Distribution: Brazil; Uruguay; Argentina.

Notocactus rudibuenekeri

DATA

Form: Simple. To 2.4 in (6 cm) broad and 7.8 in (20 cm) high.

Spines: Very fine; to 1.4 in (3.5 cm) long; densely covering the plant; white.

Flower: Yellow. To 1.2 in (3 cm) across. July in cultivation.

Flowering time from seed: 3–4 years.

Distribution: Brazil (Rio Grande do Sul, Pedra do Segredo).

In habitat plants of this attractive soft-spined species resemble white organ pipes projecting from vertical cliffs. It was first offered by the German firm of Uhlig as *Notocactus scopa* var. *longispinus n. n.*, and it occurs only a short distance from populations of *N. scopa*. Unlike that species, which is common in collections, *N. rudibuenekeri* is rarely seen, but it is worth seeking out for its attractive spination.

The plant illustrated is a vegetative propagation from a plant collected south of Segredo, HU1000.

Notocactus scopa

nis widely distributed species consists of widely scattered populations, each of which often has a distinctive set of characteristics. Some of these populations e received names, while others (equally distinct) are simply lumped under *ocactus scopa*. One of the most handsome forms is var. *machadoensis*, whose sely spined heads can reach 5.1 inches (13 cm) across and 19.6 inches cm) high. In var. *marchesii* the individual heads remain small but they cluster ifically to form striking white clumps, while var. *cobrensis* is noted for its very rt, bristly spination.

plant illustrated is a vegetative propagation from a plant collected from Pedras s, Rio Grande do Sul, Brazil, and is similar to what you will probably receive if order an undocumented plant of Notocactus scopa *by mail order.*

DATA

Form: Simple or clumping. Heads to 11.8 in (30 cm) high and 3.9 in (10 cm) broad.

Spines: Radials to 40; to 0.3 in (0.7 cm) long; white. Centrals 3–4; usually brownish red.

Flower: Yellow. 1.6 in (4 cm) broad. June–July in cultivation.

Flowering time from seed: 3–4 years.

Distribution: Southern Brazil; Uruguay.

Notocactus sellowii

DATA

Form: Simple. 5.9–7.8 in (15–20 cm) high and broad.

Spines: Radials 5–7; to 1 in (2.5 cm) long. Centrals often only 1; to 0.8 in (2 cm).

Flower: Yellow. To 2 in (5 cm) across. June–July in cultivation.

Flowering time from seed: 4–5 years.

Distribution: Southern Brazil; Uruguay; Argentina.

This has the densely white-woolly crown typical of plants formerly placed in the genus *Wigginsia* (*Malacocarpus*). It is very variable, and it is doubtful that it is really specifically distinct from the very similar *Notocactus erinaceus*. Both species make very handsome plants for the first 10 years or so from seed, after which they start to become elongated. Their appearance is then gradually marred by the increasingly unattractive corky state of the old base. Burying the plant so that only its topmost third is above the compost is probably the best solution.

The plant illustrated above was grown from seed that was collected near Pedras Altas, Brazil, AH358.

Notocactus succineus

its typical form this species grows quite quickly into a densely spined golden
olumn. Less often seen is a form (var. *albispinus n. n.*, var. *albus n. n.*) in which
spines are softer, denser, and pure white. The latter plant is not as vigorous as
normal golden-spined plant and is more prone to lose its roots. *Notocactus*
ccineus is a close relative of *N. scopa* and is often listed as a subspecies of it (as
arodia). In habitat the plants grow among stones and grasses on rocky hilltops.

e plant illustrated was grown from seed collected on the Cerro do Ouro.

DATA

Form: Simple. 4.9–5.9 in
(10–15 cm) high and
1.6–3.2 in (4–8 cm)
broad.

Spines: Radials 15–20;
to 0.3 in (0.6 cm) long.
Centrals 8–12; to 0.8 in
(2 cm); yellow.

Flower: Yellow. 1.4 in
(3.5 cm) across. May–
June in cultivation.

**Flowering time from
seed:** 2–3 years.

Distribution: Brazil (Rio
Grande do Sul, between
São Gabriel and Lavras).

Notocactus uebelmannianus

Form: Simple. To 6.7 in (17 cm) across and 4.7 in (12 cm) high.

Spines: Radials 6; 0.4–1.2 in (1–3 cm) long. Centrals 0.

Flower: Purple. 1.6–2.8 in (4–7 cm) across. June in cultivation.

Flowering time from seed: 3–4 years.

Distribution: Brazil (Rio Grande do Sul, Minas do Camaquã).

Most of the plants seen in collections exhibit the striking purplish flower seen above. Less often seen is the forma *flaviflorus* with yellow flowers, both colo having occurred together in the original habitat, which has now been destroyed. In var. *nilsonii* the flower is always a pale purplish pink and the plants are flatter, with more ribs and paler spination. The most distinctive form is the prolifically offsettin var. *pleiocephalus* that grows some 30 miles (50 km) away at Arroio del Velhaco. The flower is only 1.6 inches (4 cm) broad, purple, or (in forma *gilviflorus*) yellow.

The plant illustrated is var. nilsonii *grown from seed collected near Camaquã, Rio Grande do Sul.*

Notocactus warasii

or many years after its original discovery nobody knew where the original plants of this attractive species had been collected from the wild, but they were ntually tracked down to the Rio Pardo, growing on steep-sided gorges. In earance this species lies intermediate between *Notocactus leninghausii* and *magnificus*, but in cultivation it is more vigorous than either, being a particularly ust plant able to cope with a wide variety of composts and maltreatment.

e plant illustrated below is a vegetative propagation from a plant that was ected near Soledade.

DATA

Form: Clumping. Heads to about 31.5 in (80 cm) high and 7.8 in (20 cm) or more across.

Spines: 15–20. Radials and centrals similar; to 1.6 in (4 cm) long; yellow.

Flower: Pale yellow. 2–2.4 in (5–6 cm) across. July–August in cultivation.

Flowering time from seed: 4–5 years.

Distribution: Brazil (Rio Grande do Sul, Rio Pardo).

Obregonia denegrii

DATA

Form: Simple; flat-topped; covered in scalelike tubercles. To 4.7 in (12 cm) across.

Spines: 3–4; thin. To 0.6 in (1.5 cm) long; soon dropping off.

Flower: White or pale pink. To 1 in (2.5 cm) across. June–July in cultivation.

Flowering time from seed: 5–6 years.

Distribution: Mexico (Tamaulipas, valley of Jaumave).

Having been illegally removed from habitat in large numbers over many years to satisfy the demand from collectors for something a little different, this species is now becoming more freely available from seed-grown plants, as shown here. These are not too difficult to raise, and they flower well once they reach maturity. A shallow pot to accommodate the rather sparse, weak roots is one of the main requirements, together with some shade in hot weather. Plants raised from seed do much better than imported field-collected material, which (apart from being illegal to acquire under CITES regulations) often fails to reestablish in cultivation and eventually dies a long, lingering death.

Opuntia microdasys

s can be seen from the photograph taken just outside the city of San Luis Potosí, in habitat this species—popularly known as "bunny's ears"—forms almost penetrable low thickets. In these wild plants the tufts of glochids are usually low, and plants raised from field-collected seed seem to flower very well in tivation. Most commercially raised material is propagated from a limited number vegetative clones, few of which flower. Plants with reddish glochids are also ailable, as well as a clone with much softer, white glochids. This is certainly the st clone for a windowsill or where children are present, since the easily detached chids in the yellow and reddish forms can be unpleasant. In fact, some growers w only stock the white form.

DATA

Form: Segments oval; to 5.9 in (15 cm) long (usually smaller in cultivation), forming clumps to 24.5 in (60 cm) high.

Spines: Absent. Tufts of glochids are dotted around on the pad.

Flower: Yellow. 1.6–2 in (4–5 cm) across. June–July in cultivation.

Flowering time from seed: 5–6 years.

Distribution: Mexico (widespread).

Opuntia platyacantha

DATA

Form: Forming clumps 5.9 in (15 cm) high. Segments oval; 1.4–2 in (3.5–5 cm) long and broad.

Spines: Mostly 3–4. Usually pointing downward; bent and twisted; to 2 in (5 cm) and more long; flattened.

Flower: Yellow. 2–2.4 in (5–6 cm) across. June in cultivation; November–December in habitat.

Flowering time from seed: 6–10 years.

Distribution: Originally described as Argentina only.

This is one of several plants that are often lumped together into *Maihueniopsis darwinii*, usually as var. *hickenii*. However, attempts to cross-pollinate these two species in cultivation have ended in failure, so it would seem wiser to retain *Opuntia platyacantha* (there is no combination available in *Maihueniopsis*) as a good species until more evidence to the contrary is available. In cultivation it makes a more handsome plant than any of the *M. darwinii* forms, and has the advantage over them of being consistently free-flowering. Like them, however, it needs no heat in winter, no matter how hard the frost.

The plant illustrated is a vegetative propagation from a collection made between Mazán and Aimogasta, La Rioja, Piltz 033.

Opuntia polyacantha hystricina

This is a very widespread plant, occurring over much of the western United States and north into southern Canada. Over most of this area the winters are extremely cold, with long periods below zero, so it is not surprising that this is a very cold-hardy cactus. The subspecies illustrated is noted for its striking thatch of long white spines, and the plant shown below is a vegetative propagation from field-collected material, but without precise locality. In cultivation it grows relatively tall and upright, whereas in habitat the plants soon begin to sprawl.

DATA

Form: Segments round to broadly obovate; 2–4.9 in (5–12.5 cm) long and 1.4–3.9 in (3.5–10 cm) wide, forming low sprawling groups that reach 3.3 ft (1 m) or more across.

Spines: 6–10; curving downward; white. To 3.9 in (10 cm) long.

Flower: Yellow. 1.8–3.2 in (4.5–8 cm) across. April–May in habitat; June in cultivation.

Flowering time from seed: 8–10 years.

Distribution: United States (northern Arizona and Colorado).

Opuntia stenopetala

Form: Segments to about 4.7 in (12 cm) across; almost circular, forming low, creeping mounds.

Spines: 1–2; blackish then gray. To 2 in (5 cm) long.

Flower: Orange. 0.8 in (2 cm) across. July–August in habitat.

Flowering time from seed: 8–10 years.

Distribution: Central Mexico.

In parts of San Luis Potosí state, on either side of the Pan-American highway, this a relatively common plant. It creeps its way across stony hillsides in a manner that is not unattractive given the rather distinctive spination on the flat, pale green pads. The flowers are really unusual. They have very short orange petals, as can be seen in the illustration of a plant photographed south of Matehuala, San Luis Potosí. Seeds germinate readily in culture and form handsome multipadded plants after just a few years, although they take up a fair amount of space. For best effect they should be grown in an indoor bed or planted outside in a garden. Beware, however—it is not as hardy as many of the opuntias from the United States.

Oreocereus celsianus

The author once drove around the bend of an Andean dirt road and came upon the magnificent sight of hundreds of multibranched specimens of this elegant species scattered across a steep hillside and glowing silver in the setting sun. The stems are the thickest in the genus and are fairly abundantly covered with long whitish hairs, from which the flowers protrude somewhat inconspicuously. In cultivation growth is strong and reasonably quick. You may be lucky enough to start seeing flowers after 15 years or so, although not all plants oblige in this respect.

The plant illustrated was photographed at Cieneguillas in Bolivia, where this species grows with Lobivia ferox longispina *and* Parodia commutans maxima.

DATA

Form: Stems to more than 9.9 ft (3 m) high and 7.8 in (20 cm) thick; branching from the base.

Spines: Radials about 9; to 0.8 in (2 cm) long. Centrals 1–4, to 3.2 in (8 cm) long; yellow to orange.

Flower: Dull pink; tubular. To 3.5 in (9 cm) long. June–July in cultivation; November–January in habitat.

Flowering time from seed: 15–20 years.

Distribution: Highlands of southern Bolivia and northern Argentina.

Oreocereus leucotrichus

Form: Stems to about
4.9 ft (1.5 m) high and
3.9 in (10 cm) across;
branching from the base.

Spines: Radials 8–9; to
0.6 in (1.5 cm) long.
Centrals mostly 4; to
2.8 in (7 cm) long;
yellowish or reddish.

Flower: Carmine; tubular.
2.8 in (7 cm) long. June–
July in cultivation.

**Flowering time from
seed:** Not known;
probably 15–20 years.

Distribution: Highlands
of southern Peru and
northern Chile.

Often seen for sale under various other names, but most often as *Oreocereus
hendriksenianus*, this makes a very attractive plant in cultivation thanks to the
dense white wool that almost covers the body. It grows well but relatively slowly,
forming stems that are a little curved, so if it starts leaning don't try to make it grow
upright in the mistaken belief that this is how it should be. This species comes from
rather drier areas than the other members of the genus, so more care in watering
is needed at all times. It also seems less willing to flower in cultivation, but is so
attractive in its own right that this really does not matter.

*The plant illustrated above was photographed beside the winding road from Nazca
to Puquio in Peru.*

Oreocereus pseudofossulatus

or many years known as *Oreocereus fossulatus*, dense thickets of this plant can be found in the valleys near La Paz, where they tend to prefer the more level und rather than the steeper slopes. The amount of hair on the stems varies, some nts being more or less naked in this respect, making the color of the spines more ⁻ious. In cultivation growth is relatively rapid but the stem bases are more slender ⁻ in habitat and may not support the weight of the branching plant above, so king will often be necessary. Once flowering starts it is usually repeated every r, although the flowers are a little dull.

⁻ plant illustrated was grown from seed collected near La Paz, PM145.

DATA

Form: Stems to 8.25 ft (2.5 m) high and 3.2 in (8 cm) across; branching from various points.

Spines: Radials to 16; about 0.2 in (0.6 cm) long. Centrals 1–4, to 1.6 in (4 cm) long; yellowish to brownish.

Flower: Dull reddish. About 3.9 in (10 cm) long. July–August in cultivation; October in habitat.

Flowering time from seed: 15–25 years.

Distribution: Bolivia (central highlands).

Oreocereus trollii

DATA

Form: Stems to about 23.6 in (60 cm) high and 5.9 in (15 cm) across; branching from the base.

Spines: About 10–15. Radials and centrals similar; to about 2 in (5 cm) long; horn colored.

Flower: Pinkish red. About 1.6 in (4 cm) long. June–July in cultivation; October–January in habitat.

Flowering time from seed: 10–20 years.

Distribution: Southern Bolivia to northern Argentina.

The popular name of "old man of the Andes" seems to have died out now for th' attractive woolly cactus that makes its home among rocks and tufts of tough grasses in the cold, arid highlands of the Andes. Some people feel that this may be simply a high-altitude form of *Oreocereus celsianus*, and it is true that in some places in northern Argentina there are populations to which it is difficult to assign name. In cultivation *O. trollii* makes a squatter, hairier, more attractive plant that h' a good chance of flowering, although some specimens are better at this than othe'

The plant illustrated below was photographed at Cuchu Ingenio south of Potosí, Bolivia, PM169.

Oroya borchersii

The large, rather flattened amber-spined barrels of this hardy plant often occur in hundreds among grass in the high Andes, sometimes sitting in water during the summer rainy season. In this sunny environment flowers are usually produced in abundance, followed by dozens of plump fruits. In cultivation the story is different, and it is a very shy-flowering plant, although the handsome spination helps make up for this. Unfortunately, under glass the spines are not dense enough to protect the plant beneath from burning. Bearing in mind therefore the plant's high-altitude and truly cool habitat, make sure you provide shade in really hot weather.

The plant photographed was grown from seed collected near Huaráz, PM069.

Form: Simple. To 11.8 in (30 cm) or more across and high.

Spines: Radials 15–25; scarcely differentiated from the 1–5 (or more) centrals. To 1 in (2.5 cm) long; all amber colored.

Flower: Lemon yellow. 0.4 in (1 cm) across. June in cultivation; November–December in habitat.

Flowering time from seed: 15–25 years.

Distribution: Peru (Cordillera Blanca and Cordillera Negra).

Oroya peruviana

DATA

Form: Simple or clumping. Heads to 15.8 in (40 cm) high; 7.8 in (20 cm) across.

Spines: Radials 10–30; to 0.6 in (1.5 cm) long. Centrals 0–5; to 0.8 in (2 cm) long.

Flower: Usually pink or red outside, yellow inside; also plain lemon yellow. To 0.8 in (2 cm) long. June–July in cultivation; October–December in habitat.

Flowering time from seed: 3–10 years.

Distribution: Central Peru.

Such is the variability of this species that it has received several different names. Since most of them are still used commercially, it is convenient to use them here to describe the more extreme forms. In *Oroya gibbosa* the spines are a little sparse, exposing the glossy dark green body, and flowers are common in cultivation. Flowers are often hard to come by in *O. neoperuviana* (= *laxiareolata*), which has the most handsome spination, being densely covered in generally golden comblike spines that are closely pressed against the body. Various forms lie somewhere between these two extremes, and most of them usually flower well in a greenhouse.

The plant illustrated above was grown from seed that was collected about 12 miles (20 km) southeast of Chincheros. This form flowers freely at only three to four years from seed.

Pachycereus pringlei

habitat this is one of the tallest of all cacti, forming huge, multibranched
ecimens with stout woody trunks. Large numbers of seedlings are grown for
horticultural trade, since small plants are very attractive (see illustration). These
w relatively quickly into neatly spined and handsome plants. Like all the larger,
like cacti, this species does much better if planted in a bed with free root run
—even better—outside if the climate will allow it. It is somewhat more winter-
dy than the glossy green red-spined *Pachycereus pecten-aboriginum,* which
st be kept well above freezing in winter.

DATA

Form: To about 36 ft
(11 m) high with a woody
trunk; branching. Stems
to 11.8 in (30 cm) across.

Spines: About 20. Radials
and centrals similar;
mostly about 0.8 in (2 cm)
long; to 7.8 in (20 cm) in
big old plants.

Flower: White; bell-shaped.
To 3.2 in (8 cm) long.

**Flowering time from
seed:** Many years.

Distribution: Mexico
(Sonora to Nayarit;
Baja California and
neighboring islands).

Parodia aureicentra

Form: Heads to some 15.8 in (40 cm) or more high and 5.9 in (15 cm) across; clumping from the base.

Spines: Radials up to 40; bristlelike. Centrals 6–10; thicker; to 1 in (2.5 cm) long; some curved at the tip or even hooked; amber to gold to reddish orange to chocolate brown in color.

Flower: Pale orange, blood red, or yellow. 1.6 in (4 cm) across. August–September in cultivation; January–March in habitat.

Flowering time from seed: 4–6 years.

Distribution: Northern Argentina (Salta).

With its dense spination a well-grown plant of this species is a real asset to a collection. As with most cacti, there is plenty of variability, and several varieties have been named, although they tend to grade into one another. The form illustrated is the golden-spined var. *omniaurea*, grown from seed collected at Cachi (PM349). This is the author's favorite form, closely followed by var. *muhrii* (formerly *Parodia muhrii*) from much farther south, near Molinos. The latter has much darker brown spines and forms very large multiheaded clumps, with very tall main stems, flowering yellow. Ritter's var. *albifusca* has distinctive orange spination and very pale orange flowers. They all grow well in cultivation but should be watered with care.

Parodia aureispina

otanically speaking, there are two ways you could consider this plant and
several of those on the following pages. They are either forms of a very variable
odia microsperma or they are "microspecies," all with valid names. Most of them
amply distinct, and they form the so-called *P. microsperma* complex. The latter
roach is the most useful horticulturally and is the one used here. With its dense
ow spination, *P. aureispina* is probably the most attractive member of the
nplex, although it is very similar to the orange-spined *P. mutabilis*. Both are
ely grown in the trade, and they flower well (like all parodias), but these two
e a nasty habit of losing their roots during the winter dry spell.

plant illustrated was grown from seed collected near Salta.

DATA

Form: Simple. To about
2.8 in (7 cm) tall and
broad.

Spines: Radials about 40;
bristly and fine; white.
Centrals about 6; to 0.6 in
(1.5 cm) long; bright
yellow; several hooked.

Flower: Yellow. About 1.2 in
(3 cm) across. June–July
in cultivation; November–
December in habitat.

**Flowering time from
seed:** 2–3 years.

Distribution: Argentina
(near Salta city).

Parodia ayopayana

DATA

Form: Clumping. Heads to 3.2 in (8 cm) high and 3.5 in (9 cm) across; fresh green.

Spines: Radials 10–11; to 0.8 in (2 cm) long; white. Centrals 4; to 1.4 in (3.5 cm); brown.

Flower: Yellow. 0.4 in (1 cm) across. June–July in cultivation.

Flowering time from seed: 3–4 years.

Distribution: Bolivia (Puente Pilatos and surrounding area).

Although Cardenas gave the type locality for this species as Puente Pilatos, it is also found in a number of other localities. For example, the plant illustrated was grown from seed collected by Friedrich Ritter near Santa Rosa, FR746b, and named by him provisionally as var. *depressa,* since it has rather flatter heads than the type. It grows in the gorge of the Sacambaya River, about 27 miles (45 km) from Puente Pilatos. In cultivation it offsets prolifically, forming a handsome, multiheaded clump that must be kept well above freezing in winter, otherwise it will mark or die

Parodia chrysacanthion

When the author saw this species on steep, open, sunny slopes at Volcán, the plants appeared as golden balls half-buried among large gray clumps of omietella bromeliads. At another site, at a much lower altitude, the plants were aller and grew on cliffs that were densely shaded (at least in summer) by trees. ultivation this lovely plant seems to grow reasonably well whatever the ditions, and even on a windowsill fair-sized, well-spined specimens can be ined through a policy of benign neglect.

plant illustrated was grown from seed collected at Volcán, where thousands eeds lay in the crowns of the plants, PM268.

DATA

Form: Simple. To 4.3 in (11 cm) broad and high.

Spines: Golden yellow. Radials numerous; bristlelike. Centrals numerous; slightly thicker; to 0.8 in (2 cm) long.

Flower: Yellow. 0.6–0.8 in (1.5–2 cm) across. June–July in cultivation.

Flowering time from seed: 3–4 years.

Distribution: Argentina (Jujuy).

Parodia comarapana

DATA

Form: Simple. To 2 in (5 cm) high and 3.2 in (8 cm) broad.

Spines: Radials 18–23. Centrals very similar, but 3–4 are slightly longer than the radials; to 0.8 in (2 cm) long; yellow, tipped brown.

Flower: Egg-yolk yellow. 0.2 in (0.5 cm) across. June in cultivation; November–December in habitat.

Flowering time from seed: 3–4 years.

Distribution: Bolivia (north of Comarapa).

This is a compact, low-growing species that does best if confined within a pot only slightly larger than the diameter of the plant. The flowers are rather small although a tuft of them usually opens at any one time, and the spination is neat and attractive. Friedrich Ritter described a var. *paucicostata* that differs by being more slender and upright, having fewer ribs, and offsetting prolifically from the base. It was found near Mataral, some 24 miles (40 km) as the crow flies from Comarapa.

The plant illustrated is a vegetative propagation from a plant collected from habitat by Martin Cardenas, who first described this species.

Parodia commutans maxima

The habitat of this giant form of *Parodia commutans* lies some way distant from the locality where the type is found, which is near Impora. In habitat the [or]nation tends to be longer and denser than in cultivation, where the body also [ten]ds to elongate rather more at an early stage than it does on the high windswept [slo]pes of its Andean homeland. The spines are long and curving, remaining yellow [und]er the protection of glass, but turning grayish brown in the wind and rain of its [nat]ural habitat. Cultivation is easy.

[Th]e plant illustrated was grown from seed collected at Cieneguillas, PM183.

DATA

Form: Simple. To about 9 in (23 cm) broad and 19.6 in (50 cm) or more high.

Spines: Radials 18–28; 0.6–2 in (1.5–5 cm) long. Centrals 2–4; curved; 2–4.3 in (5–11 cm) long, sometimes to 5.5 in (14 cm).

Flower: Yellow. 1.6 in (4 cm) across. June– July in cultivation; October in habitat.

Flowering time from seed: 6–8 years.

Distribution: Bolivia (dept. Tarija, Cieneguillas).

Parodia gracilis

Form: Simple. 2–4.9 in (5–10 cm) across; spherical at first, then elongated.

Spines: Radials 14–22; to 0.6 in (1.5 cm) long. Centrals 4–10; to 0.4 in (1 cm) long; pale brown.

Flower: Yellow. 1 in (2.5 cm) across; strongly perfumed; June in cultivation.

Flowering time from seed: 3–4 years.

Distribution: Bolivia (province of Mendez, Alta España).

With its densely white-woolly crown and equally woolly areoles, this is a neat-looking species that flowers freely over several weeks. It is a close relative of *Parodia procera*, and indeed is lumped in with it by some people. In cultivation *P. procera* is a very different-looking plant, growing to 19.6 in (50 cm) high, with longer spines and larger, scentless flowers of a different shade of yellow. It grows on almost inaccessible cliffs at the mouth of the Río Challamarca. Both plants are worth a place in the greenhouse.

The plant illustrated is a vegetative propagation from a plant grown from seed collected at the type locality, FR740.

Parodia hausteiniana

Seedlings of this attractive little plant are very precocious and will start to flower abundantly at only two years from seed. Growth is relatively slow, and a fairly small pot will be all that is ever needed, although the globular body eventually starts to elongate and become columnar, after which some plants start to offset around the base. This is a close relative of *Parodia laui* but, unlike that species, does not seem to be particularly tender in winter.

The plant illustrated is a vegetative propagation from a plant collected by Alfred Lau at the type locality, Lau 321.

DATA

Form: Spherical to columnar. 2–4.9 in (5–10 cm) across.

Spines: Radials 26–30; 0.4 in (0.8 cm) long. Centrals 4; yellow; to 0.5 in (1.3 cm).

Flower: Yellow. 0.4 in (1 cm) across. June in cultivation.

Flowering time from seed: 2–3 years.

Distribution: Bolivia (near Mizque).

Parodia laui

DATA

Form: Simple; bright green. To 2.8 in (7 cm) high and 3.5 in (9 cm) across.

Spines: Radials 20; to 0.6 in (1.5 cm) long; white; tipped brownish. Centrals 6; 3 hooked; 0.8–1 in (2–2.5 cm) long; reddish brown.

Flower: Red. 1.6 in (4 cm) across. June–July in cultivation.

Flowering time from seed: 3 years.

Distribution: Bolivia (Mine Asientos, above the Río Caine).

After being described in 1973 from a discovery by Alfred Lau this fast-growing plant rapidly became popular in cultivation and was grown commercially in large numbers (as illustrated), but its star has faded a little over the years, and it is not often seen these days. With its softish, bright green body it is a distinctive plant that produces large numbers of its colorful flowers over several weeks of summer. Unlike most members of the genus, it is unable to cope with hard frosts, and should be maintained a few degrees above freezing at all times.

Parodia maassii

aving the largest north–south range of any member of the genus, it is not surprising that this species is very variable. In some populations the plants are all, in others very large; in some the spines are all glassy and straight, in others ow and very twisted. In most populations the flowers are orange, but in some y are bright red, often allied to black spines, although these may be yellow on the ghboring plant. Numerous names have been coined, but the plants themselves all very obviously just *Parodia maassii*. This species has earned a reputation for ng shy-flowering in cultivation. This is undeserved, however—it just needs to be ttle older than most other parodias before flowering begins, and the strongest-ned plants are worth bench space in any collection.

e plant illustrated below was photographed in pouring rain on the Pampa Lecori, Bolivia.

DATA

Form: Simple or clumping from the base. To 5.9 in (15 cm) or more across and 11.8 in (30 cm) high.

Spines: Radials 8–15, 0.2–1.2 in (0.5–3 cm) long. Centrals 4; much thicker; to over 2.8 in (7 cm) long; usually more or less hooked at the tip; sometimes very sinuous.

Flower: Orange to red. 0.8–1.2 in (2–3 cm) across. June–July in cultivation; October–January in habitat.

Flowering time from seed: 5–6 years.

Distribution: Bolivia to northern Argentina.

Parodia mairanana

DATA

Form: Head to 2 in (5 cm) across; fairly flat; offsetting prolifically; dark green.

Spines: Radials 9–14; 0.1–0.4 in (0.3–1.2 cm) long. Centrals usually 1; more or less hooked; dark brown.

Flower: Orange to golden yellow. To 1.4 in (3.5 cm) across. July–August in cultivation.

Flowering time from seed: 2–3 years.

Distribution: Bolivia (Mairana).

Although the very dark glossy green body of this plant is distinctive, the most characteristic feature is its habit of producing large numbers of offsets around the base of plants only three to four years from seed. These can be detached easily and rooted up if you want more plants. But they are best left in place, since a large clump covered in its bright, rather metallic-sheened orange flowers is quite something. Some nurseries raise this plant in large quantities (see illustration), hoping that the flamelike flowers will catch the eye of the public.

Parodia nivosa

the spectacular surroundings of the Quebrada del Toro this species usually grows
n rather inaccessible cliffs. The author once spent some time vainly trying to hold
amera in one hand above his head to photograph a flowering plant just out of
ch—while pricking his chest on dozens of nonflowering specimens lower down.
st of these plants were far smaller than the maximum size given here. Higher up
Toro the white-spined plant gives way to a flatter one with shorter, darker spines
t grows in thousands on gently rolling, almost bare ground in a much more arid
e. This has been called *Parodia faustiana*. It has a superb flame-orange flower,
nore difficult to grow, and is probably simply a form of *P. nivosa*.

e plant illustrated was grown from seed collected near El Candando, PM344.

DATA

Form: Simple. To 5.9 in
(15 cm) high and 3.2 in
(8 cm) broad.

Spines: Radials numerous;
bristly fine; white. Centrals
4; 1 in (2.5 cm) long;
snow white.

Flower: Scarlet. To 2 in
(5 cm) broad. July in
cultivation; December–
February in habitat.

**Flowering time from
seed:** 3–4 years.

Distribution: Argentina
(Salta, Quebrada del Toro).

Parodia penicillata

DATA

Form: Simple. To 4.7 in (12 cm) across and about 27.6 in (70 cm) long.

Spines: Radials about 30; thin. Centrals 15–20; very difficult to distinguish from the radials; 1.6–2 in (4–5 cm) long. All glassy whitish.

Flower: Scarlet. 1.2 in (3 cm) across. July in cultivation.

Flowering time from seed: 3–4 years.

Distribution: Argentina (Salta, near Cafayate).

In habitat this species often hangs down from steep cliffs from where, in some places, it has been extirpated by local people who collect the plant for decorative use at Christmas time. It is doubtful if they realize that this plant grows just around their town and nowhere else in the world. In cultivation it is a far more vigorous and fast-growing plant than the closely related *Parodia nivosa* and, unlike that species does not exhibit the slightest tendency to lose its roots. The flowers are among the best in the genus and appear over several weeks.

The plant illustrated was grown from seed collected near Cafayate.

Parodia ritteri

With its dense spination this is an attractive species which is very variable in habitat. All the plants in some populations clump strongly, with 100 or more heads packed into a mound 3.3 feet (1 m) or more across, while at other localities every plant will be simple. Spine color also varies, sometimes within a single population. Because of this variation several other names have been coined, including *Parodia camarguensis* (golden brown spines) and *P. roseoalba* (pinkish to pale yellow spines). In cultivation this is a more tricky plant than the similar *maassii* and requires more care with the watering can.

The plant illustrated was photographed at Puente San Pedro, south of Camargo.

Form: Simple or strongly clumping. Heads to 19.6 in (50 cm) high and 3.9 in (10 cm) across.

Spines: Radials 8–14; 0.6–1.6 in (1.5–4 cm) long. Centrals 1–4; to 2.8 in (7 cm) long. All spines white to pinkish to brown.

Flower: Brownish red. 1 in (2.5 cm) across. July in cultivation; November–December in habitat.

Flowering time from seed: 4–6 years.

Distribution: Southern Bolivia.

Parodia sanguiniflora

DATA

Form: Simple. To 2.4 in (6 cm) broad and 3.9 in (10 cm) high.

Spines: Radials bristly; to 0.3 in (0.8 cm) long; white. Centrals to 0.8 in (2 cm) long; the lowermost one hooked; brownish.

Flower: Blood red. 1.6 in (4 cm) across. June in cultivation; November–December in habitat.

Flowering time from seed: 2–3 years.

Distribution: Argentina (Catamarca, Cuesta del Totoral).

The original description was based on plants of unknown origin in a European collection, but this species has now been confidently equated with plants growing among mosses and ferns on the Cuesta del Totoral, where it can be found right on the roadside. It is one of the best of the *Parodia microsperma* complex (see page 371). It has a superb flower and is a relatively strong grower in a group for which this cannot always be said. As with all these plants, it is a relatively short-lived species, becoming rather columnar and ugly after about 15 years, when it is fit only for beheading and vegetative propagation (or the compost heap). Growing it really hard will keep it small for much longer.

The plant illustrated above was grown from seed that was collected on the Cuesta del Totoral, PM294.

Parodia stuemeri

The main habitat for this species is in the Quebrada del Toro, where plants up to nearly 3.3 feet (1 m) long may be found occasionally, growing along the ground and clumping from the base. Most plants are much smaller than this, but they vary in size from one locality to another. Lower down the Toro, just beyond Chorrillos, every plant flowers red, but farther up, around 50 miles (75 km) from Salta, the flowers can be red, dark yellow, or the bronzy shade illustrated here (on PM323). In cultivation this species needs to be grown hard if you are to get the best out of the dense spination, while any tendency to overwater is likely to kill the plant.

Form: Mostly simple. Usually elongate-globular; to 7.8 in (20 cm) high and 5.9 in (15 cm) across.

Spines: Radials about 25; about 0.8 in (2.2 cm) long; thin and interlacing. Centrals mostly 4; thicker; to 1 in (2.5 cm) long; pinkish brown to violet gray, sometimes blackish.

Flower: Red to coppery orange or brownish yellow. 1.2 in (3 cm) across. August in cultivation; November–January in habitat.

Flowering time from seed: 4–5 years.

Distribution: Argentina (Salta).

Parodia subterranea

DATA

Form: Simple. Flattened-spherical. To 2.4 in (6 cm) across.

Spines: Radials about 10; to 0.3 in (0.8 cm) long; horn colored. Centrals mostly 1; thicker; to 0.6 in (1.4 cm), black; often hooked.

Flower: Deep red. About 1 in (2.5 cm) across. July–August in cultivation; December–January in habitat.

Flowering time from seed: 3–4 years.

Distribution: Bolivia (La Cueva, near Culpina).

This is a dwarf, slow-growing species that will never outgrow a smallish pot and is therefore ideal for a greenhouse with limited space. With its charcoal-black spines it is an interesting and attractive plant, at its best when its deep blood-red flowers appear. In habitat it often occurs in thousands on river terraces, as shown in the photograph above, taken near Inca Huasi during a day of virtually nonstop rain. *Parodia occulta* is an even smaller plant, restricted to a very special type of bare gravely habitat scattered here and there to the west of Culpina, as at Caña Cruz.

Parodia taratensis

The accompanying description was based on plants in habitat and includes *Parodia bilbaoensis,* which Cardenas described later from the same area. Why should have done this when two years earlier he had described the same plant *P. taratensis* is something of a puzzle. In cultivation growth often becomes rather more columnar—up to 3.9 inches (10 cm) or more high—and the spines are a pale golden brown. This species seems to appreciate plenty of water in the summer when growth is rapid. Flowering continues over several weeks, although the individual blooms are not large.

The plant illustrated was grown from seed collected at La Viña.

DATA

Form: Head to 2 in (5 cm) high; to 2.4 in (6 cm) across; clumping around the base.

Spines: Radials 18–20; to 0.2 in (0.5 cm) long. Centrals 4; to 1 in (2.5 cm) long; white to brownish.

Flower: Golden yellow. 0.6 in (1.5 cm) across. June–July in cultivation.

Flowering time from seed: 3–4 years.

Distribution: Bolivia (road from Tarata to Río Caine).

Parodia tuberculata

Form: Simple. To 4 in (10 cm) high and 5.5 in (14 cm) across.

Spines: Radials 7–11; 0.1–0.4 in (0.4–1.2 cm) long. Centrals 1–4; to 1 in (2.5 cm) long; hooked downward, brown to blackish.

Flower: Carmine. To 1.2 in (3 cm) across. June–July in cultivation; December–January in habitat.

Flowering time from seed: 3–4 years.

Distribution: Bolivia (mainly between Sucre and Zudañez).

Take the rough dirt road from Sucre to Zudañez and you will see this species in hundreds of thousands. It changes somewhat over that distance, but is still identifiably the same species, although several other names have been given to it. The plant illustrated, photographed near Tarabuco, probably corresponds to *Parodia otuyensis*. A rather more erect form with a salmon-pink flower was named by Bra as *P. salmonea*. Despite any small differences, these are both still *P. tuberculata*. In cultivation it is an easy species to grow, perfect for a beginner.

Pediocactus paradinei

his is a species that will normally only be available from dealers who specialize in raising difficult-to-grow plants (such as *Pediocactus* and *Sclerocactus*) from d. Few people manage to grow this plant for long on its own very rot-prone ts, although certain individuals seem to have the knack, using a gritty compost , in some cases, leaving the pots outside for the summer. Most people rely on fting the small plants (or offsets from decapitated plants) onto a stock that has re vigorous roots. This is the case with the plant in the photograph below, which a vegetative propagation from a plant raised from seed collected many years ago louse Rock valley. Several other dwarf species of the genus, such as *P. bradyi* P. knowltonii,* are also usually supplied on grafts.

DATA

Form: Simple. To 3 in (7.5 cm) high and 1.5 in (3.8 cm) across; grayish green.

Spines: Radials about 20; short. Centrals to 6; to 1.1 in (2.8 cm) long; thin and glasslike.

Flower: Creamy white. To 1 in (2.5 cm) across. April in cultivation and in habitat.

Flowering time from seed: 2–3 years.

Distribution: United States (Arizona, House Rock valley and Kaibab plateau).

Pediocactus simpsonii

Form: Simple or forming large clumps of 50 or more heads. Heads to 5.9 in (15 cm) wide and high.

Spines: Radials 15–35; to 0.7 in (1.9 cm) long; white to cream. Centrals usually 5–8, sometimes more; 0.2–1.1 in (0.5–2.8 cm) long; reddish brown to blackish.

Flower: Yellowish, white, pinkish white, or magenta. To 1 in (2.5 cm) across. June in cultivation; April–May in habitat.

Distribution: United States (from the Southwest northward to Washington State and Oregon).

Growing much larger than any other member of the genus, this species has an extraordinarily wide distribution. It is taken here to include *Pediocactus nigrispinus*. As with other members of the genus, *P. simpsonii* is more likely to survive in the long term on a graft rather than on its own roots. Bear in mind that although this species is completely cold-hardy, the stock on which it is grafted may not be. The flowers are interesting, having sensitive stamens that respond to touch by instantly curving inward over the stigma.

The plant illustrated above was photographed beneath oaks in the Abajo Mountains in Utah.

Pelecyphora aselliformis

ecause of its rarity, restricted habitat (part of which has been destroyed by
highway construction), and extensive illegal collecting of wild plants, this
cies is now listed in Appendix 1 of the CITES legislation. Its dwarf size, unusual
chetlike tubercles, and rarity value have always made it an object of great desire
ong collectors. Readers of this book should on no account purchase illegally
ected habitat material. Instead, they should make every effort to propagate
m their own plants or (if lucky enough) to acquire one of the old, multiheaded
cimens that are available from time to time as collections are sold off. It comes
l from seed, although growth is relatively slow.

e plant illustrated is an old (illegally) collected import not in the author's collection.

DATA

Form: Simple or clumping. Globular, covered in hatchet-shaped tubercles. 0.8–2 in (2–5 cm) across.

Spines: 40–60; comblike; very short.

Flower: Pinkish purple. To 0.9 in (2.2 cm) across. May–June in cultivation.

Flowering time from seed: About 6–10 years (ungrafted).

Distribution: Mexico (San Luis Potosí).

Peniocereus viperinus

Form: Shrubby, with many branches. To 9.9 ft (3 m) high. Stems 0.3–0.8 in (0.8–2 cm) in diameter; trailing.

Spines: Centrals 3–4; black; to 0.2 in (0.6 cm) long; soon falling off. Radials 8–9; to 0.2 in (0.4 cm) long; pressed against the surface of the stems.

Flower: Red. To 1.6 in (4 cm) across. July in cultivation.

Flowering time from seed: 8–10 years.

Distribution: Mexico (Morelos and Puebla).

With its long, trailing, whiplike stems this plant needs plenty of room in which attain full size. It can most usefully be trailed across large neighboring plants such as various cerei. The thin twiglike stems are useless for storing water, which is achieved by means of a large underground tuber—so a pot large enough to accommodate this will be needed. The stems are sensitive to low temperatures and will die off if subjected to frost, but usually regrow the following year. Flowering is little hit-and-miss, occurring in some years and not in others. *Peniocereus greggii*, the "Arizona queen of the night," has large white nocturnal flowers.

The plant illustrated was grown from seed collected near Zapotitlán de Salinas, Puebla, Lau 1517.

Pereskia bahiensis

With its large green leaves and nonfleshy stems, this very uncactuslike cactus looks like just another thorny tree in habitat. It is only when the flowers appear that its true nature becomes obvious. In cultivation it is a very vigorous plant and does well indoors, making a showy houseplant as long as it is given enough light. The flowers last only a single day and are often produced in tufts of two to 12.

The plant illustrated below was photographed in the caatinga in Bahia, flowering during the rainy season.

DATA

Form: Treelike. 3.3–20 ft (1–6 m) high with thin twiggy branches bearing leaves 2–4.7 in (5–12 cm) long and 0.8–2.8 in (2–7 cm) wide.

Spines: Up to 40; 0.8–3.5 in (2–9 cm) long.

Flower: Pink. 1.6–2.8 in (4–7 cm) across. November–December in habitat.

Flowering time from seed: 8–10 years.

Distribution: Brazil (Bahia, in the caatinga).

Pilosocereus arrabidae

DATA

Form: 3.3–13 ft (1–4 m) high; branching from the base. Stems to 3.7 in (9.5 cm) across; green.

Spines: Radials 7–10; to 0.8 in (2 cm) long. Centrals normally 2–4; to 1.6 in (4 cm) long; yellowish brown at first, fading to grayish.

Flower: Off-white; funnel form. To 2 in (5 cm) across.

Flowering time from seed: 15–20 years.

Distribution: Brazil (Rio de Janeiro; Espírito Santo; southeast Bahia).

As one of the green-stemmed members of the genus, this attractive species is not grown as often as it deserves to be. With its somewhat gingery-brown spines, often mixed with a few white hairs, and glossy, angled stems it makes a very distinctive plant that merits a place in the greenhouse. Unfortunately, like all members of the genus, it is not hardy in winter and needs to be kept at a minimu of 50°F (10°C), although it will take brief spells below this. Older plants flower we with rows of buds appearing up the stems.

The plant illustrated was photographed in coastal sand dunes at Marica near Rio de Janeiro, PM106.

Pilosocereus aurisetus

Form: Shrubby, branching from the base; 3.3–9.8 ft (1–3 m) high. Stems to 2.8 in (7 cm) across.

Spines: 17–25; translucent; white to yellow; to 1 in (2.5 cm) long (twice as long in the flowering zone).

Flower: Whitish; funnel form. To 0.9 in (2.2 cm) across.

Flowering time from seed: 10–15 years.

Distribution: Brazil (Minas Gerais).

The description at right applies to subspecies *aurisetus*, a fairly large-growing, mainly blue-stemmed plant often sold as *Pilosocereus werdermannianus*. The plant illustrated, subspecies *densilanatus*, is far more often seen in cultivation and is a smaller plant in all its parts (although the name you are most likely to see on it is still the illegitimate *P. saxatilis densilanatus*). Its main attraction versus the type plant is its densely white-woolly, much more slender stems, very similar to those of *Espostoopsis* or the more slender-stemmed species of *Espostoa*.

The plant illustrated was photographed growing in quartz sand at the type locality, Grão Mogol, Minha de França.

Pilosocereus catingicola

Form: Branching above the base; 9.8–33 ft (3–10 m) high. Stems to 4.7 in (12 cm) across; olive green to greenish blue.

Spines: Radials 8–12; to 0.5 in (1.3 cm) long. Centrals 1–11; to 1.6 in (4 cm) long. All spines yellowish brown.

Flower: White. 1.9–2.8 in (4.7–7 cm) across; opening widely.

Flowering time from seed: 15–20 years.

Distribution: Brazil (widespread in the caatinga of the northeast).

As depicted in the accompanying photograph, this will be the most common cactus in the flat caatinga that rolls out into the distance on both sides of the road if you drive westward from the large bustling city of Salvador in Bahia. As with most cacti, its appearance varies from place to place, the stems being noticeably blue-green in some localities and plain green in others. In cultivation growth is rapid and, like many of the taller cacti, this species really only shows what it can do in terms of growth and flowering when planted out in a bed with free root-run.

Pilosocereus chrysostele

t first glance anyone seeing this strikingly golden-spined plant in a collection would take it to be a *Haageocereus*, but this species grows far larger than y member of that genus. Given the correct compost and plenty of light and rmth, growth is very rapid. Planting it out in a bed will do wonders for the nual increment in length of the stems, as is the case with most members of s genus, especially the larger-growing species.

e plant illustrated was grown from seed collected in habitat.

DATA

Form: Branching from the base; to 9.8 ft (3 m) high. Stems to 2.8 in (7 cm) across; pale green.

Spines: Radials 9–12; to 0.4 in (1 cm) long. Centrals 6–8; to 0.5 in (1.2 cm) long. All spines thin and bright yellow.

Flower: Pinkish or brownish. 1.5 in (3.7 cm) across.

Flowering time from seed: 15–20 years.

Distribution: Brazil (near the borders of Ceará, Paraíba, and Pernambuco).

Pilosocereus fulvilanatus

DATA

Form: Branching above the ground; 6.6–13 ft (2–4 m) high. Stems to 4.7 in (12 cm) across; blue.

Spines: Yellowish brown to black. Radials 8–10, to 0.6 in (1.5 cm) long; pressed against the stem. Centrals 1–7; to 1.2 in (3 cm) long.

Flower: Greenish. To 1.6 in (4 cm) across.

Flowering time from seed: 20–25 years.

Distribution: Brazil (Minas Gerais).

The biggest attraction in this species is the bright blue epidermis and the long reddish brown hairs that adorn the areoles, which are crammed in along the ri[?] so tightly that you can scarcely tell one from another. In cultivation this is one of t[?] slowest-growing members of the genus. Don't worry if you find that for the first fe[?] years from seed your plant is green. You haven't been sold the wrong thing—the striking blue color of the epidermis only develops in older plants. This is even mor[?] evident in habitat, where the larger plants are a brilliant blue and the younger one[?] are dull green and look like a different species.

The plant illustrated (PM113) was photographed at the type locality, Grão Mogol, where this lovely plant can be found right outside the town.

Pilosocereus gounellei

DATA

Form: Shrubby; richly branched; to 13 ft (4 m) high. Stems to 3.5 in (9 cm) across.

Spines: Radials 12–15; to 1.2 in (3 cm) long. Centrals 1–5, up to 5 in (13 cm) or more long, but usually much shorter.

Flower: Greenish to pinkish; funnel form. To 2.4 in (6 cm) across.

Distribution: Northeast Brazil.

ejoicing in the local name of *xique-xique*, this is one of the most characteristic plants of the vast area of caatinga vegetation that still covers much of northeast zil. It is unusual in the genus in that the stems often branch outward in a more ess horizontal fashion, forming dense, spiny, often low-growing bushes. In ivation growth is relatively rapid, but care is needed in watering, since this cies seems more intolerant of excess moisture than most. It is also particularly d-sensitive and needs to be kept well above freezing in winter.

• *plant illustrated was photographed at Milagres, Bahia, PM124.*

Pilosocereus lanuginosus

Form: Treelike; to 33 ft (10 m) high. Stems to 3.9 in (10 cm) across; blue to blue green.

Spines: Radials 9–15; to 0.8 in (2 cm) long. Centrals 1–4; 0.8–2.8 in (2–7 cm) long; spines yellow to black, fading to gray.

Flower: Creamy white; bell-shaped. To 1.6 in (4 cm) across.

Flowering time from seed: 15–20 years.

Distribution: Netherlands Antilles; Trinidad (only on offshore islands such as Chacachacare); Colombia; Venezuela; Ecuador; Peru.

This widespread species is rather variable and has received a number of alternative names. These are based on differences in spination and body color. The latter is variable according to the age of the plant—younger growth being a lovely bright blue fading to a dull greenish blue in age, although in some populations even the younger growth is dull greenish. The most distinctive and beautiful supposed variant is *Pilosocereus tillianus*, but this seems different enough to merit the full treatment that it is given on page 403.

The plant illustrated was photographed on the coast at Coro in Venezuela, PM136.

Pilosocereus pachycladus

you ever see a member of this genus on sale in a florist or garden center, it
s most likely to be this species, although it will almost certainly be labeled as
socereus azureus, a form with about 11 ribs and bright blue stems that are
ular with the general public. The form illustrated has only five ribs, and the
ms are a pale shade of blue.

*plant illustrated was grown from seed collected from near the Rio Jacaré
st of Jequie, Bahia, PM131.*

DATA

Form: Mostly treelike; to
33 ft (10 m) or more high.
Stems erect; to 4.3 in
(11 cm) across; blue to
blue green to gray green.

Spines: Radials 8–18;
0.2–0.6 in (0.5–1.5 cm)
long, pressed against
the stem. Centrals 1–12;
to 1.3 in (3 cm) long.

Flower: White. 1.6–2.8 in
(4–7 cm) long and
0.9–1.8 in (2.2–4.5 cm)
across. July in cultivation.

**Flowering time from
seed:** About 20 years.

Distribution: Widespread
in northeast Brazil.

Pilosocereus pentaedrophorus

Form: Upright, branching from low down; blue. Stems to 20 ft (6 m) high and 2.2–4.3 in (3–7.5 cm) across.

Spines: Radials 8–18; 0.2–0.6 in (0.5–1.5 cm) long. Centrals 1–12; to 1.2 in (3 cm) long.

Flower: White. To 1.1 in (2.8 cm) across.

Flowering time from seed: About 15–20 years.

Distribution: Brazil (Minas Gerais, Pernambuco, and Bahia).

In this widespread and often very common species the stems are extremely slender, particularly in cultivation, and are usually an attractive shade of blue, sometimes tinged with green. In the caatinga of northern Brazil it often grows with the green-stemmed *Pilosocereus catingicola* and the low spiny bushes of *P. gounel* *Pilosocereus pentaedrophorus* grows quickly from seed, but suffers from the problem often seen in columnar plants in cultivation of inadequate development of the stem base. The slender stems will often need some support as they get taller.

The plant illustrated was photographed in the caatinga near Milagres, Bahia, PM1.

Pilosocereus tillianus

recent works this beautiful species has been relegated (probably correctly) to synonymy with *Pilosocereus lanuginosus*. It is distinctive enough, however, both in habitat (see illustration) and in cultivation, for it to be retained as a species here. Seedlings of this species have been available for many years and are noticeably more attractive than in *P. lanuginosus*, partly because they generally have more ribs and partly because the spines are such an attractive golden yellow color. Growth is relatively rapid, and this is certainly one of the easier members of the genus to grow well, quickly making a fine specimen.

DATA

Form: Treelike; to about 20 ft (6 m) high. Stems branching; to 3.9 in (10 cm) across; dark green to blue.

Spines: 25–26. Radials and centrals indistinguishable; to 0.8 in (2 cm) long; yellow.

Flower: Cream. To 1 in (2.5 cm) across.

Flowering time from seed: 15–20 years.

Distribution: Venezuela (near Mérida).

Pilosocereus ulei

Form: Treelike; to 16.4 ft (5 m) high, with a cluster of branches above a woody trunk. Individual stems to 4.7 in (12 cm) or more across; gray green to blue.

Spines: Radials 8–18; to 0.4 in (1 cm) long. Centrals 1; 0.5–0.7 in (1.2–1.8 cm) long.

Flower: White. About 1.2 in (3 cm) across.

Flowering time from seed: Probably 25 years or more.

Distribution: Brazil (Rio de Janeiro, in a very restricted dry zone on the coast at Cabo Frio).

The maximum size given here is drawn from the original description, updated by subsequent authors, but it can be updated again here, since several individuals seen by the author at Cabo Frio were the biggest cacti he has ever seen, being easily twice as high (or more) than the figure given here, with a huge woody trunk. In habitat younger plants (as illustrated, PM108) are very attractive, with sturdy, bright blue stems. In cultivation they grow well from seed, although the blue coloration takes a few years to appear. Seeds or plants tend to be available only at sporadic intervals, so it may take a while to obtain a plant of this fairly rare species.

Pterocactus araucanus

his species has the most obviously succulent stems in the genus, the pear-
shaped segments perching one on top of the other. In their sandy habitat,
ever, this is not always obvious, and the topmost segments are often the only
s visible above the surface of the sand. In cultivation it is probably the slowest-
wing species of all, and the segments tend to be less plump than in habitat and
efore less attractive. Even so, it is an interesting and completely hardy plant,
ough not always easy to get hold of.

e plant illustrated was photographed beside Laguna Blanca and was in fruit
early February.

Form: Stems more or less
pear-shaped; grayish
brown; 1.2–1.6 in
(3–4 cm) long; 0.4–0.6 in
(1–1.5 cm) broad.

Spines: About 8; comblike.
To 0.1 in (0.3 cm) long.

Flower: Brownish red.
To 1.6 in (4 cm) across.
May–June in cultivation.

**Flowering time from
seed:** 5–6 years.

Distribution: Argentina
(Neuquén).

Pterocactus australis

DATA

Form: Stem segments globular to pear-shaped to elongate; blackish brown; to 3.2 in (8 cm) long and 0.6 in (1.5 cm) across.

Spines: Radials 10–15; short; white. Centrals 1–2; to 0.8 in (2 cm) long.

Flower: Brownish yellow with a satiny sheen. About 1.2 in (3 cm) across. In May in cultivation.

Flowering time from seed: Probably about 5–6 years.

Distribution: Argentina (Santa Cruz; Río Negro and Chubut).

In plants of this genus the above-ground stems arise from substantial underground storage tubers. In this species the stems are very variable—sometimes long, slender, and almost spineless, at other times with a mass of rather papery spines. The form illustrated is of the latter type. It is a very free-flowering vegetative propagation from WP89-39 51/4 from the Cerro Morro on Route 61, Río Negro Province. This is probably the most attractive form of the species in cultivation. Like most members of the genus, it is propagated mainly from cuttings, although seed is sometimes available.

Pterocactus fischeri

this slow-growing species the stems are rather more obviously spiny than in
most members of the genus. Flowers are less often in evidence, however, and
the plants never seem to flower at all, while others do so only at irregular
intervals. This plant does not like being pushed and will lose its roots if given too
much water, so take care not to be too generous in this respect.

*The plant illustrated is a vegetative propagation from material collected near
ta Ranquil, Neuquén, FK93-238-722.*

Form: Stem segments
rather slim and cylindrical;
to 5.9 in (15 cm) long and
0.9 in (1.5 cm) across.

Spines: Radials 12 or
more; whitish; bristlelike;
0.2 in (0.6 cm) long.
Centrals mostly 4; papery;
0.4–2 in (1–5 cm) long.

Flower: Mostly coppery
yellow; also amber or
purple. 1 in (2.5 cm)
across. May–June
in cultivation.

**Flowering time from
seed:** 5–6 years.

Distribution: Argentina
(Mendoza and Neuquén).

Pterocactus megliolii

DATA

Form: Stem segments blackish brown; elongate; to 1.2 in (3 cm) long and 0.8 in (2 cm) across.

Spines: Radials 10–20; glassy; hugging the stems; to about 0.1 in (0.2 cm) long. Centrals 4–5; very short.

Flower: Yellow. About 1.2 in (3 cm) across. June in cultivation.

Flowering time from seed: 5–6 years.

Distribution: Argentina (north of the city of San Juan).

Growth in this species is extremely slow, making it ideal for anyone with restricted space. It needs a pot large enough to house its tuberous root, which dwarfs the above-ground stems and is prone to rot away if too much water is allowed to soak the compost for too long in prolonged periods of dull, damp weather. It is not always as free-flowering as some other members of the genus—the flowers tend to appear in some years and not in others.

The plant illustrated above is a vegetative propagation from a plant that was collected near San Juan.

Pterocactus reticulatus

he rhomboidlike tubercles that make an attractive pattern on the grayish purple
to brown or even olive-green stems are a characteristic feature of this species,
nce the specific name. The flowers are probably the most attractive in the genus
d are borne at the tips of the stems, leaving a clearly visible scar when they
ther and fall off. Growth is fairly slow. Take care not to overwater, otherwise the
ge tuberous roots may rot. They can reach up to 7.9 inches (20 cm) long, so they
ed a fairly large pot to accommodate them.

e plant illustrated was grown from seed collected west of Pismante, San Juan.

DATA

Form: Clumping. Stems
globular to pear-shaped;
0.8–1.2 in (2–3 cm)
long and 0.4–0.8 in
(1–2 cm) across.

Spines: Radials 6; comblike
(pectinate); whitish to
brownish; to 0.2 in
(0.5 cm) long. Centrals
0–1, to 0.2 in (0.5 cm)
long.

Flower: Pearly white with a
pink flush. To 2 in (5 cm)
across. June in cultivation.

**Flowering time from
seed:** 4–5 years.

Distribution: Argentina
(San Juan and Mendoza).

Pterocactus tuberosus

DATA

Form: Stems twiglike, slender; to 7.9 in (20 cm) long and 0.2–0.6 in (0.5–1.5) across; blackish brown.

Spines: Whitish. 8–12; 0.2–0.4 in (0.5–1 cm) long.

Flower: Brownish yellow to coppery to more or less lemon yellow. About 2 in (5 cm) across. June in cultivation.

Flowering time from seed: 5–6 years.

Distribution: Argentina (widespread, from Salta in the north to Neuquén and Río Negro in the south).

This has the longest and most slender stems in the genus and is also the most vigorous in cultivation, putting on plenty of new growth each summer and being less sensitive to generous amounts of water than the rest. As befits its extensive natural range, it is variable. In the form often supplied as *Pterocactus decipiens* the stems are shorter and thicker and the plants are somewhat slower growing. They are equally free-flowering, however, and this species is notable in that respect.

The plant illustrated was grown from seed collected from Los Colorados, La Rioja.

Puna subterranea

though described here in *Puna* and often listed as such in plant and seed
catalogs, the characteristics of its seeds and fruits probably mean that *Puna*
uld be included in *Maihueniopsis*. In habitat this plant is often partially buried in
ground, the above-ground stems being very inconspicuous until the beautiful
vers appear. Sometimes they are all that can be seen, apparently arising from
bare soil, and the plant beneath being invisible. In cultivation growth is slow
reliable, and flowers usually appear every year. Propagation is often carried
by cuttings rather than seed.

e plant illustrated below is a vegetative propagation from material that was
lected east of La Quiaca.

Form: Segments ovoid to
elongate; 0.8–1.6 in
(2–4 cm) long; arising
from a stout taproot to
4.8 in (12 cm) long.

Spines: 1–10; all radials;
very short.

Flower: Rose pink to
brownish to yellowish
rose. About 1.2 in (3 cm)
across. June–July
in cultivation; November–
January in habitat.

**Flowering time from
seed:** 5–6 years.

Distribution: Argentina
(Jujuy).

Pygmaeocereus bylesianus

Form: Clumping strongly. Stems to 3.2 in (8 cm) long and 0.8 in (2 cm) across; dark green.

Spines: Short; numerous; dark brown fading to gray.

Flower: White; nocturnal; on a long slender tube. To 1 in (2.5 cm) across. June–July in cultivation.

Flowering time from seed: 5–6 years.

Distribution: Southern Peru.

In habitat plants of this genus tend to be almost buried beneath loose earth and sand and can be very difficult to spot when not in flower. In cultivation the heads cluster closely together to form a compact clump that stands well proud of the compost. Watering should always be done with care because growth is slow. In the natural habitat rainfall is often absent for long periods, and the plants survive on condensation from the often dense and prolonged coastal mists.

The plant illustrated is a vegetative propagation from material collected near the Pan-American highway in southern Peru.

Pyrrhocactus bulbocalyx

ccurring in scattered but often large colonies, this is a variable species—so much so that plants in some localities may be four to five times as bulky as se from other places. The plant illustrated was growing at Los Colorados in La ja. Many of the plants here reach the maximum size for the species, and all wer yellow. Near Marayes the plants are far smaller and very densely covered in nes that are often black, and the flowers are often pink and small. In cultivation it a notoriously tricky and slow-growing plant, needing careful attention to watering d compost. It also has a nasty habit of losing its roots when repotted, and refusing grow any new ones. Some people lump *Pyrrhocactus* into *Erioscyce*, but not every ecialist is convinced, and for convenience it is kept separate here.

DATA

Form: Simple. To about 1.5 ft (45 cm) high and 7.5 in (20 cm) across.

Spines: Radials 5–12; to 0.8 in (2 cm) long. Centrals usually 4; to 1 in (2.5 cm) or more long; curve upward.

Flower: Usually pale yellow, also pink. To 2 cm (0.8 in) across. May–June in cultivation; November–December in habitat.

Flowering time from seed: 5–8 years.

Distribution: Argentina (San Juan and La Rioja).

Quiabentia verticillata

Form: Plants treelike or shrubby; 6.6–49 ft (2–15 m) high. Branches to more than 1.2 in (3 cm) across.

Spines: Several; to 2.8 in (7 cm) long.

Leaves: Oval to lance-shaped; to 2 in (5 cm) long and 0.8 in (2 cm) across.

Flower: Pale red. 0.6 in (1.5 cm) long.

Flowering time from seed: Many years.

Distribution: Bolivia; Paraguay; northwest Argentina.

If you like cacti that are a little bit out of the ordinary, this unusual member of the opuntia tribe is for you. With its leafy stems it looks a little like a *Pereskia*. It is much rarer in cultivation, however, and it is only relatively recently that plants have become widely available. In habitat this is one of the tallest-growing of all cacti, although large plants look much like the other thorny trees that grow with them. In cultivation growth is rapid, but greater care is needed in winter, when this plant will certainly need some extra warmth.

The plant illustrated is a vegetative propagation from material collected by Roberto Kiesling near Ingeniero Juarez, Formosa, Argentina (ISI200-35).

Rebutia albiflora

To find this very small-headed species Friedrich Ritter traveled on foot for many hours down the gorge of the Río Pilaya, into a subtropical region. Despite numerous searches, nobody has since been able to follow his precise route and discover this plant in the wild. In cultivation it is surprisingly hardy, in spite of subtropical origins. Older clumps often start to die out in the center, however, and need to be started again from a few offsets (seed not normally being set on this self-sterile species).

The plant illustrated resulted from a single tiny offset of FR766a given to the author (aged 15) many years ago by Ritter's sister, Frau Winter, at her nursery in Germany, with the comment, "This is something new."

Form: Clumping strongly. Heads pale green; globular to semi-elongated; 0.7–1 in (1.8–2.5 cm) in diameter.

Spines: Soft. Radials up to 15. Centrals about 5. All to 0.2 in (0.5 cm) long; glassy whitish.

Flower: White, often with a pink midstripe. To 1 in (2.5 cm) across. May in cultivation.

Distribution: Bolivia (province of Mendez, in the Río Pilaya gorge below Cajas).

Rebutia albipilosa

DATA

Form: Heads flattened-globular, to about 2 in (5 cm) across; offsetting near the base.

Spines: Radials 25–35; hairlike; soft and white; 0.4–0.6 in (1–1.5 cm) long. Sometimes a single central spine; to 1.6 in (4 cm) long; tipped brownish.

Flower: Orange to red. To 1.2 in (3 cm) across. May–June in cultivation; December in habitat.

Flowering time from seed: 2–3 years.

Distribution: Bolivia (province of O'Connor, Narvaez).

Discovered by Friedrich Ritter in 1958, authentic material of this attractive plant is scarce in cultivation, and the plants seen in collections are usually someone else's interpretation of this species. It has to be admitted that they are usually far more attractive than Ritter's original specimens, a good example being the plant illustrated above, which was grown from seed collected by the Ramirez brothers on the Río Pilaya, RBC500. In reality, these all seem to be self-pollinated clones of *Rebutia fiebrigii*, which tend to behave as self-reproducing "microspecies."

Rebutia albopectinata

hen the author saw this species growing in rocky clefts above a river, it occurred as tiny, scattered, and hard-to-find single heads nestling among ns and mosses. In cultivation it seems to throw off some restriction imposed on it ts natural home, and forms large clusters of dozens or even (if you are a skillful wer) hundreds of heads. They cover themselves in flowers to such an extent that plant is often invisible, swamped beneath a tide of red.

e plant illustrated was grown from seed collected between Culpina and ahuasi, PM181.

DATA

Form: Simple in habitat. Heads globular; to 0.6 cm (1.5 cm) in diameter.

Spines: Radials to 13; white, comblike and flattened against the stem; to about 0.1 in (0.3 cm) long. Centrals 0–2; shorter.

Flower: Red. To 1.8 in (4.5 cm) across. May–June in cultivation; October–November in habitat.

Flowering time from seed: 2–3 years.

Distribution: Bolivia (near Culpina).

Rebutia aureiflora

DATA

Form: Clumping. Stems flattened-globular; to 2.4 in (6 cm) across.

Spines: Radials 10–16; white to brownish; to 0.3 in (0.7 cm) long. Centrals 1–4; grayish white, to 0.8 in (2 cm) long.

Flower: Yellow, orange, or pinkish violet. To 1.6 in (4 cm) across. May–June in cultivation; December–January in habitat.

Flowering time from seed: 2–3 years.

Distribution: Argentina (Salta, Quebrada del Toro).

If you want to see this plant in habitat you will need to climb up the steep slopes near the village of Chorrillos in the spectacular surroundings of the Quebrada de Toro. Here it was rediscovered in 1965 by Walter Rausch, who was already tramping through the cactus habitats while the author was still at school. Rausch comments that this species grades into *Rebutia einsteinii*, a narrower-stemmed plant that is very difficult to grow in cultivation, since it often loses its roots. *Rebutia aureiflora*, by contrast, is extremely easy, growing and flowering with no problems at all. About 25 years ago rather long-spined forms of this species were supplied under the provisional names of *R. longiseta* and *R. albilongiseta*.

The plant illustrated above is a vegetative propagation from WR158, collected near Chorrillos.

Rebutia buiningiana

he description given here follows that given by Rausch when this plant was first
described as a new species. When the author stood and gazed at the steep cliffs
the other side of a dried-up riverbed near Iruya, he saw that dozens of quite large
sters of this species were in full flower, well out of reach (as always). This is at
s with Rausch's statement that offsetting was rare, although (like all rebutias) in
ivation the plants offset prolifically. Standing in flower on the same cliff were lots
Rebutia deminuta, very different both in plant body and flower, and making a
nsense of the recent "lumping" of *R. buiningiana* into this species.

e plant illustrated was grown from seed collected on a cliff near Iruya, PM298.

DATA

Form: Body simple, rarely
offsetting. Light green.
To 2 in (5 cm) across.

Spines: Radials 14–16;
glassy whitish; 0.3–0.4 in
(0.6–1 cm) long. Centrals
2–3; to 0.6 in (1.4 cm)
long.

Flower: Pink. 1.2 in (3 cm)
across. May–June in
cultivation; November–
January in habitat.

**Flowering time from
seed:** 2–3 years.

Distribution: Argentina
(Salta, near Iruya).

Rebutia deminuta

DATA

Form: Heads globular to short-cylindrical; to 2.4 in (6 cm) high and about 1.6 in (4 cm) across; dark green.

Spines: 10–12. White with brown tips or all brown. To 0.3 in (0.6 cm) or more long.

Flower: Orange red to orange. To 1.2 in (3 cm) across. May–June in cultivation; December–January in habitat.

Flowering time from seed: 2–3 years.

Distribution: Northern Argentina and southern Bolivia.

Originally described from Tucumán in Argentina, this is quite a common and widespread plant that is also found in southern Bolivia. It is even more variab than most cacti, resulting in a plethora of names, some of which are treated as species in the following pages even though they probably do not deserve such distinction. Commonly seen names not worth dealing with separately here include Rebutia pseudodeminuta, R. pseudominuscula, R. kupperiana, and R. spegazziniar In cultivation growth is rapid, and large mounds are soon formed, which smother themselves with flowers for a few weeks during early summer.

The plant illustrated was photographed nestled among mosses and ferns in the Quebrada del Toro, Salta, Argentina, PM319a.

Rebutia donaldiana

DATA

With its bright green body contrasting sharply with the deep chestnut-brown spines, this is a distinctive and attractive plant, especially when accompanied by a mass of flowers, which are an unusually pure shade of orange. In its flower and seed it is close to *Rebutia fiebrigii* and has been lumped into that species by some people, although in body form and color it seems to have a closer affinity with *deminuta*. In cultivation it makes largish clumps, although the author has yet to see a plant with a head anything like as large as quoted in the original description.

The plant illustrated is a vegetative propagation from a plant collected by Alfred Lau at the time of its discovery, Lau 348.

Form: Body globular to short-cylindrical; to 3.9 in (10 cm) high and 3.2 in (8 cm) across; bright green.

Spines: Radials 10–12; to 0.6 in (1.5 cm) long; white to brown. Centrals 4–6; 0.8–1 in (2–2.5 cm) long; deep chestnut brown.

Flower: Pure orange. Only about 0.6 in (1.5 cm) across. May–June in cultivation.

Flowering time from seed: 2–3 years.

Distribution: Bolivia (dept. Santa Cruz, Pucará).

Rebutia euanthema

DATA

Form: Heads to 2 in (5 cm) high and 1.2 in (3 cm) across; dull leaf green.

Spines: Radials 12; to 0.4 in (1 cm) long; glassy. Centrals absent.

Flower: Usually in some striking combination of orange, red, carmine, and yellow. About 1.2 in (3 cm) across. May–June in cultivation; December–January in habitat.

Flowering time from seed: 2–3 years.

Distribution: Northern Argentina (Jujuy).

As can be seen from the illustration above, in its arid stony habitat in the upper reaches of the Quebrada de Purmamarca this plant exists only as tiny single heads, and each head normally has only a single bloom open at any one time (in fact, often the only bloom on offer). In cultivation, like all rebutias, it forms clumps, although they do not grow as large as in some species—growth being fairly slow from roots that are large and tuberous. Fortunately, pampered plants in cultivation are able to produce their often spectacular bicolored or tricolored flowers in far greater numbers than in the rigorous conditions of the high Andes.

Rebutia fabrisii

This tiny-headed, mat-forming plant has become very popular in recent years since its discovery and description by Walter Rausch. The type plant has a red flower, but equally popular in cultivation is the yellow-flowered form (var. *aureiflora*). The form illustrated is var. *nana*, which has numerous tiny heads that are very densely covered in a short and noticeably neat spination. Although it comes well from seed, this species is propagated mainly from offsets.

The plant illustrated below is a vegetative propagation from material that was collected near Cortaderas.

DATA

Form: Clumping prolifically. Heads more or less globular; mainly only 0.4 in (1 cm) or less across.

Spines: Numerous; short, white, covering the plant bodies.

Flower: Red. About 0.8 in (2 cm) across. May–June in cultivation.

Flowering time from seed: 2–3 years.

Distribution: Northern Argentina (Jujuy, between Santa Ana and Valle Colorado).

Rebutia fiebrigii

DATA

Form: Heads globular to short-cylindrical; to 2.4 in (6 cm) high.

Spines: 30–40; light to dark brown; to 0.8 in (2 cm) long; erect and needlelike.

Flower: Mostly orange, sometimes almost red. To about 1.2 in (3 cm) across. May–June in cultivation; December–January in habitat.

Flowering time from seed: 2–3 years.

Distribution: Northern Argentina and southern Bolivia.

In some populations this plant seems to have softly white-spined variants that reproduce as self-pollinated "microspecies" and these are dealt with under *Rebutia albipilosa* and *R. muscula*. The plant illustrated (PM369, from seed collected at Iruya, Salta, Argentina) is a variant previously described as *R. jujuyana*. In some Bolivian populations of *R. fiebrigii* the central spines are particularly long, with reddish brown tips contrasting nicely with the white radial spines. The flower is usually fairly small—the form known as *R. kieslingii* has the largest flower, which is usually an attractive pastel shade of orange, but can also be red.

Rebutia flavistyla

Along with *Rebutia albiflora*, this is another plant from the gorges below Cajas that no-one has been able to relocate since Friedrich Ritter's original discovery, though he did describe this species as being rare. In cultivation it remains as a single head for many years, which is unusual in this genus. Eventually, however, it starts to clump and will slowly form a large cluster, on which the flowers can be spectacular, as illustrated here.

The plant illustrated is a commercial plant, one of thousands being raised to be sold in flower at garden centers.

DATA

Form: Stems 1.6–2 in (4–5 cm) across; flattened-globular; darkish green.

Spines: Radials 15–22; 0.2–0.4 in (0.5–1 cm) long; whitish. Centrals usually 1; similar to radials.

Flower: Orange. About 1 in (2.5 cm) across. May–June in cultivation.

Flowering time from seed: 2–3 years.

Distribution: Bolivia (below Cajas, province of Mendez).

Rebutia fulviseta

Form: Stems globular to short-cylindrical; dark blackish green; to 0.6 in (1.5 cm) high and 0.4 in (1 cm) across (getting bigger than this and then clumping in cultivation).

Spines: Radials 10–12. Centrals 1–3; to 0.4 in (1 cm) long; yellowish to reddish brown; tipped darker.

Flower: Dark red. 1 in (2.5 cm) across. May–June in cultivation; December–January in habitat.

Flowering time from seed: 2–3 years.

Distribution: Bolivia (Arque, near Padcaya).

With its blackish green body this plant has a dark look that is very distinctive. The flowers too are darker in shade than most other members of the *Rebutia deminuta* group to which this species belongs (see page 420). In fact, based on observations made by the author of a population of *R. deminuta* at Iscayache, *R. fulviseta* may be no more than a self-pollinated "microspecies," as is also probably the case in *R. fiebrigii* and *R. pygmaea*. Its actual status need not bother the plant enthusiast, the main point being that it breeds true from seed and gives rise to a plant that is well worth growing.

The plant illustrated is a vegetative propagation of WR319 from the type locality.

Rebutia heliosa

In its original form, as illustrated here, the coat-of-mail appearance of the tiny, neatly arranged spines gave this plant a unique look that made it highly prized from the start. In cultivation it forms handsome clumps, but in habitat you almost need to go on hands and knees to locate the tiny single heads, which are only really obvious when they flower. This form is tricky to grow, often losing its roots. The larger-headed, but rather less attractively spined var. *condorensis* and var. *cajasensis* are somewhat tougher, staying alive for much longer for most people and forming much larger clumps.

The plant illustrated is a vegetative propagation from a plant collected by the Rebutia specialist John Donald between Tarija and Jucanas, JD268.

DATA

Form: Simple in habitat; heads flattened-globular; to 0.8 in (2 cm) high and 1 in (2.5 cm) across. In cultivation heads to 2 in (5 cm) high; clumping prolifically.

Spines: All radials; 24–26; very short; white with dark bases.

Flower: Mostly orange, also red or yellow. To 1.6 in (4 cm) across. May–June in cultivation; November–December in habitat.

Flowering time from seed: 2–3 years.

Distribution: Bolivia (Tarija, road to Narvaez).

Rebutia huasiensis

DATA

Form: Solitary or clumping. Heads to about 2 in (5 cm) high and 1.2 in (3 cm) across; blackish green.

Spines: 7–9; to 0.2 in (0.5 cm) long; thin; brownish.

Flower: Bright glossy red. To 1.4 in (3.5 cm) across. May–June in cultivation; December–January in habitat.

Flowering time from seed: 2–3 years.

Distribution: Bolivia (Incahuasi, near Culpina).

This is the name now being applied to plants formerly referred to (incorrectly) as *Rebutia atrovirens*. As such, the description given here only strictly applies to Rausch's plant from Incahuasi (his *Aylostera huasiensis*). Taken over the species' complete range (from northern Argentina to southern Bolivia), there is some degree of variation in body size and spination. The plant depicted here was one of thousands in flower on a gently sloping hillside between Yavi and Santa Victoria in northern Argentina, PM373. Note how the plant body is almost buried in the soil. In this instance it is simple, but in others there can be as many as eight to nine heads

Rebutia leucanthema

The beautiful white flowers of this very dark-bodied species are unusual in this genus. In cultivation they occur early in spring—in fact, in the author's collection is usually the first of the rebutias to come into bloom. Growth is unusually slow, and it takes years for even a small cluster to form. In Ritter's var. *cocciniflora* formerly distributed under his nomen nudum of *Rebutia melachlora*) from north of Camargo the flower is a vivid, glossy lipstick red, making it well worth the effort of acquiring this seldom-seen plant.

The plant illustrated is a vegetative propagation of WR305 from the type locality.

DATA

Form: Heads short-cylindrical; to 2.8 in (7 cm) high and 1.4 in (3.5 cm) across; blackish green.

Spines: Radials 7–8; brown; to 0.3 in (0.6 cm) long, pressed close to the body.

Flower: White, sometimes with a pink midstripe. To 1 in (2.5 cm) across. April–May in cultivation.

Flowering time from seed: 2–3 years.

Distribution: Bolivia (Caña Cruz).

Rebutia mamillosa

Form: In cultivation clumping strongly. Heads spherical to elongated. To 0.8 in (2 cm) across.

Spines: Radials 8–10; to 0.2 in (0.4 cm) long; yellow; bases brown. Centrals 0–1; shorter.

Flower: Red. About 1.6 in (4 cm) across. June in cultivation.

Flowering time from seed: 2–3 years.

Distribution: Bolivia (west of Camargo).

It is the flowers that make this fairly slow-growing plant worth acquiring, for in Rausch's original form seen here (vegetative propagation from WR302) there is a beautiful but very subtle whitish violet shimmer on the petals, seen in no other member of the genus. Several other people have collected plants in this area and well to the south of it, but none of their plants seen by the author has had that lovely shimmer on their flowers. In fact, they resemble a rather nondescript-looking *Rebutia spegazziniana*, itself only a minor form of *R. deminuta*.

Rebutia muscula

his original description Ritter mentions that this plant is rare in habitat. This is probably for the reason observed by the author near Iscayache, namely that these ft-spined plants are self-reproducing clones of *Rebutia fiebrigii* and often occur th normal, strongly spined plants of that species. As with *R. albipilosa*, *R. muscula* s been variously interpreted by collectors over the years, but the plant depicted re, grown from seed collected by the Ramirez brothers near Narvaez, corresponds ry closely with Ritter's original specimens. In cultivation older clumps eventually come rather ugly, with deformed heads, and have to be started again from offsets.

DATA

Form: Heads eventually elongate; green; to 1.6 in (4 cm) across.

Spines: About 50. Thin and soft; white; about 0.1 in (2.4 mm) long.

Flower: Pale orange. About 1.2 in (3 cm) across. May–June in cultivation; December–January in habitat.

Flowering time from seed: 2–3 years.

Distribution: Bolivia (province of O'Connor, Narvaez).

Rebutia narvaecensis

DATA

Form: Clumping. Body to about 1.4 in (3.5 cm) high and broad.

Spines: 10–20 or more; thin; glassy whitish; to 0.1 in (2.5 mm) long.

Flower: Pink, sometimes white. About 1.6 in (4 cm) across.

Flowering time from seed: 2–3 years.

Distribution: Bolivia (dept. Tarija, near Narvaez).

For many years this species was raised in thousands for its stunning pink flowers usually marketed under the invalid provisional name of *Rebutia espinosae* (see illustration above). Unlike most members of the genus, it is rather slow to clump, remaining as a single head for many years, although flowers are produced in quantity every year over several weeks. A form with white flowers—the so-called var. *albiflora*—has also been distributed.

Rebutia padcayensis

iscovered originally by Walter Rausch and named for the town near which it grows, this species has particularly rich red flowers that normally envelop the ~~nt in a sumptuous mantle. In fact, the author had to remove several flowers in ~~er to reveal certain details of the plant body in the accompanying illustration, ~~ich shows a vegetative propagation of WR322 from the type locality.

DATA

Form: Clumping. Heads to 1 in (2.5 cm) high and 1.6 in (4 cm) across.

Spines: Radials 12–14; to 0.5 in (1.2 cm) long. Centrals absent.

Flower: Red. 1.4 in (3.5 cm) across. June in cultivation.

Flowering time from seed: 2–3 years.

Distribution: Bolivia (west of Padcaya).

Rebutia perplexa

Form: Heads spherical; pale grass green; to 0.8 in (2 cm) high and 0.6 in (1.5 cm) across.

Spines: 10–16. Golden; slightly upright; very short.

Flower: Lilac pink. About 1.2 in (3 cm) across. May–June in cultivation.

Flowering time from seed: 2–3 years.

Distribution: Bolivia.

There has been confusion about both the origin and identity of this species, hence the specific name. Originally said to be from Minas Asientos, nobody has been able to find anything like it there in the many years since Alfred Lau supposedly collected it along with several other species of cacti, all of which have been found again without trouble. It now seems that there was a mix-up in labeling and that the plant originated from another region, probably near Narvaez. No matter, it is a very distinctive plant, forming mounds of numerous, small globular grass-green heads and covering itself over several weeks with oodles of lovely pink blooms.

The plant illustrated above is a vegetative propagation from material that was collected in habitat, Lau 329a.

Rebutia pygmaea

Rather variable in body form and color and in flower size and color, this wide-ranging species has had a plethora of different names. Many of them are different genera (just to make things complicated), but all have now been reduced *Rebutia pygmaea*. The crux of the problem may lie in the fact that each plant within a population is often self-pollinated. When the author collected seed pods from orange-flowered plants, the seedlings all flowered orange. A pod from a nearby red-flowered, large-bodied plant produced red-flowered, large-bodied seedlings. Bees visiting the flowers did not seem to be affecting the outcome. In cultivation large many-headed clumps are soon formed, swathing themselves in flowers every year, unlike the single-headed, single-flowered plants usually seen in habitat.

The plant illustrated was grown from seed collected near Pazna, Oruro, Bolivia.

DATA

Form: Heads (in habitat) usually simple; to 1.6 in (4 cm) high and about 0.6 in (1.5 cm) across.

Spines: Radials 8–12; comblike; pressed against the body; about 0.1 in (2–3 mm) long. Centrals 0.

Flower: Orange, red, pink, yellow, or white. About 1–1.2 in (2.5–3 cm) across. May–June in cultivation; November–January in habitat.

Flowering time from seed: 2–3 years.

Distribution: From northern Bolivia (Oruro) to northern Argentina (Jujuy and Salta).

Rebutia simoniana

Form: Simple in habitat. Body bright green; to 1 in (2.5 cm) across.

Spines: Radials 11–13; glassy; to 0.2 in (0.5 cm) long. Centrals 1–4; thicker; whitish, tipped brown; to 0.3 in (0.7 cm) long.

Flower: Orange. To 1.4 in (3.5 cm) across. May–June in cultivation; November–December in habitat.

Flowering time from seed: 2–3 years.

Distribution: Bolivia (Chuquisaca, southern Cinti, La Cueva).

Described as recently as 1984 by Walter Rausch, this is a very vigorous grower that rapidly forms large clumps of bright green heads. The flowers are rather bigger than in some of its close relatives, and are a very delicate shade of pure orange. Like all the rebutias, this species is winter-hardy and can easily tolerate temperatures near freezing or even below.

The plant illustrated above is a vegetative propagation from material that was collected at the type locality, WR739.

Rebutia spinosissima

This is a relatively old name, coined by Curt Backeberg in 1935. Plants remained relatively scarce in cultivation until the advent of material of Lau 404 from Tadcaya in Bolivia. The latter became popular in the 1970s, but under a new name, *Rebutia archibuiningiana*, published by Ritter in 1978. This is the form illustrated below. It is a vegetative propagation from material collected by Lau. The white-spined, small-bodied *R. hoffmannii* from Santa Victoria in Argentina was published in 1977. This form is less often seen, although it is probably the best of all. *Rebutia walteri*, also from Santa Victoria, has very short spines that reveal the body beneath, but with similar flowers. All three names still appear widely in the trade, and all of the plants grow and flower well.

Form: Stems globular to flattened; to 1.6 in (4 cm) high and broad; bright green.

Spines: Radials numerous; fine, bristlelike, and soft; whitish; to 0.4 in (1 cm) long. Centrals 5–6; to 0.5 in (1.2 cm) long; white to yellow to brown.

Flower: Orange to red. 1.2–1.6 in (3–4 cm) across. May–June in cultivation, December–January in habitat.

Flowering time from seed: 2–3 years.

Distribution: Southern Bolivia and northern Argentina.

Rebutia steinmannii

Form: Stem simple (in habitat); globular to short-cylindrical; to 0.8 in (2 cm) or more high and 1.4 in (3.5 cm) across.

Spines: Radials about 8–13; flexible; to 0.4 in (1 cm) long. Centrals 0.

Flower: Orange to red. About 0.8 in (2 cm) across. May–June in cultivation, December–January in habitat.

Flowering time from seed: 2–3 years.

Distribution: Northern Bolivia to northern Argentina.

Another wide-ranging species that has received a plethora of names at the level of species and variety, this plant is usually recognized by its dark green body and bristly spines. In cultivation the various forms all grow rather slowly and take a while to form a sizeable clump, and some of the forms seem to have weak roots compared with most rebutias. The plant illustrated is a vegetative propagation from Rausch's *Digitorebutia cincinnata*, a fairly small-bodied version collected at Cuchu Ingenio, south of Potosí in Bolivia, WR300. A similarly rich shade of orange is seen in the flowers of a number of other forms.

Rebutia tarijensis

irst discovered by Friedrich Ritter as a single example in 1962 and provisionally named *Rebutia sphaerica*, this very dark-looking plant was later found by Walter usch and was given its current name in 1975. It has recently been lumped into *spegazziniana* (itself only a form of *R. deminuta*), although it has to be said that e flowers are quite different from the very characteristic type seen in that species.

e plant illustrated was grown from seed collected on the Pilaya River.

DATA

Form: Clumping. Heads 2–4.5 cm (0.8–1.8 in) across and high; darkish green.

Spines: 8–10; to 0.2 in (0.5 cm) long; brown.

Flower: Red. About 1.2 in (3 cm) across. May in cultivation; November–December in habitat.

Flowering time from seed: 2–3 years.

Distribution: Bolivia (Tarija).

Rebutia wessneriana

DATA

Form: Body flattened-globular; to 2.8 in (7 cm) high and 3.2 in (8 cm) across.

Spines: About 25. Stiff, bristly, interlacing, glassy white; to about 0.4 in (1 cm) long.

Flower: Blood red. 2.2 in (5.5 cm) across. May–June in cultivation; December–January in habitat.

Flowering time from seed: 2–3 years.

Distribution: Argentina (Jujuy).

This is one of the few members of this genus that forms clusters in the wild as well as in cultivation. On steep, eroded slopes at Volcán the author saw clumps some 6 inches (15 cm) across with a dozen or so heads, growing only a short distance away from the plant illustrated here. This was one of several dozen in flower, most of which could not, alas, be reached. In cultivation this species is very vigorous, quickly forming large mounds that in summer disappear beneath a blood-red veil of flowers. This species is also still often sold under the names *Rebutia calliantha* and *R. beryllioides*—these old names are taking a long time to die out.

Rhipsalidopsis rosea

Included in *Hatiora* in the most recent treatments, this species is probably going to be listed as *Rhipsalidopsis* for some time, given the conservative nature of most plantsmen. In cultivation it looks its best when grown in a hanging pot (as in the commercially raised plant illustrated). This allows the rather floppy stems—their tips decorated with an array of pink flowers—to hang down. Propagation is by cuttings rather than seed, as in all these epiphytic cacti, which do best in a nonmineral compost such as coir mixed with composted bark (peat-free compost).

Form: Freely branching. Stem segments flat or with three to five angles; 0.8–1.6 in (2–4 cm) long.

Spines: Just a few bristles present.

Flower: Pink. Broadly funnel form. 1.2–1.6 in (3–4 cm) across. June–July in cultivation.

Flowering time from seed: Probably about 5–6 years.

Distribution: Brazil (Paraná to Rio Grande do Sul).

Rhipsalis grandiflora

DATA

Form: Freely branching. Stem segments cylindrical; green; 2–5.9 in (5–15 cm) long and 0.4 in (1 cm) across, (but mostly much thinner).

Spines: Absent.

Flower: White. To 0.8 in (2 cm) across. June–July in cultivation.

Flowering time from seed: 4–5 years.

Distribution: Southeast Brazil.

Formerly included in the genus *Lepismium*, this is one of the more free-flowering species of *Rhipsalis*, some of which can be difficult to flower in cultivation. As with all these epiphytes, it is best not to expose your plant to full sun. Grow it in semishade beneath the greenhouse staging, or on the windowsill of a house where it should thrive as long as it is given plenty of water in the growing season.

The plant illustrated above is a cutting from a plant that was collected from habitat but without specific locality.

Rhipsalis trigona

s the sharply angled stem that is the main feature of this species, which should
grown in a hanging basket. This allows the stems to trail down freely, as they
ld in habitat from the branch of a tree. As with all these prolifically branched
phytes, propagation tends to be from cuttings rather than seed, although seed
arious species collected by the author in Brazil all germinated very well.

*plant illustrated below is a vegetative propagation from material that was
ected in Brazil, but without specific locality.*

DATA

Form: Stems three-angled
and richly branching.
Segments to 3.9 in
(10 cm) long and about
0.3–0.4 in (0.8–1 cm)
across.

Spines: A single bristle
often present.

Flower: White to pinkish.
To 0.8 in (2 cm) across.
June–July in cultivation.

**Flowering time from
seed:** 5–6 years.

Distribution: Southeast
Brazil.

Schlumbergera truncata

DATA

Form: Multi-branched. Stem segments flat; to 2.4 in (6 cm) long and 1.4 in (3.5 cm) wide.

Spines: A few bristles present.

Flower: Pink, red, orange, or white. 2.6–3.2 in (6.5–8 cm) long. December–January in cultivation.

Distribution: Brazil (Rio de Janeiro).

Sometimes known as the Christmas cactus, this familiar house plant was seen growing high up on the branches of forest trees within the city of Rio de Janeiro, which is fortunate enough to have a rain-forest reserve within its city lim In cultivation this plant tends to be grown in the home rather than in a greenhouse and is supplied in huge numbers for the houseplant trade (as illustrated). Arising from a rather upright, woody stem, the branches droop somewhat, but not to the extent that the plant needs to be kept in a hanging basket. This species is notorio for often dropping all its flower buds at an early stage—not moving the plant dur bud formation is said to help prevent this.

Sclerocactus parviflorus

Form: Simple or clumping from the base. Stems 2–11 in (5–27 cm) or more high; 1.6–5.1 in (4–13 cm) across.

Spines: Radials 3–17; whitish; to 1.4 in (3.5 cm) long. Centrals 4–6; lowermost one hooked; reddish to whitish; to 1.8 in (4.5 cm) long.

Flower: Purple, rose, white, or yellow. 0.8–2.4 in (2–6 cm) across. May–June in cultivation; April–May in habitat.

Flowering time from seed: 2–3 years (on a graft).

Distribution: United States (Four Corners region of Arizona, Utah, Colorado, and New Mexico).

the arid deserts of the Four Corners region this plant is often common on oadsides or even on waste lots in towns, sometimes growing with *Echinocereus* *dleri*. In cultivation all species of *Sclerocactus* are extremely difficult, often using to grow on their own roots and only surviving for any length of time en grafted. As with all plants, some people manage better than others to keep m alive ungrafted. The seeds are also usually very difficult to germinate, hough various tricks are available to encourage this. In subspecies *terrae-nyonae* the flower is bright lemon yellow.

e plant shown is subspecies intermedius, *photographed among sagebrush in Utah.*

Stenocactus coptonogonus

Form: Usually simple. Stems flattened-globular; 2–3.9 in (5–10 cm) high and 3.2–4.3 in (8–11 cm) across.

Spines: 3–7; upper ones pointing upward; broad and flattened; to 1.4 in (3.5 cm) long.

Flower: Petals white with a violet midstripe. To 1.6 in (4 cm) across. April–May in cultivation.

Flowering time from seed: 5–6 years.

Distribution: Mexico (San Luis Potosí, Zacatecas, Hidalgo, and Guanajuato).

This is the only member of the genus that lacks the narrow wavy ribs seen in all the other species. Instead, the ribs are few in number (10 to 15) and sharply keeled, and the body is a grayish green in color. In habitat the author saw this species growing in grass in areas of flat desert north of the city of San Luis Potosí. In cultivation it is the slowest-growing member of the genus and must not be overpotted or pushed, otherwise it will lose its roots.

The plant illustrated above was grown from seed that was collected north of San Luis Potosí city, but not by the author.

Stenocactus crispatus

This very widespread species occurs in a multitude of different forms, all of which grade into one another (and possibly into other species). Many of the plants supplied as this species lack the purple tones on the flowers, which are often much paler. The number of ribs varies from 25 to 60, and they are often very folded and undulate. If you are attracted by this genus, the best approach is simply to forget about names and purchase plants (or seeds) derived from material of known origin, and write the details of the habitat locality on your labels to act as a kind of name.

The plant illustrated below was grown from seed that was collected near Valparaíso, Zacatecas, Lau 1092.

DATA

Form: Flattened-globular; 3.2–4.7 in (8–12 cm) across.

Spines: Radials 2–10; 0.1–1.1 in (0.4–2.8 cm) long. Centrals 1–4; 0.4–2.6 in (1–6.5 cm) long.

Flower: Purple violet. 0.8–1.6 in (2–4 cm) across. May in cultivation.

Flowering time from seed: 3–4 years.

Distribution: North and central Mexico.

Stenocactus erectocentrus

DATA

Form: Usually simple. To 3.2 in (8 cm) high and 2 in (5 cm) across.

Spines: Radials 5–6; white, glassy. Centrals 2; to 0.8 in (2 cm) long; upper central to over 2 in (5 cm) long; flattened and thin.

Flower: Whitish. Under 0.8 in (2 cm) long. May in cultivation.

Flowering time from seed: 3–4 years.

Distribution: Mexico.

The plant illustrated here was grown from seed collected near Ascensión, Nuevo León, and supplied as this species, which was described by Backeberg without any exact locality. The illustration could equally well fit *Stenocactus lloydii*, whose upper spine is said to overtop the plant, being up to 3.2 inches (8 cm) long. The spines on the plant seen here reached to just over 3.5 inches (9 cm). In both specie the ribs are described as thin and wavy, but that applies to most stenocacti. As always with this genus, there are more questions than answers, but at least you now know more or less what you might get if you order either species, regardless of what the correct botanical name might be.

Stenocactus lamellosus

As with the previous species, this is the name that was supplied with the seed, in this case collected near Santiago, Veracruz. The plant illustrated is a reasonably good fit with the original description, having the correct number of ribs (30 to 35) and a fairly large carmine flower. It is certainly distinctive, being easily the fastest flower from seed of any member of the genus. It rapidly forms large, bright grass-green plants (also unusual) that start to offset around the base at about 10 years from seed. As before, this is shown merely to let you know what you might get under this name, rather than as a definite representation of *Stenocactus lamellosus*.

DATA

Form: To 3.9 in (10 cm) high; 3.2 in (8 cm) across.

Spines: Radials 4; white. Centrals 2; to 1.6 in (4 cm) long; the upper one flattened.

Flower: Flesh colored, carmine inside. To 1.6 in (4 cm) long. May–June in cultivation.

Flowering time from seed: 4–5 years.

Distribution: Mexico (Hidalgo).

Stenocactus multicostatus

DATA

Form: Simple. Flattened-spherical; fresh green. To 3.9 in (10 cm) across.

Spines: Radials short; mostly 4. Centrals to 1.2 in (3 cm) long, curving upward like horns; yellowish to brownish.

Flower: White, purple violet in the middle. 1 in (2.5 cm) long. April–May in cultivation.

Flowering time from seed: 4–5 years.

Distribution: Mexico (widespread in the north).

In the restricted sense used here this species is characterized by the broad flattened body and large number (more than 100) of very thin, wavy ribs that are fully exposed by the very open spination. The plant illustrated was grown from seed collected at Los Imagenes, Nuevo León, and half the seedlings produced adult plants with more than 100 very thin ribs, while the other half had only about 70 much thicker ribs. In cultivation this species is often the first *Stenocactus* each year to open its flowers, often in early April. For many people it is their favorite member of the genus on account of the large number of wavy, fully exposed ribs.

Stenocactus ochoterenanus

The plant illustrated was grown from seed collected near Jeréz in Zacatecas, and it seems to be intermediate between *Stenocactus ochoterenanus* and *zacatecasensis*. It is closer to the former in the number (about 26), length 5 inches/1.2 cm), and breadth of the radial spines. Its flower is also closer to *ochoterenanus*, but its central spines are closer to *S. zacatecasensis* in color and length. This is typical of the problems constantly encountered in defining species in this difficult genus, with intermediates often cropping up to complicate matters.

DATA

Form: Simple. Flattened-globular; bluish green. To 3.2 in (8 cm) high and 3.9 in (10 cm) across.

Spines: Radials 22 or more; needlelike; white; to 0.5 in (1.2 cm) long. Centrals 4; yellow; upper ones 2–2.4 in (5–6 cm) long; broad and flattened.

Flower: Pale pink or white with purplish midstripes. May in cultivation.

Flowering time from seed: 3–4 years.

Distribution: Mexico (Guanajuato and Querétaro).

Stenocactus phyllacanthus

Form: Usually simple. Flattened-globular. 1.6–3.9 in (4–10 cm) across.

Spines: Radials 2–7; white; 0.2–0.4 in (0.4–0.9 cm) long. Centrals 1.2–3.2 in (3–8 cm) long; upper one flattened.

Flower: Yellowish white with brownish red throat. About 0.6 in (1.5 cm) across. May in cultivation; July–August in habitat.

Flowering time from seed: 3–4 years.

Distribution: Mexico (Hidalgo, Zacatecas, San Luis Potosí, and Guanajuato).

The small yellowish flowers of this species are said to be diagnostic, but many years ago the author collected a single seed pod near Río Verde, San Luis Potosí. It produced plants with both the typical yellow flowers and also white flowers with brownish pink midstripes—and not a hint of yellow (PM028, illustrated). In its most typical body form, as seen here, it is quite easy to recognize, but as always, numerous intermediates seem to exist between this and other species. In habitat this cactus sometimes grows in areas where it is partially immersed in water during the height of the summer rainy season.

Stenocactus zacatecasensis

this attractively spined species the rather narrow, bluish green ribs number about 55 and contrast nicely with the blackish central spines. Unlike in the original scription, the flowers do not seem to be yellow with darker midstripes, but white th a brownish violet stripe. The author is totally mystified as to why this species s been lumped into *Stenocactus multicostatus* in recent years.

e plant illustrated was grown from seed collected near the city of Zacatecas, this ecies apparently being common in the hills near the city.

DATA

Form: Simple. To about 3.9 in (10 cm) broad; in cultivation higher than 3.9 in (10 cm).

Spines: Radials 10–12; 0.3–0.4 in (0.8–1 cm) long; white. Centrals 3; 0.8–2.4 in (2–6 cm) long; curving upward; blackish brown.

Flower: Yellow with a brownish midstripe. 0.6 in (1.5 cm) long. May in cultivation.

Flowering time from seed: 4–5 years.

Distribution: Mexico (Zacatecas).

Stenocereus eruca

DATA

Form: Clumping. Stems to 9.8 ft (3 m) long and 3.2 in (8 cm) across.

Spines: Radials 10–17; whitish; 0.4–0.6 in (1–1.5 cm) long. Centrals 1–3; grayish; flattened and daggerlike; to 1 in (2.5 cm) long.

Flower: Cream to pinkish white. 3.9–4.7 in (10–12 cm) long.

Flowering time from seed: About 15–20 years.

Distribution: Mexico (Baja California, Magdalena plain).

Known as the creeping devil, or caterpillar cactus, and perhaps more familiar as *Machaerocereus eruca*, in habitat the long stems of this plant sprawl across the ground in great spiny tangles. In cultivation it is grown for its striking, daggerlike spines rather than for flowers, which open at night and are not particularly attractive (although they appear regularly on old plants in cultivation, even in dull climates). Cultivated plants take a long time to cluster, and most people grow their specimen as a single stem creeping along a long narrow tray of gravel or grit.

The plant illustrated above is a vegetative propagation from a plant that was collected on the Magdalena plain.

Stenocereus thurberi

Known popularly as the organ pipe cactus, this species has its own reserve named for it: the Organ Pipe Cactus National Monument in southern Arizona. This is where the plant illustrated below was photographed, growing beside the green trunk of a *palo verde* tree (*Cercidium microphyllum*). In cultivation this is not a very winter-hardy plant, and it should be kept well above freezing. The flowers open at night and remain open for 24 hours, but are not very likely to be seen under greenhouse conditions.

DATA

Form: Stems 3.3–26 ft (1–8 m) high and 2–7.9 in (5–20 cm) across; branching; yellowish green.

Spines: Radials 7–9; to 0.4 in (1 cm) long; grayish. Centrals 1–3; to 2 in (5 cm) long; grayish to blackish.

Flower: White; funnel form. 1.6–3.2 in (4–8 cm) long.

Flowering time from seed: Probably 20 years or more.

Distribution: United States (southern Arizona); Mexico (Sonora, Sinaloa, and Baja California).

Stephanocereus leucostele

DATA

Form: Stems usually simple; 6.6–16 ft (2–5 m) high; 1.6–3.2 in (4–8 cm) broad.

Spines: Radials 15–20; to 0.6 in (1.5 cm) long. Centrals 1–4; to 1.6 in (4 cm) long. All spines yellow to white.

Flower: White. 2.4–2.8 in (6–7 cm) long.

Flowering time from seed: 10–20 years.

Distribution: Brazil (Bahia).

The solitary white columns of this species (see photograph) can be seen scattered around like tall white sticks among the thorny bushes and trees of the caatinga. The bell-shaped or tubular flowers are usually borne from a ringlike mass of bristle forming a crownlike cephalium at the apex of the plant. Since the following year's growth starts on top of the cephalium, a series of bristly rings is formed as the plant grows, eventually comprising a series of segments stacked on top of each other. In cultivation this can be quite a demanding plant, needing lots of heat throughout the year, but in the right compost and with adequate warmth, growth is very rapid, although flowering is difficult to achieve.

Stetsonia coryne

Form: Forming massive trees to 26 ft (8 m) high, consisting of numerous upright blue-green stems up to 3.9 in (10 cm) across, perched atop a substantial woody trunk.

Spines: Radials 7–9; to 1.2 in (3 cm) long. Centrals 1; to 2 in (5 cm) long.

Flower: White. To 5.9 in (15 cm) long; opening at night and remaining open for most of the next day. November–December in habitat.

Flowering time from seed: Probably 20 years or more.

Distribution: Northwest Argentina; neighboring areas of Bolivia and Paraguay.

The tall stems of this species are a common sight, sticking out of the thorny scrublands around the city of Catamarca in Argentina, where the accompanying photograph was taken. Unfortunately, thousands of plants are bulldozed annually as this relatively flat (and therefore easily farmed) habitat is increasingly being converted for growing crops. Seedlings of this species are attractive, with their long black spines and blue-green bodies, and this was one of the first cacti that the author ever purchased, from a local florist. It is not so often seen these days, perhaps because it needs to be kept rather warmer in winter than most cacti .

Strombocactus disciformis

Form: Stems more or less flattened; to 3.5 in (9 cm) across; pale green; covered in small tubercles.

Spines: 1–4; gray; bristly; soon falling off.

Flower: Pale yellow. About 1.3 in (3.2 cm) across. May–July in cultivation.

Flowering time from seed: 6–8 years.

Distribution: Mexico (Hidalgo and Querétaro).

This plant has a very localized distribution, and large numbers have been removed illegally from habitat for the cactus trade. As well as being a crime, this is a pity, since it grows well enough from seed, as evidenced by the plant illustrated. This plant is about 20 years old, but started flowering after eight years or so. The flowers are self-fertile, so masses of the tiny seeds are always available, and once the seedlings are past the first year or two, they are easy to grow. In fact, this is a particularly tough cactus that thrives on neglect and is seemingly immune to attack by pests such as red spider mites. In the recently discovered subspecies *esperanzae* the flowers are magenta.

Sulcorebutia alba

After first being subsumed into *Weingartia*, which seems to have been correct, the sulcorebutias are all now usually listed in *Rebutia*. However, they are maintained as separate here—as they still appear in most seed and plant lists. This popular species—although described as single-headed in the wild—adds extra heads at a prolific rate under the pampered conditions of cultivation, and eventually forms large, handsome, white-spined clumps with dozens of heads. The flowers are very vivid red, as seen here, or a showy magenta. In recent works this species has been treated as a form of *Sulcorebutia canigueralii* (but as a *Rebutia*).

The plant illustrated was grown from seed collected between Sucre and Los Alamos.

DATA

Form: Simple. Heads to 0.8 in (2 cm) high and 1.4 in (3.5 cm) across.

Spines: Radials 20–24; 0.2 in (3–4 mm) long; white, with darker bases. Centrals usually 0.

Flower: Magenta to red. 1.2 in (3 cm) across. May–June in cultivation; October–November in habitat.

Flowering time from seed: 2–3 years.

Distribution: Bolivia (along the road from Sucre to Los Alamos).

459

Sulcorebutia arenacea

DATA

Form: Heads simple or forming cushions; to 1.4 in (3.5 cm) high and 2 in (5 cm) across.

Spines: 14–16; short; closely pressed against the plant body; white. To 0.2 in (0.5 cm) long.

Flower: Golden yellow or a more orange yellow. To 1.2 in (3 cm) across. May–June in cultivation.

Flowering time from seed: 3–4 years.

Distribution: Bolivia (Dept. of Cochabamba, near Tiquipaya and between Quiacollo and Kami on the road to Independencia).

The description given here covers this name as originally applied and as illustrated above—a vegetative propagation of a plant from Tiquipaya. However, *Sulcorebutia arenacea* is now taken to include a number of other former species, namely *S. glomeriseta*, *S. candiae*, *S. menesesii*, and *S. muschii*. Within an overall pattern they all look rather different from the plant illustrated here and from each other, and no matter how sound the purely botanical arguments might be for a reduction in names, in horticultural terms it is very unhelpful. Fortunately, most of these names will probably continue to be used for many years to come, enabling people to distinguish what they are getting.

Sulcorebutia canigueralii

DATA

When the author saw this plant in habitat, not far from the rather faded old city of Sucre, it occurred as clumps of about five to 12 heads almost buried in the earth with only their tops showing. In cultivation it eventually grows in much larger clumps than this, often with dozens of heads forming mounds up to about 2 inches (8 cm) high. The bicolored flowers are particularly rewarding and are produced with great abandon, even on small specimens.

The plant illustrated below is a vegetative propagation from Krahn 217, collected near Sucre.

Form: Clumping. Heads more or less spherical; about 0.8 in (2 cm) across.

Spines: Radials 11–14; comblike; pressed against the plant; very short. Centrals normally 0.

Flower: Golden yellow below, orange above. 1.6 in (4 cm) across. May in cultivation, October–November in habitat.

Flowering time from seed: 2–3 years.

Distribution: Bolivia (near Sucre).

Sulcorebutia crispata

DATA

Form: Simple or clumping. Heads to 1 in (2.5 cm) tall and 3.5 cm (1.4 in) across.

Spines: Radials 20–30; glassy white to brownish; 0.1–0.8 in (0.4–2 cm) long.

Flower: Pale to dark magenta. About 1.2 in (3 cm) across. May–June in cultivation.

Flowering time from seed: 3–4 years.

Distribution: Bolivia (Chuquisaca, at Tomina).

In cultivation this species always forms clumps on which the spination is particularly variable. In some plants the spines are only about 0.1 inches (4 mm) long and are pressed closely against the body. In others the spines are wavy, up to 0.8 inches (2 cm) long, and curling away from the plant. Plants with brownish spines are far less attractive than those in which the spination is white, but the flowers always appear in masses and are very showy.

The plant illustrated above is a vegetative propagation from material that was collected near Sopachuy, Lau 390.

Sulcorebutia kruegeri

n recent works this plant is treated as a subspecies of *Sulcorebutia steinbachii*, (but as a *Rebutia*) but it is more convenient here to keep it at the level of species, sing the "microspecies" concept. In habitat it forms clumps of small heads uggled down low on grassy, stony hillsides. In cultivation it tends to get much rger, eventually forming clumps with dozens or even hundreds of heads. Although sually yellow, the flowers often have orange margins to the petals, especially in ar. *hoffmanniana*, which generally has much darker brown spination, frequently ith prominent central spines up to 0.6 inches (1.5 cm) long.

he plant illustrated below was grown from seed that was collected right on the dge of Cochabamba city, PM151.

DATA

Form: Clumping. Heads 1.2–1.6 in (3–4 cm) across.

Spines: Radials 20–25; thin; about 0.1 in (3 mm) long; whitish to pale brown. Centrals 0–2; short.

Flower: Yellow. About 1 in (2.5 cm) across. May–June in cultivation; November–December in habitat.

Flowering time from seed: 2–3 years.

Distribution: Bolivia (near Cochabamba).

Sulcorebutia mizquensis

Form: Clumping. Heads more or less spherical; about 1.2 in (3 cm) across.

Spines: Radials to 20; about 0.2 in (0.4 cm) long. Centrals 0.

Flower: Magenta. 1 in (2.5 cm) across. May–June in cultivation.

Flowering time from seed: 2–3 years.

Distribution: Bolivia (near Mizque).

As can be seen from the above photograph, which is of a vegetative propagation from a plant collected near Mizque (WR194), the flowers on this species are a striking shade of magenta. The surface of the body is more or less concealed by a close-knit array of spines that lies against the surface below. At their tips the spines are white, then pink in the center, and blackish at the base. In some recent works this plant has been reduced to a form of *Sulcorebutia steinbachii* (as a *Rebutia*).

Sulcorebutia oenantha

When the author visited the type locality for this plant in mid-December most of the specimens were single-headed, but some were forming small clumps. A few just-ripe fruits were present and provided the seed from which the plant illustrated below was grown (PM162), while every plant had a crop of new flower buds that were about two weeks away from opening. In cultivation this is a vigorous plant that can eventually form clumps some 7.8 inches (20 cm) across. Some recent works treat it as a form of *Sulcorebutia steinbachii* (as a *Rebutia*).

DATA

Form: Heads flattened-spherical; to 2.4 in (6 cm) high and 3.9 in (10 cm) across.

Spines: Radials 24. Centrals 4; similar to the radials; about 0.5 in (1.2 cm) long; thin; yellowish.

Flower: Brownish red. 1.4 in (3.5 cm) across. June in cultivation; October and again in December in habitat.

Flowering time from seed: 2–3 years.

Distribution: Bolivia (south of Totora).

Sulcorebutia pampagrandensis

Form: Simple. Heads to 1.6 in (4 cm) high and 2.8 in (7 cm) across.

Spines: Radials 17–21; to 0.4 in (1 cm) long. Centrals usually 1; to 0.6 in (1.5 cm) long.

Flower: Lively bright pink. 1.8 in (4.5 cm) across. May–June in cultivation; October and again in December in habitat.

Flowering time from seed: 2–3 years.

Distribution: Bolivia (south of Totora).

You don't have to drive for long past the site of *Sulcorebutia oenantha* before you come to the similar-looking rocky habitat of *S. pampagrandensis*. They are probably forms of the same species, but they grow isolated from one another, so they are treated separately here. As with *S. oenantha*, this species seems to have a double round of flowering in the wild—most plants in mid-December having both recently ripened fruits and immature flower buds. In habitat and in cultivation it seems to remain simple. The plant illustrated (PM163 from seed collected at the type locality) is 20 years old, has reached 4.3 inches (11 cm) across (larger than the size given in the original description), and is still simple.

Sulcorebutia rauschii

It did not take long from the date of its first description for this striking species to become the most sought-after member of the genus. With its short, black, clawlike spines and violet-tinted bodies, its appearance is so distinctive that its instant appeal is not surprising. Various clones are in cultivation, one of which has green bodies allied to golden yellow spines, while in some clones the body surface is almost black, with an attractive velvetlike quality. Fortunately, this is an easy plant to grow, either from seeds or offsets.

The plant illustrated is a vegetative propagation from a plant collected at the type locality by its original discoverer, Walter Rausch (WR289).

DATA

Form: Clumping. Heads to 1.2 in (3 cm) across; blackish green to violet.

Spines: Radials about 11; very short; pressed against the body; black; clawlike.

Flower: Magenta. About 1.2 in (3 cm) across. May–June in cultivation.

Flowering time from seed: 2–3 years.

Distribution: Bolivia (Zudañez).

Sulcorebutia steinbachii

Form: Clumping. Heads to about 2 in (5 cm) across and high.

Spines: Radials 6–8; to 1 in (2.5 cm) long. Centrals 1–3; to 1.2 in (3 cm).

Flower: Scarlet, yellow, or magenta. About 1.2 in (3 cm) across. May–June in cultivation; November–December in habitat.

Flowering time from seed: 2–3 years.

Distribution: Bolivia (widespread in the mountains around Cochabamba).

When the author visited the Cuesta de Huakani near Cochabamba one sunny day in early December this species was in full glorious flower, exhibiting a range of colors. The plants themselves also varied from large single heads with a fierce mass of black spines to flat-topped clumps of dozens of heads with thinnish, pliable spines pressed against the bodies. Although the flowers were being freely visited by bees, a single seed pod collected by the author produced only yellow-flowered plants from the 20 or so that germinated. In some recent works *Sulcorebutia steinbachii* (as a *Rebutia*) has gobbled up a large number of other species, being taken to be a single, very variable, taxon.

Sulcorebutia swobodae

The soft, interlacing, rather wavy golden spination of this species quickly made it popular (although some clones have dark brown spines). In the mountainous terrain of the area inhabited by this plant, the cacti tend to grow on hilltops, each one isolated from the next and each local population having its own distinctive set of characteristics. Some people regard these isolated populations as distinct species (as in the separate treatment here for *Sulcorebutia swobodae*). Others claim they are simply forms of one variable species, in which case this plant—along with the stiffer-spined *S. flavissima*—becomes a form of *S. mentosa*.

The plant illustrated below is a vegetative propagation from material that was collected by Heinz Swoboda at the type locality, HS27a.

DATA

Form: Simple (usually clumping in cultivation). Heads flat-globular; to 1.6 in (4 cm) wide.

Spines: Radials and centrals intermixed; 28–30; thin; yellow; to 0.6 in (1.6 cm) long.

Flower: Pink. 1.4 in (3.5 cm) across. May–June in cultivation; December in habitat.

Flowering time from seed: 2–3 years.

Distribution: Bolivia (between Aiquile and Mizque).

Sulcorebutia tarabucoensis callecallensis

Form: Clumping. Heads to about 1.6 in (4 cm) tall and 1 in (2.5 cm) across.

Spines: About 12. To 0.2 in (0.5 cm) long; white with brown bases.

Flower: All-yellow, yellow with red margins to the petals, or all-red. About 1.6 in (4 cm) across. May–June in cultivation; November in habitat.

Flowering time from seed: 2–3 years.

Distribution: Bolivia (Tarabuco).

Originally described as *Sulcorebutia verticillacantha* var. *auriflora*, this is a deservedly popular plant in cultivation. It rapidly forms large clusters of dozens (even hundreds) of rather small heads packed in tightly together, but not so tightly as to prevent the eruption of masses of flower buds. The flowers open in a massed display that envelops the plant and is quite breathtaking. In habitat the heads are few in number and barely protrude above the surface of the ground.

The plant illustrated was grown from seed collected near Tarabuco, PM166. Some plants from the single pod collected flowered pure red.

Sulcorebutia tiraquensis

This is a variable plant. The specimen illustrated, raised from seed collected near Lopez Mendoza Bridge (PM157), has longish spines. The most beautiful form is the so-called var. *bicolorispina*, with heads up to 7.1 inches (18 cm) high, densely covered with an array of white radial spines and red-brown centrals. In var. *electracantha* the spines are supposed to be yellow and the flower orange, but in some plants seen in its type locality, the flowers were magenta and the spination was similar to *bicolorispina*. Botanically speaking, these names can probably be ignored, but they can be useful in selecting plants to buy, and *Sulcorebutia tiraquensis* itself is now often treated as a subspecies of *S. steinbachii* (in *Rebutia*).

DATA

Form: Single or offsetting from high up on the body. Heads to 2 in (5 cm) high and 4.7 in (12 cm) across.

Spines: To over 30. Radials and centrals often difficult to differentiate; 0.2–1.2 in (0.5–3 cm) long.

Flower: Purplish pink. 1.2 in (3 cm) across. May–June in cultivation; October–December in habitat.

Flowering time from seed: 2–3 years.

Distribution: Bolivia (in various places along the Cochabamba–Santa Cruz highway).

Tacinga inamoena

Form: Segments oval;
1.2–1.6 in (3–4 cm) long;
forming low clumps.

Spines: Normally absent.

Flower: Orange to reddish.
To 1.6 in (4 cm) broad.
June–July in cultivation;
October–December
in habitat.

**Flowering time from
seed:** 4–5 years.

Distribution: Brazil
(Pernambuco, Bahia).

Since it comes from a tropical region with persistently high temperatures, this is a species that needs to be kept well above freezing in winter. However, its small, attractive, spineless pads and, above all, its shiny, orange, plastic-looking flowers, earn it a place in any collection. Seeds germinate well, and growth is relatively rapid—nice compact little clumps are soon formed. If these get too big, it is easy enough to detach one or two pads, root them up, and start all over again. In subspecies *subcylindrica* the stem segments are oblong—up to 2.8 inches (7 cm) long and 0.8–1.2 inches (2–3 cm) wide—and the whole plant is much taller.

The plant illustrated was photographed near Milagres, Bahia.

Tephrocactus alexanderi

The plant illustrated here was photographed near Villa Mazan in Catamarca province, flowering just on the edge of the area being used as the village garbage dump. In cultivation it is a slow-growing plant, often adding only a single segment each year. Along with some forms of *Tephrocactus articulatus,* it suffers (at least in a damp climate) from a fungal infection that causes oozing black lesions, eventually leading to the death of the segment. If you can avoid this problem, this is a worthwhile plant to keep, and its slow growth precludes the need for a rapid increase in pot size.

Form: Segments often spherical; also to 2 in (5 cm) long and 1.2 in (3 cm) broad; bright green; forming groups to about 19.6 in (50 cm) high and broad.

Spines: 12–15; 0.4–1.6 in (1–4 cm) long.

Flower: Pinkish white. About 1.6–2 in (4–5 cm) across. November–December in habitat; July in cultivation.

Flowering time from seed: About 8–10 years.

Distribution: Argentina (La Rioja and Catamarca).

Tephrocactus aoracanthus

Form: Segments spherical; to 3.2 in (8 cm) across; pale green; forming large clumps to about 19.6 in (50 cm) high and broad.

Spines: 1–7; thick and stiff; brown to blackish; to 5.9 in (15 cm) or more long.

Flower: White. About 2.4 in (6 cm) across. June–July in cultivation; November–December in habitat.

Flowering time from seed: Probably 10 years or more.

Distribution: Argentina (San Juán, La Rioja, Mendoza, and Córdoba).

With its large pale green spherical segments, this is a pretty impressive species, especially when bearing its large white flowers, as seen here in habitat near San Juán. Whereas most of the globular cacti seem to grow on mountain slopes, this species seems to prefer river valleys, often growing among gravel and shingle where no other cacti are present. In cultivation growth is very slow, one extra segment being added every couple of years or so. One problem is that each new segment is often smaller than the previous one, although giving plenty of root run seems to alleviate this, and planting out in a bed may be the best answer.

Tephrocactus articulatus

Although abandoned by most recent workers on cactus classification because they grade into one another all the time, there are a number of named varieties of this immensely variable species. They differ in spination, stem size, and stem shape. The names can help identify what you might receive if you order a plant by mail. For example, if you specify var. *inermis,* you should get a more or less spineless plant with segments up to 3.9 inches (10 cm) long and 1 inch (2.5 cm) across. Ordering var. *polyacanthus* should get you a similar plant but with spines up to 3.9 inches (10 cm) long, and a "frosted" surface.

The plant illustrated is a very attractive form with incredibly broad, papery spines, up to 0.3 inches (0.7 cm) wide at the base. It is often seen in cultivation and this photograph was taken near Chilecito, La Rioja.

DATA

Form: Segments subglobular to short-cylindrical, covered in tubercles. To 3.9 in (10 cm) or more long; pale green to gray green.

Spines: 1–4 (often absent); flattened, papery, and flexible to relatively stiff. To 3.9 in (10 cm) long, gray to white.

Flower: White to pale pink. About 1.6 in (4 cm) across. July in cultivation; November–December in habitat.

Flowering time from seed: 7–10 years.

Distribution: Argentina (widespread in the northwest).

Tephrocactus molinensis

DATA

Form: Clumping. Segments globular to ovoid; to 1 in (2.5 cm).

Spines: None. Conspicuous tufts of glochids present.

Flower: Pinkish cream. Up to 1 in (2.5 cm) across. June–July in cultivation.

Flowering time from seed: 6–7 years.

Distribution: Argentina (Salta, along the Calchaqui valley from Molinos and southward to the Quebrada de Cafayate).

Several different forms of this variable plant are in cultivation. The one from the Quebrada de Cafayate is probably the most attractive, with numerous small, rounded segments densely covered in tufts of bright ginger glochids. Around Molinos the segments on the plants are far larger but fewer in number, and the glochids are a dull grayish brown. Some clones also flower better than others, but the flowers are somewhat disappointing, as can be seen in the illustration of FK91-37-239, a vegetative propagation from material collected near the pass at Molinos.

Tephrocactus weberi

ow mats of this plant often almost cover the ground in habitat, and from their rather dingy appearance it is hard to imagine what an attractive plant this makes in cultivation. In most forms the spines are long and relatively dense, varying n color in a very collectible way. Clones often available for sale include the lovely 'iltz 50 (white spines) from the Sierra de Quilmes and Piltz 50a (yellow spines) from he same area. The plant pictured is var. *deminuta*, a vegetative propagation of 'R241 from Cachipampa-Amblayo. It has shortish segments and a rather dark, ntidy, and sparse spination. Although far less attractive than most other forms, t is unusual in that it is very free-flowering in cultivation.

Form: Segments cylindrical; 1.2–3.9 in (3–10 cm) long. May clump to form plants up to 7.9 in (20 cm) high, but often low and sprawling.

Spines: Usually 5–10. Needlelike; 1.2–2 in (3–5 cm) long; white to yellow to pinkish to dark brown.

Flower: Yellow to orange. About 1.2 in (3 cm) across. June in cultivation; January–February in habitat.

Flowering time from seed: 4–5 years.

Distribution: Argentina (Salta, Tucumán, San Juán, Catamarca, and La Rioja).

Thelocactus bicolor

DATA

Form: Simple or clumping from the base. Stems globular to elongate; 0.6–15 in (1.5–38 cm) high and 0.8–7.1 in (2–18 cm) across; bright green.

Spines: Radials 8–17; 0.4–1.1 in (1–2.8 cm) long (sometimes even longer). Centrals 0–5; 0.6–1.3 in (1.4–3.3 cm) long.

Flower: Magenta, usually with a reddish center. 1.6– 3.2 in (4–8 cm) across. May in cultivation; July–August in habitat.

Flowering time from seed: 4–6 years.

Distribution: Northern Mexico and southern Texas.

This widespread species is relatively easy to grow in cultivation. It will produce its gorgeous flowers every year without fail, but it is a little touchy if given too much water and it does not like being overpotted. Some plants quickly grow tall, while others remain squat and domelike, depending on where the seed originated. It is also very variable in the density and color of its spination, from open and pale pinkish purple on the plant illustrated (near Saltillo, Coahuila) to very dense and all-yellow in subspecies *flavidispinus* from Texas. In the rare subspecies *schwarzii* from Tamaulipas, which is difficult to grow, central spines are absent.

Thelocactus buekii

This plant was originally described as a species, but for many years it was treated as a variety of *Thelocactus tulensis*. A recent study found that, based on microscopic details of the seed, *T. buekii* is distinct after all. In cultivation it is slow-growing, taking years to get to about 2 inches (5 cm) across, but flowering every year once it is old enough. The body is covered in rather low, flat-sided tubercles. In subspecies *matudae* these are taller with curved sides, and it has a bigger flower, up to 3.2 inches (8 cm) across. This too was originally described as a species, then as a variety of *T. tulensis*, but it is now considered a subspecies of *T. buekii*.

The plant illustrated was grown from seed collected near La Ascensión.

DATA

Form: Simple. 1–2.4 in (2.5–6 cm) high and 2.8–7.1 in (7–18 cm) across.

Spines: Radials mostly 4–5; 0.3–0.7 in (0.6–1.8 cm) or more long. Centrals 1–4; 0.6–2.2 in (1.5–5.5 cm) long.

Flower: Magenta. About 1.6 in (4 cm) across. May–June in cultivation.

Flowering time from seed: 5–6 years.

Distribution: Mexico (Nuevo León).

Thelocactus conothelos

Form: Usually simple. Stems globular to slightly cylindrical; mostly to 4.7 in (12 cm) high and 6.7 in (17 cm) across.

Spines: Radials 10–23; 0.2–0.8 in (0.5–2 cm) long. centrals 1–4, 1–5.5 cm (0.4–2.2 in) long.

Flower: Various shades of magenta; sometimes white. About 1.6 in (4 cm) across. May–June in cultivation.

Flowering time from seed: 4–5 years.

Distribution: Mexico (widespread in San Luis Potosí, Tamaulipas, and Nuevo León).

The plant illustrated, grown from seed collected near Tula, Tamaulipas, is fairly typical and is what you will probably get if you obtain a plant without provenance. The main variations lie in the number of spines, the size of the tubercle that cover the body, and the intensity of the flower color. In subspecies *aurantiacus* from a limited area near Aramberri in Nuevo León, the flower is bright yellow to yellowish orange. In subspecies *argentatus* the spines are creamy white and cover the body densely, while the flower is vivid magenta. It grows only in pine forests near La Ascensión, also in Nuevo León.

Thelocactus heterochromus

Normally growing on hilltops in limestone soils, this species is somewhat variable. Some forms have only a few, longish, thick spines that curve back over the body, while in others the spines are thinner, more numerous, and project outward from the plant. In the most extreme of the latter forms there is a very close resemblance to the more squat forms of *Thelocactus bicolor*, and in the author's collection there are plants that are impossible to assign with certainty to either of these two species.

The plant illustrated was grown from seed collected near Santiago Papasquiaro, Durango, and is the form most distant from Thelocactus bicolor.

DATA

Form: Simple. Globular to flattened-globular. To 2.8 in (7 cm) high and 5.9 in (15 cm) across; gray green.

Spines: Radials 6–9; 0.8–1.2 in (2–3 cm) long. Centrals 1–4; 0.8–1.2 in (2–3 cm) long.

Flower: Magenta. 2.2–3.9 in (5.5–10 cm) across. May–June in cultivation.

Flowering time from seed: 4–5 years.

Distribution: Mexico (Chihuahua and Durango).

Thelocactus hexaedrophorus

DATA

Form: Simple, sometimes making clumps of 5–6 heads. These mostly flattened-globular; to 3 in (7.5 cm) high and 5.9 in (15 cm) across.

Spines: Radials 4–8; to 1 in (3.5 cm) long. Centrals 0–3; 0.6–1 in (1.5–2.5 cm) long.

Flower: White. About 2 in (5 cm) across. May–June in cultivation.

Flowering time from seed: 4–5 years.

Distribution: Mexico (San Luis Potosí, Tamaulipas, Nuevo León, and Zacatecas).

Both in habitat and in cultivation this is a very distinctive plant, being a little flattened and a distinct shade of bluish green. Like most cacti, it varies somewhat, even over a limited area. The plant illustrated was in flower (note the bee in one flower) in early August on the east side of the large city of San Luis Potosí. On the southwestern side of the city the plants were much more dome-shaped and had a smaller number of far less tuberculate, more smoothly rounded ribs and longer, more clawlike spination. In cultivation growth is slow but without any special problems, and flowers appear every year without fail.

Thelocactus leucacanthus

his is the most prolifically clumping member of the genus. Clumps up to 31.5 inches (80 cm) across are often found, containing dozens of heads. The lant illustrated is a fairly typical specimen, photographed between Zimapán and .miquilpán—one of hundreds that were in flower in early August. While yellow the predominant flower color in Hidalgo, it is replaced in most of Querétaro by agenta, in the subspecies *schmollii*. This also tends to have narrower, longer eads, eventually making quite large clumps in cultivation.

Form: Clumping prolifically. Heads to 5.9 in (15 cm) high and 2 in (5 cm) across; yellowish green.

Spines: Radials 6–20; to 0.3 in (0.7 cm) long. Centrals 0–1; 0.4–2 in (0.9–5 cm); pale yellow to almost black.

Flower: Yellow. 1–2.1 in (2–4.5 cm) across. May–June in cultivation; July–August in habitat.

Flowering time from seed: 3–4 years.

Distribution: Mexico (Hidalgo and Querétaro).

Thelocactus macdowellii

DATA

Form: Simple or clumping. Heads to 3.7 in (9.5 cm) high and 4.7 in (12 cm) across.

Spines: Radials 15–25; 0.3–0.5 in (0.8–1.2 cm) long; white, fading to yellow. Centrals 2–4; whitish; 0.4–1 in (1.1–2.5 cm) long.

Flower: Pink. About 1.6 in (4 cm) across. May–June in cultivation.

Flowering time from seed: 5–6 years.

Distribution: Mexico (Coahuila and Nuevo León).

Until *Thelocactus conothelos argentatus* was discovered, this was the only member of the genus in which the bodies were almost concealed beneath a dense mass of whitish spines. In the author's opinion this is still the more attractive plant, forming very handsome globular heads that may start to form offsets from the base at around 10 to 12 years from seed. In habitat it grows only on limestone, and some people add this to the compost, but it seems to grow well enough even without this addition.

The plant illustrated was grown from seed collected from Arteaga, Coahuila.

Thelocactus rinconensis

With its blue-green body covered in large angular tubercles, this makes a superb specimen in cultivation, especially as a big old plant. The longer-spined form, subspecies *nidulans*, is the most impressive (often labeled as *Thelocactus nidulans*), while the shorter-spined form (sometimes the spines are more or less absent) is often marketed as *T. phymatothelos*. It is this form that is illustrated here, growing among limestone rubble on the roadside at Arteaga Canyon, south of Saltillo. In subspecies *freudenbergeri* the body lacks the bluish tone seen in the other forms, and the flower is large and magenta. In cultivation *T. rinconensis* is a slow-growing species that plods along at its own pace and is seemingly immune to attack by red spider mites, even when stressed.

DATA

Form: Simple. Body 1.6–5.9 in (4–15 cm) high and 3.2–7.9 in (8–20 cm) across; bluish green.

Spines: Radials 0–5; 0.1–1.4 in (0.3–3.5 cm) long. Centrals 0–4; 1.6–2.4 in (4–6 cm) long.

Flower: White to pink to pale yellow. About 1.2–1.6 in (3–4 cm) across. May–June in cultivation; July–August in habitat.

Flowering time from seed: 5–6 years.

Distribution: Mexico (Coahuila and Nuevo León).

Thelocactus tulensis

DATA

Form: Simple or clumping. Stems to 9.8 in (25 cm) high and 7.1 in (18 cm) across.

Spines: Radials 4–12; 0.3–0.6 in (0.7–1.5 cm) long. Centrals 1–7; 0.6–3.2 in (1.5–8 cm) long.

Flower: Pink to white to yellow. 1.2–1.6 in (3–4 cm) across. May–June in cultivation.

Flowering time from seed: 5–6 years.

Distribution: Mexico (Tamaulipas and San Luis Potosí).

This is another slow-growing plant but, unlike in the previous species, the bodies are green, with no hint of blue. In *Thelocactus tulensis* the tubercles that cover the plant are also more rounded and less angular than in *T. rinconensis*. Of the two, *T. tulensis* is definitely the more tricky plant to grow. It lacks the robust constitution of the other species and sometimes loses its roots for no apparent reason (although some forms are more prone to this than others). The most attractive form in the author's collection is a yellow-flowered plant from east of Huizache.

The plant illustrated above is a vegetative propagation from a plant that was collected at Tula, Tamaulipas.

Trichocereus atacamensis pasacana

This slow-growing species is unlikely to flower in most collections grown under glass in dull climates, although planting it out in a bed will speed up growth and therefore make flowering more likely. In its natural homeland it often stands in thousands across the arid stony hillsides, and its durable timber is used for a number of purposes by the local people in a landscape that is otherwise treeless. Plants for sale are still most often labeled as *Trichocereus pasacana*, but *T. atacamensis* was described first (from Chile), and so at subspecies level the name *pasacana*, applying to plants from Argentina and Bolivia, must be subordinate to the older name.

The plant illustrated was photographed near Amaicha del Valle, Tucumán, Argentina.

DATA

Form: Treelike; to 33 ft (10 m) high. Stems to more than 11.8 in (30 cm) broad.

Spines: Spines 50–100, not split into radials and centrals. Up to 5.5 in (14 cm) long; golden brown to white; often wavy.

Flower: White. To 4.7 in (12 cm) long. November–January in habitat.

Distribution: Northern Argentina; southern Bolivia; Chile.

Trichocereus bertramianus

Form: Stems erect, cylindrical; branching from near the base. To 16 ft (5 m) high and 9.8 in (25 cm) across.

Spines: Up to 35. Whitish to yellowish to golden brown. 0.8–3.9 in (2–10 cm) long.

Flower: Creamy whitish to yellowish. 4.7–5.1 in (10–14 cm) long. October–November in habitat.

Flowering time from seed: 25 years or more.

Distribution: Bolivia (from La Paz to Oruro).

On the high, bleak altiplano of Bolivia this impressively spined species is scattered across numerous valleys and hillsides, often in very localized populations. Some of them have been given names, including *Trichocereus antezanae*, *T. orurensis*, and *T. conaconensis*, but these are all included here in *T. bertramianus*, the earliest name that can usefully cover all these very variable plants. In cultivation growth is rapid, and at about 10 years from seed you should have a nice spiny specimen, although not perhaps as wildly spined as the juvenile plant illustrated here, photographed just outside Oruro, PM142.

Trichocereus camarguensis

With its fairly short stems, forming a compact clump, this is the ideal plant for a smallish greenhouse, although it does best when planted out with full root run in a bed, where it is more likely to flower. Plants confined in pots seem a little shy in this respect, although they seem to grow well enough. In habitat it is something of a local species, seemingly restricted to a limited area to the south of Camargo, where the plant illustrated was photographed in flower in the third week of December.

DATA

Form: Plant shrubby. Stems to 19.6 in (50 cm) high and 2 in (5 cm) across; clumping sparingly from the base.

Spines: Radials 12–13; to 1.2 in (3 cm) long. Centrals 2–3; to 2 in (5 cm) long. All spines thin and needlelike.

Flower: White. To 7.8 in (20 cm) long. June–July in cultivation; November–December in habitat.

Distribution: Bolivia (Camargo).

489

Trichocereus candicans

Form: Stems erect or spreading; to 23.6 in (60 cm) long and 5.5 in (14 cm) across; forming clumps up to 9.9 ft (3 m) across.

Spines: Radials 10 or more; to 1.6 in (4 cm) long. Centrals mostly 4; to 3.9 in (10 cm) long.

Flower: White; nocturnal. 4.3–7.5 in (11–19 cm) across. June in cultivation; October–December in habitat.

Flowering time from seed: About 15 years.

Distribution: Argentina (widespread in the north).

The kind of large clumps of this species seen in habitat would be very unwelcome in most greenhouses, but fortunately this plant does not have to be very large to flower—the specimen illustrated above flowered at just 14 years old and about 17.7 inches (45 cm) high. It was grown from seed collected at Capilla del Monte, Córdoba, PM267a. It now flowers every year, although the flowers last only a single night and into the following day, filling the air in the large greenhouse with an amazingly powerful perfume. One useful bonus is that this is a very cold-resistant species that can withstand extended periods below freezing.

Trichocereus chiloensis

This plant occurs in several forms, varying clinally from south to north. In the most southerly populations from near Villa Prat (var. *australis*) the spines are usually fairly short and neat and the stems are relatively slender. In the hills around Santiago you will easily find var. *chiloensis*, with rather longer spines and fatter stems. In the most northerly populations, from a far more arid region, the stems are shorter and fatter and the central spines can be spectacularly long, up to about 7.8 inches (20 cm). This is var. *borealis* and is the form illustrated below, in the Elqui valley. In cultivation the spines do not get as amazingly long as seen here, but they can be pretty impressive—although this is also by far the slowest-growing of the three named forms.

DATA

Form: To 26 ft (8 m) high; branching from near the base. Stems to 4.7 in (12 cm) across.

Spines: Radials 8–12; to 1.6 in (4 cm) long. Centrals 1; 1.6–2.8 in (4–7 cm) or more long.

Flower: White. To 5.5 in (14 cm) long. July in cultivation; November–December in habitat.

Flowering time from seed: 20–30 years.

Distribution: Chile (widespread).

Trichocereus coquimbanus

DATA

Form: Stems to 3.3 ft (1 m) high and 3.2 in (8 cm) across; branching from the base to form dense thickets.

Spines: Radials 8–12; 0.4–0.8 in (1–2 cm) long. Centrals 3–4; to 2 in (5 cm) long.

Flower: White. To 4.7 in (12 cm) long. July in cultivation; November–December in habitat.

Flowering time from seed: 20–30 years.

Distribution: Chile (along the coast near Coquimbo).

When the accompanying photograph was taken of a plant (PM428) in flower on the coast a few minutes' drive south of Vallenar, the whole area was enveloped in dense fog and the massed ranks of plants looked dark and rather gloomy. In cultivation this is an attractively spined species, but it is extremely slow-growing (far more so than the species on the next page) and it will take correspondingly longer to attain flowering size, even though it is a relatively low-growing plant. Of course, this makes it ideal for someone with limited space who grows plants for themselves rather than just for their flowers.

Trichocereus deserticolus

DATA

Form: Stems upright; branching from the base. To 4.9 ft (1.5 m) high and 2.8 in (7 cm) across.

Spines: Radials 15–25; 0.4–0.6 in (1–1.5 cm) long. Centrals 1–3; to 4.7 in (12 cm) long.

Flower: White. About 3.2 in (8 cm) long. July in cultivation; December–February in habitat.

Flowering time from seed: 15–20 years; a good flowerer in cultivation.

Distribution: Chile (coastal hills from Caldera to Tocopilla).

For fans of long-spined cacti this is another "must have" species (although it is often labelled as *Trichocereus fulvilanus*). Even in dull climates the central spines reach 4.7 inches (12 cm) long. The young spines in active growth in the crown of the plant are strikingly attractive, with bright yellow bases, while the rest of the spines are gray. In habitat this species often depends for long periods on dense sea mists that condense on the plants as water droplets, visible in the accompanying illustration (of PM208) taken in Pan de Azúcar National Park near Taltal. The plants are often clothed with dense festoons of lichens also taking advantage of the mists.

Trichocereus litoralis

DATA

Form: Upright or sprawling, branching from the base. Stems to 6.6 ft (2 m) high and 4.7 in (12 cm) or more across.

Spines: Radials 15–29. Centrals 2–6, to 0.9 in (2.4 cm) long.

Flower: White. To 10 cm (3.9 in) across. November–December in habitat.

Flowering time from seed: 20 years or more.

Distribution: Chile (along the coast from north of Valparaíso to north of Los Vilos).

It is doubtful that this really is a distinct species, since going inland from the coast it seems to change gradually into *Trichocereus chiloensis*, and there are populations that are difficult to assign to either species (although they could be hybrid populations between two "good" species). On the clifftops by the Pacific Ocean and brushed by its spray *T. litoralis* is distinct enough, and is generally the more attractive of the two species, with a neater, shorter, and far denser spination. In cultivation it is slow-growing and, like all these Chilean species, very frost-resistant.

The plant illustrated was photographed in flower south of Los Vilos.

Trichocereus santaensis

DATA

Form: To 16.4 ft (5 m) high, branching from the base. Stems to 5.9 in (15 cm) across.

Spines: Radials 2–3; 0.8–1.2 in (2–3 cm) long. Centrals 1; to 1.6 in (4 cm) or more long.

Flower: White. About 7.5 in (19 cm) long and 7.8 in (20 cm) across. December–January in habitat.

Flowering time from seed: 20 years or more.

Distribution: Peru (Ria Santa valley).

A s with any of the larger treelike cacti, this species cannot really be expected to flower in cultivation unless it is planted out in a large bed under glass in a tall greenhouse or grown outside where the climate permits. It is closely related to *Trichocereus pachanoi*, *T. cuzcoensis*, *T. puquiensis*, and a number of other similar-looking tall-growing species that are scattered around the Peruvian highland valleys, possibly all representing forms of a single species.

The plant illustrated was photographed on a roadside in the Santa valley.

Trichocereus schickendantzii

Form: Usually branching from the base. Stems cylindrical to oblong to club-shaped; 5.9 in–3.3 ft (15 cm–1m) long and up to 5.9 in (15 cm) across.

Spines: Radials 9. Centrals 4, sometimes more. All spines thin; up to 0.4 in (1 cm) long.

Flower: White. 7.9–8.7 in (20–22 cm) long. June–July in cultivation; October–December in habitat.

Flowering time from seed: 10–15 years.

Distribution: Northwestern Argentina.

This can be considered either as a single very variable species or as several related but isolated species scattered around northwest Argentina. Some of the more distinct forms have been given names, while others have not. In some recent works they are all included in *Trichocereus schickendantzii*, but for some unfathomable reason the various populations lack the status of subspecies and therefore there is no way of distinguishing them. The form illustrated here was grown from seed collected in the Quebrada del Toro, Salta, PM318. This is a free-flowering plant in cultivation, each flower having a beautiful fragrant perfume that fills the greenhouse, but alas only for a single night.

Trichocereus shaferi

DATA

Form: Branching from the base. Stems to about 19.5 in (50 cm) high and 4.7 in (12 cm) broad; fresh green.

Spines: About 10; thin. Radials and centrals not distinguishable; to 0.4 in (1.2 cm) long.

Flower: White. To 7.1 in (18 cm) long. June in cultivation.

Flowering time from seed: 6–7 years.

Distribution: Argentina (Salta, near San Lorenzo; according to Ritter also near León and near the city of Jujuy).

This plant is often considered as simply a form of the previous species (without the status of a name, even at subspecies level). If its merits are to be recognized, it is difficult to treat it here as anything but a species. The main advantage of this plant for the cactus enthusiast is the remarkably small size and age at which it will start producing its large flowers, which seem very top heavy sitting near the tips of the rather slender stems.

The plant above was grown from seed collected north of the city of Salta, DJF295.

Trichocereus smrzianus

Form: Clumping from the base. Stems to 15.8 in (40 cm) long and 7.8 in (20 cm) across.

Spines: Variable. 7–14; all thin and needlelike; to 3.5 in (9 cm) long.

Flower: White, yellow, or pink. 3.5–7.1 in (9–18 cm) long. July in cultivation; November–December in habitat.

Flowering time from seed: 10–15 years.

Distribution: Argentina (Salta, Cuesta del Obispo, and on the road to Amblayo).

If the previous species could be considered to be a rather slender form of *Trichocereus schickendantzii*, then this could just as easily be taken to be a plumpish manifestation of the same variable species. In cultivation *T. smrzianus* grows very quickly, and within about 10 to 12 years from seed it should make a mound of six to seven heads that will fill a 12-inch (32-cm) pan. At this stage it should start to produce flowers. They are usually white, as seen in the photograph, taken on the Cuesta del Obispo right at the end of the flowering season. However, those fortunate enough to visit this area a little earlier in the month have found flowers in glorious shades of yellow or pink as well as white.

Trichocereus tacaquirensis

This plant is common over a wide area of Bolivia, such as along the main road between Sucre and Potosí, where this photograph was taken. When not in flower, the tall green branching columns can be surprisingly inconspicuous, because this species usually grows among trees and bushes. But when present, the large white flowers grab your attention, even from a distance. Over the course of a day's journey from here, the spination gradually changes and the plant becomes *Trichocereus taquimbalensis* (recently made a subspecies of *T. tacaquirensis* but—correctly—changed to *Echinopsis tacaquirensis taquimbalensis*). In cultivation growth is rapid, and this is one of the more handsome members of the genus.

DATA

Form: Branching near the base. Stems to 8.8 ft (2.5 m) high and 5.9 in (15 cm) across.

Spines: Up to 13. Often not easily differentiated into radials and centrals. To 3.2 in (8 cm) long.

Flower: White. To 9.1 in (23 cm) long. June–July in cultivation; November–December in habitat.

Flowering time from seed: 15–20 years.

Distribution: Bolivia (widespread around Sucre).

Trichocereus tarijensis

DATA

Form: Branching from the base. Stems to 16.4 ft (5 m) high and 13.8 in (35 cm) across.

Spines: Brown to glassy whitish. Radials to 50 or more. Centrals 1–4; to 3.9 in (10 cm) long.

Flower: Red to pink. To 3.5 in (9 cm) across. December–January in habitat.

Flowering time from seed: Probably 20 years or more.

Distribution: Northern Argentina (Tilcara) to Bolivia (south of Potosí).

When its clusters of sensational pink or red flowers are present in colorful tufts in the crown of the plant, this species is indeed a spectacular sight. It crops up in numerous localities scattered across its large range, the most southerly forms often being labeled in cultivation as *Trichocereus poco*. Even within a single locality, however, the spination can vary. For example, the plant illustrated, photographed at Cuch Ingenio, south of Potosí, has long, stiff, straight, glassy spines that are whitish yellow. Just out of the picture there was another plant in flower, but this one had long, wavy, soft pure white spines. In cultivation growth is relatively rapid, but flowering is not assured and even old plants often do not oblige.

Trichocereus terscheckii

Often occurring in thousands on stony hillsides over a wide area of northwest Argentina, this is the tallest cactus of the region, with its sturdy, candelabra-like stems perched on top of a substantial woody trunk up to 17.7 inches (45 cm) across. In cultivation it is worth growing for its rather distinctive spination. Growth is slow, however, and it takes a good many years for plants to become columnar, and in the average greenhouse flowering is very unlikely to occur.

The plant illustrated was photographed in flower on the Cuesta de Portezuelo, near Catamarca city.

DATA

Form: Treelike. Stems columnar; to 39 ft (12 m) high and 7.9 in (20 cm) or more across.

Spines: 8–15 or more. 0.4–2.8 in (1–7 cm) long.

Flower: White. To 4.9 in (12.5 cm) across. November–December in habitat.

Distribution: Northern Argentina (widespread).

Tunilla chilensis

Form: Branching.
Segments rather rounded
in cross-section; to 2 in
(5 cm) long and 1.2 in
(3 cm) broad.

Spines: Up to 9 or more.
To 1.2 in (3 cm) or more
long. Brownish red.

Flower: Orange. 1.6 in
(4 cm) across. June
in cultivation.

**Flowering time from
seed:** 4–5 years.

Distribution: Chile
(from Arica north to
the Peruvian border).

With its chunky little bluish green segments, beadlike manner of branching,
attractive reddish spination, and nonsprawling way of growing, this is probably
the most worthwhile member of the genus to have in your collection. The only
drawback is the relatively small chance that you will ever see any flowers on your
plant, since they are not produced with any great frequency. You should not be too
put off by this, because it is a rewardingly ornamental little plant at all times, and
flowers are just a bonus. As with the plant illustrated, most cultivated material is
derived from vegetative propagations of plants collected in habitat, in this case
without a precise locality.

Tunilla corrugata

ormerly included in *Airampoa* or *Opuntia*, this attractive little species is a
common sight in its arid homeland, its strings of segments trailing across the
ound in low mats. For a few weeks each year these are adorned with brilliant
d flowers, as seen here on a plant photographed near Andalgalá in Catamarca
ovince. In cultivation it needs to be given a low pan that is broad enough to enable
to sprawl, and then it should flower readily every year. As with all these small
puntias," propagation is mainly from cuttings, although seed germinates well.

DATA

Form: Stem segments flat to rather cylindrical; to 1.4 in (3.5 cm) long and 0.5 in (1.2 cm) across; bright green.

Spines: 6–8. Needlelike, with barbed tips. To 0.5 in (1.2 cm) long.

Flower: Red or orange. 1.6–2 in (4–5 cm) across. June in cultivation; November–December in habitat.

Flowering time from seed: 4–5 years.

Distribution: Northwestern Argentina (widespread).

Tunilla erectoclada

Form: Low and creeping. Segments to 2 in (5 cm) long and 1.6 in (4 cm) broad.

Spines: 4–7. To 0.4 in (1 cm) long.

Flower: Deep carmine. 1.6 in (4 cm) across. June in cultivation; November–December in habitat.

Flowering time from seed: 4–5 years.

Distribution: Argentina (Salta, Cachipampa).

It is a long way from Cachipampa to the locality where the original material of the plant illustrated was collected, on the Cuesta Miranda in La Rioja province. It is possible, therefore, that more than one species is involved, but not inconceivable that one single, widespread species occurs at a number of scattered, isolated localities. This plant has also been distributed as STO 399/92; whatever the doubts about its correct name, it is well worth making the effort to acquire, since the flower is delightful and is freely produced every year from very small plants.

Tunilla longispina

This is another widespread plant that is often common in the mountainous regions of northwestern Argentina. The plant illustrated was photographed in the upper reaches of the Quebrada del Toro, above Puerta Tastil in Salta province. From a distance the thousands of plants covering a steep hillside looked like a carpet of dead, bleached grass. Closer investigation revealed that what appeared to be grass was, in fact, great interwoven masses of long golden spines shining in the sun on the matlike plants. At this locality all the plants had orange flowers, but in other places they were yellow or pink on white-spined plants. Cultivated plants generally flower well.

Form: Segments oblong to subcircular; 0.6–1.4 in (2–3.5 cm) long; forming dense colonies.

Spines: Numerous. Variable in coloration. To about 1.2 in (3 cm) long.

Flower: Yellow to orange to pink to red. About 1.2 in (3 cm) across. June in cultivation; November–January in habitat.

Flowering time from seed: 4–5 years.

Distribution: Northwestern Argentina.

Turbinicarpus beguinii

DATA

Form: Simple. Globular to slightly cylindrical. To 3.9 in (10 cm) high and 1.8 in (4.5 cm) across.

Spines: Radials 12–16; to 0.2 in (0.6 cm) long. Centrals 2–3, to 0.6 in (1.5 cm); whitish with darker tips.

Flower: Pale magenta or violet. To 0.7 in (1.8 cm) across. May in cultivation.

Flowering time from seed: 2–3 years.

Distribution: Mexico (Coahuila, Nuevo León, San Luis Potosí).

Until relatively recently this attractive, very densely spined plant was included in *Gymnocactus*, along with several other species. These are all now included in *Turbinicarpus* and are likely to stay there for good. The length of the spines varies somewhat, the longest-spined plants often being offered under the commercial name of var. "*senilis.*" The flowers are apricot colored in another of the forms that is often seen in cultivation—Lau 1035 from the Sierra de la Paila in Coahuila (shown above). In cultivation *T. beguinii* is very intolerant of excess moisture, so it should be watered with care and kept in the smallest pot that looks reasonable.

Turbinicarpus lophophoroides

Whereas most of the plants in this genus grow among limestone rocks on sloping hillsides, this species is unusual in making its home in the very hot, un-baked environment of flat dried-out lake beds that have a high salt content. During the driest parts of the year the plants retreat into the ground, but after heavy summer rains they can be temporarily immersed in water. In cultivation this species is a little more prone than most to root rot if overwatered, so be careful with the watering can. The commercial plant illustrated below is one of hundreds that are being raised from seed.

DATA

Form: Simple. Flattened-globular. To 1.4 in (3.5 cm) high and 1.9 in (4.7 cm) across.

Spines: Radials 2–4; about 0.4 in (0.9 cm) long. Centrals 1; about 0.4 in (1 cm).

Flower: White to very pale pink. To 1.4 in (3.5 cm) across. May–June in cultivation.

Flowering time from seed: 3–4 years.

Distribution: Mexico (San Luis Potosí, near Las Tablas).

Turbinicarpus pseudomacrochele

Form: Plants mostly simple. To 1.6 in (4 cm) high and 1.4 in (3.5 cm) across.

Spines: 5–8. Radials and centrals are indistinguishable; bristly and twisted; 0.6–1.2 in (1.5–3 cm) long.

Flower: White to magenta to yellowish green. 0.8–1.4 in (2–3.5 cm) across. May–June in cultivation.

Flowering time from seed: 3–4 years.

Distribution: Mexico (Hidalgo, Querétaro).

Years ago this species was collected illegally from its natural home in large numbers for export to (and eventual useless death in) countries such as the U.K., Germany, and the United States. A similar fate has befallen other members of this genus, which is unfortunate enough to be considered "choice" by certain collectors. Fortunately most "turbinis" are now grown in large numbers from seed or are propagated on grafts from (illegally) field-collected material. The commercial plant shown here was taken from one of numerous large trays filled with thousands of *Turbinicarpus* seedlings.

Turbinicarpus pseudopectinatus

DATA

Form: Simple. To 1.2 in (3 cm) high and 1.4 in (3.5 cm) across.

Spines: About 50. Very short. White and comblike.

Flower: White with reddish or magenta midstripes. 0.7–1 in (1.8–2.5 cm) across. May–June in cultivation.

Flowering time from seed: 4–5 years.

Distribution: Mexico (Tamaulipas and Nuevo León).

Because of a superficial and misleading resemblance to *Peleceyphora aselliformis*, this plant was included for many years in that genus. It was then reassigned to the newly created genus *Normanbokea*, before finding its natural (and final) resting place, where it now stands. With its neat white comblike arrangement of spines it is an elegant plant. Because of its slow growth and miniature size, it will never outgrow a small pot, although care in watering is essential. As with all members of this genus, it is included in Appendix I of CITES and under no account should readers break the law by knowingly purchasing plants that have been collected illegally from the habitat in which they belong.

Turbinicarpus schmiedickianus

Form: Simple. 1–3 cm (0.4–1.2 in) high and 0.6–2 in (1.5–5 cm) across.

Spines: Usually 3; to 1 in (2.5 cm) long, curving like a ram's horns, and interlacing; one upper spine flattened.

Flower: Pink. 0.7 in (1.8 cm) broad. May in cultivation.

Flowering time from seed: 3–4 years.

Distribution: Mexico (Tamaulipas, near Miquihuana).

The accompanying description covers subspecies *schmiedickianus*, a particularly slow-growing form that is not common in cultivation. The form illustrated, subspecies *macrochele*, is easy to get hold of—often being grown in thousands, as in the commercial product illustrated. It has as many as six rather pliable, corky spines, white flowers, and hails from the region of Matehuala in San Luis Potosí. In the yellow-flowered subspecies *flaviflorus* the body gets quite large, while subspecies *gracilis* is a tiny form with very thin spines. All these and several other subspecies were originally described as species, and in the author's opinion they fully merit that status.

Turbinicarpus viereckii

Formerly included in *Gymnocactus*, this is one of the larger-growing members of the genus. Growth is faster than in any of the smaller species, but it still takes many years for a clump to form. Subspecies *major* (below) has white flowers on heads that remain simple and reach 2.5 inches (6.5 cm) in diameter. The plant illustrated is Lau 1243, grown from seed taken from plants growing in humus between limestone rocks on the road from Santa Rita to Dr Arroyo, San Luis Potosí. *Turbinicarpus saueri* is a broadly similar-looking plant, also with a white flower (but with reddish midstripes). It comes from the valley of Jaumave in San Luis Potosí.

DATA

Form: Simple or clumping. Stems globular to globular-cylindrical; to 2.8 in (7 cm) high and 2.5 in (6.5 cm) across.

Spines: Radials 13–22; to 0.5 in (1.2 cm) long. Centrals 3–5; white with dark tips; to 0.8 in (2 cm) long.

Flower: Magenta or white. 0.6–1.4 in (1.5–3.5 cm) across. May–June in cultivation.

Flowering time from seed: 3–4 years.

Distribution: Mexico (Tamaulipas, Nuevo León, San Luis Potosí).

Uebelmannia gummifera

DATA

Form: Plants gray green. Globular to slightly elongate. To 3.9 in (10 cm) high and 2.4 in (6 cm) across.

Spines: Radials 3; one pointing downward; to 0.2 in (0.5 cm) long. Centrals 1; similar to radials; pointing slightly upward.

Flower: Yellow. 0.6 in (1.5 cm) across.

Flowering time from seed: 6–8 years.

Distribution: Brazil (Minas Gerais, Serra de Ambrosia).

From a distance the slopes of the Serra de Ambrosia gleam white in the sun. When you arrive, you discover that this is because the whole hillside is covered in sandlike quartz crystals. It is among these crystals that this species grows (see photograph), and in pretty large numbers, from tiny seedlings to large old elongate specimens. In cultivation all members of this genus need to be kept well above freezing. They do best when grafted, making very attractive specimens, the most different from *Uebelmannia gummifera* being *U. pectinifera* with its reddish brown bodies and short black spines.

Weberbauerocereus weberbaueri

A common sight alongside the roads that radiate out from the large city of Arequipa, this species, with its slightly curving stems, makes an attractive, though fairly slow-growing plant in cultivation. The plant illustrated, grown from seed collected just 3 miles (5 km) north of the city (PM467), had reached a height of about 22 inches (56 cm) at 10 years from seed. The young spines in active growth are particularly attractive, the lower half being yellow, the upper half brown. In the very popular *Weberbauerocereus winterianus* the stems are more slender and are densely covered in golden-yellow spines.

DATA

Form: Plant shrubby; to about 13 ft (4 m) high. Stems to 3.9 in (10 cm) across.

Spines: Radials about 20; thin; to 0.6 in (1.5 cm) long. Centrals 6–8; brownish; to 2.4 in (6 cm) long.

Flower: Chocolate brown outside, white within. To 4.3 in (11 cm) long and 2.2 in (5.5 cm) across. October–December in habitat.

Flowering time from seed: Many years.

Distribution: Southern Peru.

Weingartia fidaiana

DATA

Form: Usually simple. Stem globular to oblong; gray green; to 7.8 in (20 cm) high and 5.9 in (15 cm) across.

Spines: Radials 9–14; to 1.2 in (3 cm) long. Centrals 3–4; to 2 in (5 cm) long.

Flower: Yellow. To 1.2 in (3 cm) long. June in cultivation.

Flowering time from seed: 3–4 years.

Distribution: Bolivia (Potosí and Chuquisaca).

The plant illustrated is the form originally described as *Weingartia westii* and was grown from seed collected south of Potosí. On the Pampa de Lecorí you can find particularly large, fine plants, sometimes forming clumps and often still listed as *W. lecoriensis*. Farther south toward Camargo the plants are quite tiny, often only 1.2 inches (3 cm) across, wedged into cracks in the rocks. South of Camargo, especially around Puente San Pedro, there are huge mounds of subspecies *cintiensi* (originally *W. cintiensis*). All these forms are available as seed or plants, usually under their old species names, and all are far slower-growing in cultivation than *W. neocumingii* and its many forms.

Weingartia neocumingii

DATA

Form: Simple or clumping. Stems globular to oblong; to 9.8 in (25 cm) high and 11.8 in (30 cm) broad.

Spines: Radials 5–24; to 0.4 in (1 cm) long. Centrals 2–8; to 0.8 in (2 cm).

Flower: Yellow. To 1 in (2.5 cm) across. Often more than one from a single areole. May–June in cultivation.

Flowering time from seed: 3–4 years.

Distribution: Bolivia (widespread).

In recent works *Weingartia* has been included in *Rebutia*, but for convenience it is maintained separately here, as it no doubt will be for many years in sales catalogs. This is a very widespread species that exhibits a perplexing range of variation, leading to a number of subspecies, all of which were originally described as species (and are usually still listed as such). The plant shown above was once known as *W. sucrensis*. It is a rather broad, flattened form, and this one was grown from seed collected close to Betanzos, near Potosí. One of the most popular forms, subspecies *trollii*, has red flowers, making a change from the otherwise ubiquitous yellow.

Other Cactus Genera

To assist the reader who is a complete beginner with cacti and is faced with a bewildering array of names on a mail order list, the following is a selection of genera that are not included here, along with brief reasons why.

Acanthocereus—large, rather ugly plants needing warmth in winter; seldom grown.

Arthrocereus—small, difficult-to-get, rather tricky-to-grow plants with nocturnal flowers; need warmth.

Austrocactus—hard to get and can be tricky to keep going.

Aztekium—much beloved of those desiring "choice" plants, but very slow-growing, often grafted; only offered by a small number of dealers.

Bergerocactus—a single, rather sprawling species, golden-spined, slim-stemmed, rather out of fashion at present.

Blossfeldia—a single species, tiny plants; usually grafted, when they become bloated and abnormal.

Brasilicereus—nondescript warmth-loving cerei.

Calymmanthium—shrubby, untidy plants with strange flowers.

Carnegiea—the "saguaro," seedlings take for ever to start getting columnar and are not particularly attractive.

Cipocereus—rather nondescript warmth-loving cerei.

Coleocephalocereus (including *Buiningia*)—some are quite attractive, but need lots of warmth and do not usually flower in most collections.

Dendrocereus—treelike plants, seldom available.

Discocactus—flattened-globular species, usually grafted, nocturnal white flowers, needing warmth; some people dote on them, most cannot be bothered.

Escontria—a single species, nice seedlings but need warmth and soon outgrow their welcome.

Facheiroa—warmth-loving cerei, can be difficult to keep going; seldom offered.

Geohintonia—see comments on *Aztekium*.

Hylocereus—long trailing warmth-loving plants with gorgeous flowers, but few people have room for them.

Lasiocereus—similar to *Haageocereus*; seldom offered.

Leocereus—warmth-loving, slender-stemmed, nondescript cerei.

Leptocereus—treelike or epiphytic cerei, very varied; seldom available.

Neobuxbaumia—very large, often unbranched cerei from Mexico; need warmth; not recommended for greenhouse cultivation.

Ortegocactus—one species; some people love it, but to most it is a small, rather dingy-flowered plant that is difficult to get to flower or even to keep alive; seldom offered.

Pereskiopsis—similar to *Pereskia*.

Polaskia—large treelike plant; two species, of which one (*P. chichipe*) is often seen in flower shops; makes nice seedling but soon grows into a nondescript plant.

Praecereus—thin-stemmed untidy-looking cerei.

Pseudorhipsalis—similar to *Rhipsalis*.

Samaipaticereus—tall, slim-stemmed plants with unusual flowers.

Selenicereus—long thin trailing stems, often huge white nocturnal flowers; need too much room and warmth for most people to bother with.

Weberocereus—epiphytic cerei with long pendant stems, seldom available.

Yavia—single tiny species, difficult on own roots; grafted plants become abnormally bloated; difficult to flower.

Yungasocerus—slim-stemmed untidy-looking plants, seldom available.

Glossary

Areole The cushion producing spines, leaves (sometimes), and flowers.

Axil The depression between the tubercles in *Mammillaria*, from where the flowers arise.

Caatinga Drought-resistant, mainly scrublike vegetation of northeastern Brazil.

Cephalium Specialized flowering zone of some cacti, usually densely hairy.

Cerei/cereoid Columnar cacti/columnar in growth.

Clumping With several stems.

Clustering With several stems.

Cristate With the growing point extended into a line, often giving a brainlike appearance to the plant.

Cylindrical Shaped like a cylinder; columnar.

Elongate Lengthened.

Epiphyte/epiphytic A plant growing on another plant.

Extrafloral nectary Nectar-producing gland situated above the areole in certain cacti such as *Ferocactus* and *Coryphantha*.

Felt Dense mass of short hairs.

Forma A distinctive form of a species, usually not occupying a separate range.

Glaucous Blue-green.

Globular Shaped like a globe.

Glochid Tiny, barbed spines, usually in tufts in the *Opuntia* group of cacti.

Head Single stem of a cactus, usually used only for globular types.

Microspecies A group of plants of a species that reproduce asexually to produce genetically identical plants.

Nectary Nectar-producing part of a flower.

Nomen nudum (n. n.) A proposed name that has not been published with an adequate description.

Offset Growing stems that appear at some place other than at the main growing tip of the plant.

Pectinate Comblike.

Pubescent Hairy or downy.

Rib A vertically arranged ridge on the stem.

Simple With just a single stem.

Solitary With just a single stem.

Spines, central Spines that project outward from the areole; may sometimes be difficult to distinguish from radial spines.

Spines, radials Spines arranged around the areole like the hands of a clock.

Subspecies A distinctive form of a species, usually occupying a separate range from the remainder of the species of which it is a part.

Tubercle A conical or cylindrical outgrowth on the stem, most often seen in *Mammillaria* (see *Mammillaria longimanna*).

Tuberculate Covered in bumps.

Type The original specimen(s) on which the description of a new species or subspecies is made.

Variety In cacti, a term formerly used for what is now usually treated as a subspecies. At present, both terms are having to be used concurrently until enough varieties have been formally changed to subspecies.

Vegetative propagation Increasing the stock of a single plant by taking and rooting cuttings or offsets.

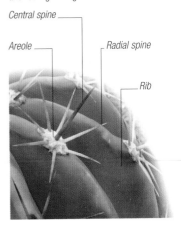

Central spine

Areole

Radial spine

Rib

Further References

Anderson, E. F., *The Cactus Family*, Timber Press, Portland, Oregon, 2001.

Anderson, M., *The Complete Guide to Growing Cacti and Succulents*, Lorenz Books, London, UK, 2004.

Bell, S-A., *Success with Cacti and Other Succulents*, Guild of Master Craftsmen Publications Ltd., Lewis, E. Sussex, UK, 2005.

Ellis, J., *Beginner's Guide to Cacti and Other Succulents*, Sterling, New York, 2004.

Fischer, P., *Mysterious Beauty: Desert Plants and Cacti of the Americas*, Squarebooks, Santa Rosa, California, 2003.

Hewitt, T., *The Complete Book of Cacti and Succulents*, Dorling Kindersley, New York/London, UK, 1997.

Hewitt, T., *Garden Succulents* (RHS Wisley Handbook), Cassell Illustrated, London, UK, 2003.

Hunt, D., Taylor, N., and G. Charles (eds.), *The New Cactus Lexicon*, David Hunt Publications for International Cactaceae Systematics Group, 2006.

Mace, T., *Cactus Basics: a Comprehensive Guide to Cultivation and Care*, Hamlyn, London, UK, 2006.

Pilbeam, J., *Mammillaria* (A Cactus File Handbook), Cirio Publishing Services, Southampton, UK, 1999.

Pizzetti, M., and S. Schuler (ed.), *Simon & Schuster's Guide to Cacti and Succulents*, Simon & Schuster, New York, 1995.

Preston-Mafham, R., and K. Preston-Mafham, *Cacti—the Illustrated Dictionary*, Timber Press, Portland, Oregon, 1997.

Quinn, M., *Cacti of the Desert Southwest*, Rio Nuevo Publishers, Tucson, Arizona, 2002.

Rogers, R., *Crazy about Cacti and Succulents*, Brooklyn Botanic Garden, Brooklyn, New York, 2006.

Sajeva, M., and M. Costanzo, *Succulents II*, Timber Press, Portland, Oregon, 2000.

Cacti and Succulents (101 Essential Tips), Dorling Kindersley, London, UK, 2004.

www.cactus-mall.com
The Cactus and Succulent Plant Mall has links to just about anything to do with cacti.

www.cssainc.org
Cactus and Succulent Society of America Web site.

www.bcss.org.uk
British Cactus and Succulent Society Web site.

Index